Knitty gritty

KNITTING FOR THE ABSOLUTE BEGINNER
and THE NEXT STEPS

Dedication

This book is dedicated to Everyone

Thank You and Thank Me

This edition first published in Great Britain in 2013

Bloomsbury Publishing Plc
50 Bedford Square
London WC1B 3DP

www.bloomsbury.com

ISBN: 978-1-4725-2994-7

CIP Catalogue records for this book are available from the British Library and the U.S. Library of Congress.

Commissioning editor: Susan James
Assistant editor: Agnes Upshall
Cover design: Eleanor Rose
Page layout: Susan McIntyre
Photography: Peter Schiazza

This book is produced using paper that is made from wood grown in managed, sustainable forests. It is natural, renewable and recyclable. The logging and manufacturing processes conform to the environmental regulations of the country of origin.

Printed and bound in China

Knitty gritty

KNITTING FOR THE ABSOLUTE BEGINNER and THE NEXT STEPS

by Aneeta Patel

photography by Peter Schiazza

BLOOMSBURY

LONDON • NEW DELHI • NEW YORK • SYDNEY

Contents

Knitting for the Absolute Beginner

Welcome to the wonderful world of knitting	9
Your Essential Knit Kit	14
How to Knit Workshop	16
Project 1: Chunky Scarf	30
Decreasing Workshop	36
Sewing-up Workshop	38
Project 2: Baby Booties	42
Stitch Patterns Workshop	48
Project 3: Hats	52
Increasing Workshop	58
Project 4: Zig-Zag Scarf	60
Finishing Workshop	62
Project 5: Cardigan (baby or child)	66
Project 6: Flower	74
Cable Stitches Workshop	78
Project 7: Cable Bag	80
Project 8: Lacy Wrap	82
Project 9: Mittens	86
Project 10: Hot Water Bottle Cover	96
Project 11: Necktie	100
Project 12: Fingerless Wrist-Warmers	104
Project 13: Phone Home	108
Project 14: Manly Scarf	112
Project 15: Girly Scarf	116
Project 16: Little 'n' Large Cushions	120
Enjoy and Experiment	124
Useful Notes: Conversion Charts and Abbreviations	126
Stockists	128

The Next Steps

Introduction	131
Tension and gauge	132
The projects	134
Choosing your yarn (The Science Bit)	134
How to use this book	135

Techniques

Casting on	136
Basic two-needle cast-on	136
Thumb method	137
Basic stitches	138
How to do knit stitch	138
How to do purl stitch	139
Stitch combinations	140
Shaping: decreasing and increasing	140
Decreasing	140
Increasing	142
Casting off	144
Basic cast-off	144
Drawstring finish	144
Three-needle bind-off	145
Kitchener stitch	146
Finishing techniques	148
I-cord	148
Pick up and knit	149
Buttonholes	149
Blocking	151
Sewing up	152
Mattress stitch	152
Sewing a sleeve into a body	153
Sewing up around corners	155
Sewing up garter stitch	156
Whip stitch	156
Easing in	157

Knitting SOS! 158

    Knitting rules 158

    Frogging: how to un-knit your knitting 158

    Recognising rib stitches 160

    Saver row 161

    Turning 163

    Adding yarn 163

    Weaving in ends 164

    How to tell the right side from the wrong side 165

    Working a two-row colour change 165

    How to count rows 166

    Markers 167

    Tips for following knitting patterns 167

The projects

Adult booties 168

Ladies' raglan jumper 172

Men's bulky jumper 180

Girls' pinafore dress 186

Versatile kiddies' jumper 192

Ladies' classic cardigan 200

Gloves 210

Hats: learn to knit in the round 218

Workshop: Using double-pointed needles 227

Socks 230

Workshop: Knitting straight on circular needles 240

Lengthways-striped scarf 241

Workshop: Short row shaping 242

Table mat and coaster set 244

Twirly scarf 246

Create your own creature 248

Seasonal projects 252

    Valentine's heart 252

    Easter bunny egg cosy 254

    Christmas tree 256

Stitch library

Do (kn)it yourself 258

The stitches 262

    Wrap drop stitch 262

    Fireside lace stitch 264

    Workshop: How to cable 266

    Cable plait stitch 266

    Aneeta's six-toed cable stitch 267

    Cable twist stitch 268

    Bramble stitch 270

    Bobble stitch 271

    Loopy stitch 274

    Knitting with beads 276

    Fir tree lace stitch 278

    How to follow a chart 280

    Knit and purl motifs 282

    Moss zig stitch 283

    Fair Isle and intarsia 284

    Swiss darning 290

The stitch-library scarf afghan 292

Farewell and good luck! 293

Appendix

Conversion charts 294

Abbreviations 295

Stockists 295

Index 296

Knitty gritty

Knitting for the absolute beginner

Acknowledgments

Yarn and other knitting materials were kindly donated by the generous people at: Colinette, Debbie Bliss, Hipknits, I Knit London, Rowan and Sirdar. For contact details and more information, please see the Stockists list on page 128.

Thanks are due to my Guinea Pigs, the tireless beginner knitters who took up the challenge of testing the patterns in this book: Alison Steadman, Annabel Leathes, Annie Ng, Becky Clarke, Caroline Fonda, Catherine Alaguiry, Cathy Eatough, Charlie Kitchen, David O'Dwyer, David Vannen, Dawn Bray, Deborah Coughlin, Genevieve Grady, Guils Driver, Hannah Spencer, Hasu Patel, Hayley Dalton, Izzy Pugh, Jane Freimiller, Jayne Morgan, Jem Davis, Karen Eaton, Kate Ballinger, Kathie Schroeder, Libby Thomas, Marion Ohlson, Mary Cowin, Michelle Cain, Natalie Billington, Niki Stevens, Nutroast, Paula Ellis, Peter Brownell, Rachael Sutton, Sam Tyfield, Sarah Macleod, Seeta Patel, Sonja Petersen, Suresh Patel, Susan Neuville and Vicky Cowin. Without them I'd never have known where I was going wrong.

Thank you to all the models – born to wear knits: Adam Hilton, Alexander Whitamore, Alexis Larusson, Brie McAuley, Catherine Alaguiry, Charlie Kitchen, Daisy Beattie, Lilian Rose Wilson, Felix Ohlson, Harriet Morgan, Henry Schroeder, Isobel Morgan, Jake Stevens, Jayne Morgan, Jane Freimiller, Jem Davis, Jess Hilton, John Neuville, Jonathan Allen, Leah Bray, Lilia Larusson, Louis Strong, Lucy Neuville, Peter Brownell, Polly Adams, Rosy Hilton, Sam Neuville, Sam Tyfield and Sonja Petersen.

Everyone else – where would I be without you? Thanks to my parents and sister, Susan James (who had to work a lot harder due to my inexperience), Peter Schiazza (the handsomest, most hardworking photographer ever), everyone at 2 Bedford Row (ridiculously supportive in all I do), The Space Hijackers (for stopping me from getting old before my time), and everyone I've ever taught to knit (they taught me how to write this book).

Welcome
to the wonderful world of knitting

Hello, my name is Aneeta

I'm your knitting teacher. Have you ever knitted before? Not since you were little? Can't really remember anything? Well, don't worry – we are going to start from scratch. I have been teaching knitting classes for a few years now; I teach men, women and children of all races, ages and backgrounds. The one thing every one of these people has in common is a desire to 'make something'.

These days, our lives can be so fast-paced and the pressure to succeed (in material terms) so unrelenting that often there is little time left over for nurturing our creative and emotional wellbeing. Knitting is a craft that can be used as a creative outlet – you can produce something unique and original, and relax at the same time! I have a tendency to get a bit Zen about it, but I do truly believe that every ounce of creativity generated keeps the planet spinning. For me, one of the best things about knitting is that the whole exercise is packed full of 'instant gratification'. Within a short time, with a relatively small amount of effort, anyone can produce something wearable, practical and beautiful.

Knitting is a fantastic creative force that you can harness to produce anything from a footie scarf for your father to a wrist-cuff for your wannabe rock-star little brother. Imagine the pleasure of someone asking where you bought that pretty scarf and being able to nonchalantly say, 'I made it myself'. I hope that this book will start you on a lifetime addiction to knitting.

Knitty Gritty has been designed especially for absolute knitting-newcomers. If you follow these workshops and patterns carefully from beginning to end you will gain a solid grounding in basic knitting techniques and you will complete some very simple, enjoyable pieces of knitting as you go. If you are an 'advanced beginner' (you already understand the basics), then you can dip into the different workshops and projects to brush up your skills, learn new techniques, and knit some gorgeous projects along the way.

In the above image, both squares have been knitted using the same number of stitches and rows. They are different sizes because they were knitted on different-sized needles

The Science Bit

The absolute beginner will find knitting patterns hugely confusing, almost as though they are written in a foreign language (which of course they are – Knit!). This book provides a simple and straightforward translation and simplification service for beginners, as well as easy-to-knit patterns for items you will be happy to wear, use or to give as special presents.

You will probably learn a variety of different methods eventually, but the main focus of this book is just to help you begin to knit, so you can learn how to start (and how to stop!), create some finished knitting of your own, and, most importantly, enjoy the process without becoming bogged down in or overwhelmed by technicalities. This way you will gradually familiarise yourself with the basic techniques as a good grounding for more advanced and skilful knitting in the future.

In knitting there is not always just one right way to do something; if you asked twelve knitters to show you how to cast on, they could each feasibly show you a different way. So the techniques I teach you in this book won't provide final answers and definitive rules, they are simply the methods my beginner students find the easiest and most useful. I think that showing one straightforward method is more constructive than bombarding you with too many confusing choices – please bear this in mind when you are asking advice of other knitters (or sharing your own wisdom further on in your knitting career)!

Tension
A tension or gauge square is knitted to make sure that you are knitting to the same dimensions as the pattern designer intended, and to ensure that your garment knits up to the exact size required. Tension and gauge are very important when making precisely fitted garments.

If you are working from a true beginner's pattern (rather than a pattern for an advanced beginner who already knows the basics), knitting a tension square should not always be necessary because:

- a tension square will take so long for an absolute beginner to knit that they may become disheartened at having to work so hard before even getting stuck into a project (especially if there is more than one tension square to be knitted);

- a true beginner's pattern will not need to be made to such rigid and precise dimensions; and

- a beginner's knitting tension will be constantly changing as they get used to the process and the stitches so a tension square wouldn't be completely accurate.

I have not stated precise tensions in any of the projects in this book – only yarn weight and needle size. One of the consequences of this is that two different knitters may get two different-sized projects, so remember that all stated final sizes are approximate. For example, the child's hat may fit any head from age 3–10 years, depending on the child's head and the knitter. The key is not to get stuck with trying to make exact sizes at this stage; you should be enjoying learning a new skill and making fun things. As you gain more confidence and experience, you will find more demanding or precise patterns easier to cope with. This is why I haven't included any patterns in this book that need to fit exactly.

You will notice that I sometimes include a different needle to that suggested on a ball of yarn – there is a good reason for this. Each yarn will have an optimum needle size for knitting – this is where the tension comes in. If you use the suggested needle, the knitting should come out at the size shown on the gauge square on the yarn label. This means your knitting will work out at the same size as a pattern in that suggested gauge. However, as I have already mentioned, one of the things I notice with all beginner knitters is that their tension varies constantly throughout their work. Even during the knitting of a single scarf, a beginner's stitches will not be consistent. This is perfectly normal, and will be corrected with practice. There is no huge problem with inconsistent tension when you are just starting out, but it does mean that even if you knit an item following every single instruction correctly your knitting might still end up uneven in some places. It won't happen forever, just while you are getting used to the process of knitting. Carry on cheerfully, remembering that you are a beginner, and it will come right in time.

As this book has been written specifically for beginners, I have purposely designed patterns in which the tension won't make or break the work. This is why you'll notice that there aren't any adult garments – with adult clothes, a precise fit is often necessary, and this means knitting with an even tension throughout. With the patterns in this book, it won't matter terribly if your tension is a bit of a rollercoaster – it shouldn't make too much difference to the final piece. Always remember: knitting should be relaxing and you are supposed to be having fun!

Even in the baby and child cardigans, I have designed the patterns to have a bit of extra stretch in them (by suggesting a slightly larger needle size than that on the yarn label) so you shouldn't have a problem in making them fit the child. If anything, I have written the cardigan pattern a little on the large side – it will fit the child eventually. If in doubt about patterns for babies and children, always choose the size up.

When choosing yarn for the patterns, I have given suggestions, but I have purposely left the yarn choice up to you. The yarn weight and approximate amounts needed are shown, but you should realise that the yarn weight is a sufficient guide for the time being and finding specific yarns is something you can focus on a little later. You can work within your own budget, and have fun rummaging around yarn shops and websites to see what's out there.

The Tried-and-Tested Guarantee

There are stacks of beautiful knitting books out there, written by very talented knitwear designers and accomplished knitters. However, the main complaint I hear repeatedly wailed by my absolute beginner students is that these books often assume the reader already knows how to knit. As well as not assuming anything of the sort in this book, I have also incorporated a 'Tried-and-Tested' guarantee with my workshops and patterns – genuine beginner knitters have knitted up all of these patterns (and they haven't been shy with their constructive criticism and clever suggestions for improving the patterns for beginners' use). I hope that this road-tested approach means that you will be able to use this book productively and happily.

Your essential knit kit

Needles

Needles these days come in all shapes, sizes, materials and colours; I have a gorgeous hand-whittled pair and a glamorous diamanté pair! Most of you will have seen metal knitting needles; they are the most easily available and often the least expensive. These days, bamboo needles are very popular – they can be a little more expensive than metal needles, but they have a lovely natural feel to them, a little bit of give and, for prolific knitters, they are said to be less likely to cause hand pain. For beginners, bamboo needles are better than metal as they are less slippery, so there is less chance of dropping stitches. However, if you find that you knit very tightly, the slipperiness of metal needles might help you loosen up your stitches. For variety and help in finding your preferred needle type, also try: casein, plastic, wooden, and any others that you can easily get your hands on.

The best piece of advice here is: experiment. Every time you buy knitting needles, try them in a different material. Everyone has personal preferences and you will find your own favourites in time.

Gadgets and Gizmos

You don't need to spend a fortune to become a knitter: a ball of yarn and a pair of needles will get you going. However, if you can see yourself knitting into the future, here are a few basics you might want to collect (these are all used throughout the patterns in this book): yarn, knitting needles, darning needles, crochet hook, scissors, pencil, cable needle, tape measure. If you have these basic tools, you can acquire additional extras as and when your new projects require them.

Yarn

These days yarn is available in a huge number of materials, colours and weights. Gone are the days when hand-knitting meant suffering inside itchy lurid green acrylic sweaters! Yarn now comes in all sorts of exotic variations, as you will see when you spend some time browsing in yarn stores; this is one of my favourite pastimes, but with so many wonderful yarns on offer the longer you look the more difficult choosing just one yarn to take home becomes!

Alongside the patterns in this book, I have included suggestions for appropriate weights of yarn to use. These are mostly standard weights – just remember that the names may differ depending on which country you are shopping in. If you go into your local yarn store and ask for the weight of yarn you need, they will know exactly what you are talking about and direct you to the correct shelf of goodies.

Fine mohair (lace weight) 3.25mm

4 ply (fingering) 2.25mm

Double-knit (sport) 4mm

Aran (worsted) 5.5mm

Chunky (bulky) 7mm

Super bulky 15mm

UK name (US name) suggested needle size

How to knit Workshop

The Slipknot

Without the ever-necessary slipknot you won't get very far at all with your knitting so practice, practice and practice it again - this is the one thing you are not allowed to forget!

For the girl guides, boy scouts and sailors amongst you this won't be necessary, but for the rest, here's how to make a slipknot.

LEFT →   ← RIGHT

1

Step 1. Make the yarn into an **upside-down U-shape**. Please note that at all times I'm holding onto the ends of the yarn with my fingers – this will keep everything in place as you are making your slipknot.

HOLE

2

Step 2. Fold the upside-down U over so the **right side goes over the left.**

LEFT

3

Step 3. Fold (where the yarn crosses over itself) the **hole over the left** side.

4

Step 4. Pull out the centre section (remembering to keep hold of the ends) – this is a slipknot!

5

Step 5. Once you have your slipknot, place it onto the needle (slide the needle upward through the segment you pulled out above - totally foolproof – I hope!) and pull tight. You know that it has worked if the slipknot undoes when you pull on the two ends of the yarn. This is your first stitch.

How to Cast On

'Casting on' is the phrase used to describe making the first row of stitches on your needle, so that you can begin knitting. If you asked a dozen different knitters how to cast on, you'd get a dozen different answers. My sister, who I taught to knit, now prefers a different cast-on method to me.

There's no right or wrong way, but I've chosen the method I've been teaching for years. This is the most 'tried and tested' part of this book!

Step 1. Start with the slipknot on your **left-hand needle**. This is your first stitch.

Step 2. Pick it up. Pick up this first stitch with the right-hand needle – insert the right-hand needle into the stitch from the bottom, keep the **needles crossed left over right**.

BACK

MIDDLE

Step 3. Back and then middle. Hold both the needles between the thumb and first two fingers of your left hand – this leaves your right hand free. Wrap the long end of the yarn to the **back** of both needles and through the **middle** of the

needles.

Step 4. Underneath and to the front. Bring the tip of the right-hand needle **underneath** the loop on the left needle and to the **front** of the work.

Knitter's Notes

You will notice that I often talk about the 'back', 'middle' or 'front' of your work. Front is closest to you, back is furthest away, and middle is in between the two knitting needles when they are crossed over.

CONTINUE...

How to Cast On *continued...*

Step 5. Stand both needles up straight. Hold onto the stitches with your thumbs.

Step 6. Left needle up the right stitch. Insert the tip of the left hand needle up the stitch on the right needle.

Step 7. Then release the right needle. Pull the right-hand needle out of the work and pull on the long end of the yarn. This is your second stitch.

Continue until you have cast on as many stitches as you require to start your knitting. Please note that with this method of casting on, your work in will 'grow' in width approximately 50% between the cast-on row and the first knitted row. By this I mean that the work itself will end up wider than the width of the cast-on row (e.g. in the picture on the right, the cast-on row measures 8cm. In the first knitted row, this width will grow to approximately 12cm). This is important to remember when you are knitting your first scarf. If at this stage you are unhappy with your cast on, undo it and start again – it's all good practice!

The work will grow in width by approximately 50% between the cast-on row and the first knitted row.

66 *Words of Wisdom*
I'm sure that you are a bright, successful human being. But remember that you are now learning something completely new that might be totally outside of your previous experience. KNITTING DOES NOT COME NATURALLY! It is easy when you know how, but until then, don't be hard on yourself. Relax, engage some extra patience, and stop for frequent cups of tea and chocolate biscuits. And embrace the joy of undoing your work and starting all over again – just remember that you are getting extra use out of your yarn and needles 99

Questions & Answers

Why does the work 'grow' in the first row?
I don't know – it's just a feature of this particular cast-on method. The work will grow in width by approximately 50% between the cast-on row and the first knitted row.

How to Knit

This is the most basic stitch you can learn; using this you can be happily knitting in no time.

In a knitting pattern, knit is abbreviated to K. So K1, would mean 'knit one stitch'. And K1 row would mean 'knit one row'.

Start knitting here!

Start with your cast on stitches in your left hand and the empty needle in your right hand.

Handy HINT

Wrap the long end of the yarn once around the index finger of your right hand. Everyone has their own way of holding the yarn, but until you find yours, this is the easiest way of keeping the yarn in the correct place; it will also help even out your tension.

Step 1. Pick it up. Insert the tip of the right needle into the stitch on the left needle – from the bottom to the top. Keep needles crossed over left over right.

Step 2. Back and then the middle. Holding both the needles in your left hand (between the thumb and first two fingers) wrap the long end of the yarn to the back of both needles (away from you) and then through the middle of the needles (back towards you).

Step 3. Underneath and then to the front. Bring the tip of the right hand needle under the first loop on the left needle.

Step 4. Release. Gently push the stitch on the left needle off using your left thumb.

Repeat these moves until all the stitches are on the right needle and the left needle is empty. Then swap the needles in your hands so that the stitches are once again in your left hand and the empty needle is in your right hand. Carry on knitting in the same way.

Rule Number One

At the end of every row – COUNT YOUR STITCHES! This is a hard and fast rule for all beginners. It will mean the difference between an even, tidy piece of knitting and something very scary.

CONTINUE...

How to Knit *continued...*

Handy HINT

Remember to work away from the tip of the needle. This will help your tension and technique. Imagine the needle as having a thin part (at the tip) and a fat part (the main length of the needle). If you work too much towards the thin part, there is a risk a) of all the stitches slipping off the needles; and b) that when eventually you move the stitches down to the fat part of the needle, they will be too tight. A bit like buying an outfit that's too small for you! So at each step, move the stitch down to the fat part of the needle. This might seem like a lot of sliding the stitch up and down, but it'll be worth it in the long run!

Rule Number Two

Never put down your knitting in the middle of a row. Always finish knitting the row before you set your knitting aside or once you pick it up again you will inevitably start knitting in the wrong direction and make mistakes. If the phone rings, try to leave it – they'll call you back or leave you a message!

The Knit Mantra

Step 1 Pick it up
Step 2 Back and then middle
Step 3 Underneath and to the front
Step 4 Release

Make this your mantra. Say the words to yourself as you are knitting so you don't forget to work each step in order. Use your patience. If you take the time at this stage to work each stitch precisely and carefully, you are less likely to make mistakes and more likely to create beautiful, tidy knitting.

Garter stitch

If you knit every row, the stitch you create is called garter stitch. This looks the same on both sides and is the perfect stitch to knit your first project with.

Garter stitch. Rowan Big Wool and 15mm knitting needles used in this picture

Casting off

'Casting off' (or 'binding off') is the term used for finishing a piece of knitting so that your knitting can live independently of its needles. You must securely cast off the stitches from the needles so that your work will not unravel.

Knitter's Notes

Knitting tension: Whether you are a 'tight' or 'loose' knitter, when casting off always keep your stitches looser than you usually would. This will stop the work from 'puckering' at the cast-off edge. A tight cast-off can look ugly and will spoil your knitting.

Handy HINT

If you find it hard to keep your cast off loose, try using a knitting needle slightly bigger than you used in the rest of your knitting (in your right hand) to cast off with.

Step 1. Knit two stitches.

Step 2. Insert the tip of the left needle down first stitch.

Step 3. Using your left index finger to guide the tip of the right needle.

Lift the first stitch over the second stitch and the right needle.

Keeping the long end of the yarn secure will help.

Step 4. Remember to release the stitch you lifted over the right needle. You will then have one stitch on the right needle.

Step 5a. Then knit one more stitch so that you have two stitches on your right knitting needle again. Then repeat the move of using the left needle to lift the lower stitch on the right needle over the upper stitch and off the left needle.

Remember that you should only have one or two stitches on the right needle at any point during casting off.

CONTINUE...

Casting off *continued...*

Step 5b. You are now casting off.

Step 6. Keep casting off until you have just one stitch left on one needle and the other needle is empty. Then cut the yarn.

Step 7. Pass the cut end of the yarn through the last stitch left on your knitting needle, remove the knitting needle and pull tight.

Step 8. Then weave this end in securely using a crochet hook – if you don't, your knitting will surely unravel.

Notice how the cast-off edge looks. One side has an edge that looks like a 'plait.' This now counts as the wrong side of your work – even if you've been knitting a double-sided stitch like garter stitch. You shouldn't be able to see the 'plait' edge from the right side. (Of course, if you have been making a garter stitch scarf it will be impossible to hide the edge, so don't worry about it.) This advice is just for projects that have an inside and an outside.

When casting off on a stocking stitch piece of knitting, always cast off with the wrong side (purl side) facing you. Otherwise, the plait will form on the right side of your work; this may seem a very small point, but this kind of attention to detail will take you a long way towards giving your work a professional finish.

Questions & Answers

When casting off on the wrong side of a stocking stitch piece, should I be using purl stitch to cast off?

No this won't matter, as you will be casting off on the wrong side, so your plait edge won't be seen. But when you are using knit/purl combinations such as a rib stitch you will have to cast off slightly differently. Don't worry about this right away; we will cover this further on in the book.

My cast-off edge looks very tight and 'bunches' up so that my work doesn't lie flat. What am I doing wrong?

This means you are casting off too tightly. When casting off, try to keep your tension and the stitches on your right knitting needle much looser than you would when knitting normally. If you have trouble making these stitches looser, try casting off using a knitting needle one size bigger than the needles you have used in the rest of the work.

How to add a new colour or start a new ball of yarn

When you come to the end of a ball of yarn, you will have to add a new ball in order to carry on knitting. To do this, you follow exactly the same procedure as for adding a new colour to include a stripe in your knitting.

The illustrated instructions show the adding of new yarn as if to stripe – this is so you can see the change more easily, but it is exactly the same as if you had just come to the end of one ball and wanted to continue with more yarn of the same colour.

It's best to do a colour change at the end of a row, so make sure you do this while there is still enough of the old yarn left to add new yarn easily (about 10cm).

Please note: When you are adding new yarn of the same colour you can add it to either side of your knitting; when adding a new yarn of a different colour, you must add it to the same side each time so that all your loose ends are on the same side, and the work now has a right side (rs) and a wrong side (ws).

Step 1. Lay your work out and make a 'cross' shape with the new yarn under the old yarn.

Step 2. Tie the new yarn into a knot with itself, with the old yarn lying inside that knot. Don't tie the knot too tightly.

Step 3. Slide the new yarn knot up until it touches the knitting needle.

Step 4. Pull the ends of the new yarn to tighten the knot.

Step 5. Then simply start knitting with the new yarn.

Step 6. Where you have changed/added yarn, your work will have loose yarn ends, like little tails. These have to be woven into your knitting to secure them and stop your knitting from unravelling.

Weaving in ends

Weaving in the ends of yarn in your knitting will give you a tidy professional finish and stop your work unravelling, which is what would happen if you just cut these ends off.

You will need a crochet hook. Any size of crochet hook close to the size of knitting needle you are working with is fine – it doesn't have to be exactly the same.

If you have been knitting a colour stripe, weave the ends into the wrong side of the work (as shown in these images). If your work is all the same colour, you should still use the wrong side to weave into; and weave into the same side all the way through the piece. (Of course, a scarf doesn't have to have a wrong and a right side; if this is the case, just choose any side to weave into and stick with this choice.)

Step 1. Insert the crochet hook into the stitch next to the end you are about to weave in. Hold the 'hook' of the crochet hook facing away from you and towards the work.

Step 2. Wrap the end of the yarn **over and then under** the crochet hook.

Step 3. Use the hook to pull the end of the yarn through the stitch on your knitting.

Step 4. Once the yarn has been pulled right through the stitch, repeat the move on the next four stitches in the row.

Step 5. Cut the woven end of the yarn close to the knitted piece. Now you have woven in the blue yarn along the blue stitches.

Step 6. Next, weave in the pink yarn along the adjacent pink stitches. Of course, if all your yarn is the same colour, you will just choose the row nearest the cut end of the yarn to weave into.

Step 7. This is the back of your knitting: wrong side = ws

Your work now has a lovely professional finish!

The ends of yarn at the cast-on and cast-off edges should also be woven into your work. If you don't do this (especially at the cast-off edge), your work will eventually unravel and this is not only disheartening, but also difficult to fix and extremely messy!

How to Purl

Purl is the second stitch you need to learn. In a knitting pattern, purl is abbreviated to P. So 'P1' means 'purl one stitch.' And 'P1 row' means 'purl one row.'

The first thing to note is this: when you knit, the yarn is held to the back of the work, and when you purl, the yarn is held to the front.

Purl with yarn at front

Knit with yarn at back

Step 1. Pick it up. Insert the tip of the right needle into the stitch on the left needle – from top to the bottom. Keep needles crossed over right over left. Your yarn should be at the front of the work.

Step 2. Middle and then front. Holding both the needles in your left hand (between thumb and first two fingers), wrap the long end of the yarn through the middle of the needles and then to the front of the needles.

Step 3. Underneath and to the back.

Take the tip of the right hand needle under the first loop on the left needle and to the back of the left needle.

Step 4. Release. Gently push the stitch on the left needle off, using your left thumb.

Repeat these moves all the way to the end of the stitches on the left needle so that you have purled all the stitches onto the right needle. Then swap the needles in your hands so that the stitches are once again in your left hand and the empty needle is in your right hand – ready for the next row.

Questions & Answers

What happens if I purl every row?
Your work will look the same as if you knit every row (garter stitch), but will take a bit longer as most people are slower at purling than knitting. I've never come across a pattern that instructs the knitter to purl every row.

Stocking Stitch

If you purl one row, then knit the next row, then keep swapping the rows between knit and purl, the pattern you create is called stocking stitch.

This stitch is not double-sided; it has a right side (rs) and a wrong side (ws). The right side is the side you knitted and the wrong side is the side you purled.

Because both sides are different, the work will curl up at all ends (as you can see in the photo below). This makes it unsuitable for scarves as they will curl up into tubes. Of course, there is always the chance that you might actually want to make a tubey-scarf, in which case you should get splendid results with stocking stitch.

Knit and purl stitches are the basis of all knitting. Now you know how to knit and purl, we will move onto using different combinations of these stitches to create all sorts of wonderful patterns later in the book.

Stocking stitch. Rowan Big Wool and 15mm needles used in this picture

Questions & Answers

I'm using stocking stitch and I've forgotten which stitch I'm supposed to do for the next row.

The best way to do this is to keep a note of your rows on a piece of paper as you are working. If you haven't been doing this, there is a simple way to work out which row to work next. Hold the needles in your hands as if were about to start your row. The knitting will be in your left hand and the empty needle in your right hand. Look at the side of the work that is facing you. You should be using the same stitch as that facing you, e.g. if the knit side of the work is facing you: knit. If the purl side is facing you: purl. Now for a little memory trick: the purl side looks like waves. This reminds me of the ocean… where you find pearls (purl stitch). The knit side looks like, well, knitting.

Mistakes

This is a very difficult section to write, because every mistake is different. If I delved too deeply into all the potential knitting mistakes you might make there would be no room in this book for any patterns!

Remember that you are making something lovingly by hand – you are not a machine – so mistakes happen. Learn to embrace your mistakes as part of making something original and individual. Also, just realising that you have made a mistake is half the battle already won. So, I am going to concentrate just on a few of the mistakes that crop up most frequently in my knitting classes.

Firstly, you must always follow Rule Number One: count your stitches at the end of every row. If you are doing this, you will immediately know if you have the right number of stitches, too many, or too few.

Too many stitches

Most beginners end up with too many stitches. The official remedy is to 'frog' your knitting; this is the term used for undoing your work and starting again. However, this can be disheartening for a beginner and I think it is not always necessary when a sneaky little move can put you back on track! I hardly ever recommend 'frogging' to a beginner, as most beginners' mistakes won't happen once you are more used to knitting.

The last stitch looks as if it hasn't been knitted

That's because it hasn't. You can see that the yarn is engaged in the last but one stitch, but not the last stitch.

To fix this, hold the work in your hands so the stitches are all on your right needle and then pass the last (un-knitted) stitch back onto the left needle (without doing anything else to it).

Then treat that stitch as the last stitch on your row and knit it as normal. You will now notice that the yarn is engaged correctly on the last stitch.

One extra stitch at the beginning (at the beginning of the row)

A mistake that beginners often make is holding the yarn in the wrong place at the beginning of a row.

On this piece of knitting, there are eleven stitches when there should be ten. This is because the yarn is in the wrong place. All that you need to do is bring the yarn over the knitting needle to the front of the work and the extra stitch will disappear.

This mistake happens because of the baggy loop at the beginning of the row. Beginners' questions often feature this baggy loop – I don't know why it's there! But if you notice, it disappears in your knitting. It will only ever appear on the row you are currently working on. So don't worry about it, just ignore it – it's quite happy where it is!

CONTINUE...

Too many stitches
(in the middle of the row)

If you have too many stitches, it will probably be because you haven't been following the steps to knit each stitch precisely enough. You will notice that two of the stitches look as if they are crossed over.

Crossed over stitches and one extra stitch when counting.

Knit the next row until you get to the mistake. Then pick up and knit these crossed-over stitches together as if they were one. This will turn the two stitches into one, thus correcting the extra stitch.

How did I make that 'cross over' mistake?

✕

You created this mistake simply by losing a little concentration when knitting and not picking up the stitch precisely – remember that knitting in front of the telly is a joy still to come for now!

✓

Instead of picking up the stitch (you are about to knit) cleanly and precisely, you picked up the loop under the stitch by mistake. This isn't a huge mistake, but one that can be avoided with a little more concentration. With experience, you will notice the minute you do it; eventually you will just stop doing it altogether.

So that covers extra stitches – but beginners worry more about the infamous 'dropped stitch'. This can happen easily if you aren't working towards the fat part of the needle or if you aren't gentle when releasing your last stitch. Left to their own devices, dropped stitches would form a ladder like a snagged stocking, but they can be picked up with a little dexterity and a crochet hook and coerced back into line with the others.

Garter stitch dropped stitch

Step 1. So you've dropped a stitch and it's laddering. Don't panic, just try to fix this as soon as you notice it.

Step 2. Insert your crochet hook into the dropped stitch and keep the ladder to the front of the dropped stitch.

Step 3a. Hook the crochet hook onto the ladder and pull it through the dropped stitch.

Step 3b. That ladder then becomes the dropped stitch.

Step 4. Keep 'climbing the ladder' through each dropped stitch until you get back to the current row of knitting. Then put the final dropped stitch onto the left hand knitting needle and keep knitting the row.

Stocking stitch dropped stitch

Step 1. I find it easiest to fix a dropped stitch on a stocking stitch piece of knitting with the right side of the work facing me.

Step 2. Insert the crochet hook into the dropped stitch – with stocking stitch keep the ladder behind the dropped stitch.

Step 3. Hook the crochet hook onto the ladder behind the dropped stitch and pull it through to the front of the dropped stitch.

Step 4. Keep 'climbing the ladder' through each dropped stitch until you get back to the current row of knitting. Then put the final dropped stitch onto the left hand knitting needle and keep knitting the row.

These are not, by any means, all the mistakes it is possible to make in knitting – almost every knitter will invent a new mistake all of their very own. However, these are the mistakes that I see most commonly with beginner students, and learning how to fix them will give you a better understanding of knitting and make you a more accomplished knitter later on. If all else fails and you just can't fix your knitting, simply ask for help. There's always a more experienced knitter around every corner.

Handy HINT

One of my beginner students has a memorable way of dealing with imperfections in her knitting. She simply sews a decorative button or sequin over the offending blemish. As a result, her knitting is always beautifully unique and quirky with no mistakes in sight!

Chunky Scarf

Now it's time to start getting excited – you are about to knit your first garment. Knitting a scarf is the first project most knitters take on; I hope it will be the start of a long and enjoyable journey into knitting for you.

This first project will be quick and easy to knit. It will give you essential practice in making the basic 'knit' stitch. The important thing is not to worry too much about how it looks or any unevenness in your stitches or cast on/off. It's just important for you to know that you can start making something immediately with your newfound skills, and that you are learning so much more with each stitch. Don't forget the pleasure you will get from telling people you made it yourself!

Bulky yarn and big needles mean that your first project will be knitted up and ready to wear in no time

Chunky scarves are not just for grown-ups – this is Wendy 'Fusion', an aran-weight yarn that changes colour by itself and knits up on 6mm needles

Colinette's 'Point 5' yarn changes colour and thickness every few centimetres – a very hard-working yarn

Rule Number Three

Try to knit at least two rows once a day. This should fit into the busiest of schedules; the benefit being that you get some practice every day. For beginners this will mean that you remember how to knit quicker and easier than if you don't pick up your knitting for weeks at a time.

Choosing yarn and needles

I haven't given a specific yarn for you to use for your scarf, as I want you to be able to have a look around the yarn shops, learn about what's available and make your first design decision! I always recommend that beginners choose a thicker yarn and big fat knitting needles so that their first project grows quickly and is finished in good time for added satisfaction. This will help you feel positive about beginning your second project.

For the beginner's scarf, it's best to use only garter stitch. This does not mean that the scarf has to look dull – far from it. There are so many exciting yarns available these days that you can really 'make the yarn work for you'.

Two pairs of hands make yarn winding easier

Winding yarn

Most yarns come already wound into neat balls (or skeins) that you can use immediately. However, more and more yarns these days come in hanks that need to be wound into balls before knitting – if you don't do this you will end up in an awful tangle. The reason it comes in hanks is that this is how it is usually dyed (particularly hand-dyed yarn), and many yarns look more attractive displayed in hanks rather than balls. Beginners often find it a bit tricky to wind the yarn from hanks into usable balls. Some tips I can offer you are:

• Make sure you have an extra pair of hands to hold the yarn;

• Try to wind the yarn into an even ball by turning the ball as you create it;

• If you really have trouble making a ball, get a tennis ball and wrap the yarn around it, making sure you cover the tennis ball evenly – this is the best method for slippery silk yarns;

• Persevere – knitting with balls will be infinitely easier than trying to knit from a hank.

Knitter's Notes

Reading a yarn label:
The yarn label will tell you what size needles to use. For this project, this is a good indication of what is suitable – I suggest nothing that uses needles smaller than 6mm. The yarn label will also give the weight of your yarn, washing instructions, and how much yarn is in the ball.

Remember:

Aran, chunky, super bulky, or 'big' yarns will work best. Useful names are: Rowan 'Big Wool', Sirdar 'Bigga', Debbie Bliss 'Cashmerino Super Chunky' and Colinette 'Point 5'. Once you take a look at these, you'll start to get the idea and can work within your price range to choose a yarn for your first project.

Shop around – there are some beautiful organic and hand-dyed yarns available. And it's not all 'wool' – look out for silk, cotton, alpaca, and more.

Don't choose anything too fine or fluffy. The pretty ribbon and mohair yarns might be tempting, but it's impossible to see the stitches and to undo mistakes. Save these yarns until you have more experience with knitting!

Two or three balls of yarn should be enough for your scarf, depending, of course, on how long you want it to be. It's always better to buy more rather than less; you can always return the unused ball, donate it to someone else or, better still, save it in your 'stash' for future projects.

START KNITTING

1. Cast on the number of stitches required. Remember the general rule that the width of your knitting will grow by 50% between the cast-on row and the first knitted row. It is completely up to you how wide your scarf is. My only suggestion is that if you knit a few rows and you find your scarf is too wide or narrow, start again. I want you to be happy with your first project. And if you've chosen according to my instructions, your yarn should be thick enough to knit up so quickly that starting again will hardly slow you down at all!

2. Garter stitch (knit every row) until scarf measures long enough to keep you warm.

3. Cast off loosely. Weave in all your ends.

Wear with pride or give as a thoughtful gift.

Finishing options

Tassels

You have finished your scarf – now it's time for tassels. These are an easy way to apply a fun and funky finish to your scarf; and if, as a beginner, you aren't happy with your cast-on and cast-off edges, it's a sneaky way of hiding them until you've had a bit more practice!

Also:

- Vary your yarn.

- Experiment with needle sizes. If you use a much bigger needle than recommended with your yarn, your knitting will have an open lacy weave.

- Add tassels.

- Knit in some stripes. Add these in the same way you would add a new ball of yarn.

- Weave some ribbon through your finished knitting with a darning needle for a pretty touch.

- Add pom-poms to the ends.

Making tassels

1 Cut lengths of yarn twice as long as the length you want your finished tassels to be.

2 Fold the cut tassel yarn in half. Insert a crochet hook into the edge of your scarf, hook it onto the folded end of the tassel yarn, and pull the folded end through the edge of the scarf.

3 Then take the two ends of the tassel yarn, fold them over and bring them through the loop you just hooked through the scarf. Pull tight and there's your tassel.

Keep going along the cast-on and cast-off edges of your scarf.

Decreasing Workshop

The most basic way to decrease is by picking up two stitches and knitting them together. As you knit them, they become one stitch. When you count your stitches at the end of the row, you will have one fewer than you started with. The abbreviation for this is K2tog, also known as knit two stitches together. What you are doing is turning two stitches into one stitch.

As with everything, there are several ways to decrease. This is the simplest way.

K2tog = Knit two stitches together

When you pick up the stitch to knit or purl it, instead of putting the tip of the right hand needle into just one stitch, insert it into the first and second stitch at the same time. Then complete the stitch as normal. You will immediately see that you have only one stitch transferred onto the right hand needle.

Remember: you won't always be asked to decrease at the beginning of a row. You can decrease in the same way in the middle, or at the end of a row.

You can practise decreasing with Project 3: Hats

Sewing-up Workshop

I always find sewing up my work the least fun part of knitting. After all, if I'd wanted to sew, I'd be learning to sew!

But learning to sew up your knitting is necessary for most things you'll want to make, and learning to do it correctly can be the difference between a professional piece of knitting and something less beautiful.

That said, don't worry if it doesn't look great immediately; like knitting, sewing takes practice. So here's how to do it.

Methods for sewing up knitting are different depending on the stitch you knitted with. Here you will learn three techniques: backstitch, garter mattress and stocking stitch mattress. If you are sewing up a piece that incorporates two different knitting stitches, or something that you are not sure of, use backstitch. If both your pieces are knitted in garter or stocking stitch, then use the appropriate mattress stitch.

You will need a yarn/darning needle – this is like a normal sewing needle, but thicker and with a blunt point and a large hole so that the yarn will slip through it easily. When sewing up, you will use this darning needle and a matching yarn. I've used a contrasting colour yarn in my images so you can clearly see just how I have done it.

Backstitch

Backstitch is the easiest sewing-up stitch, and you should pick this one if you are in any doubt about which stitch to use.

This is one of the strongest stitches and also gives a neat finish with the least amount of hassle.

Start with the work laid out inside-out (right sides together). After sewing, you will turn it right-side out and not be able to see your stitches.

Secure the yarn at the beginning of the section to be sewed. This can be done in the same way you would weave in the ends (see Weaving in ends on page 24).

Then remember: One step back, two steps forward.

The stitch starts from point 1. Push the needle down into the work one step back and bring the needle back to the front moving two steps forward.

When you have sewn all the way to the end, weave in your ends and turn the work right-side out.

Backstitch

①

Stocking Mattress Stitch

This stitch will give you an invisible finish if both the pieces you are trying to sew are knitted in stocking stitch (knit one row, purl one row). It can also be used if you are sewing up knitting using a 'rib' stitch.

Start with the right side of the work facing you.

Step 1. Anchor the sewing yarn to your knitting by stitching up through one piece and down through the other. You can weave the ends in later.

Step 2. In between each column of stitches on the right side of your work, there is a horizontal 'bar.' You'll have to dig right in between the columns to find it. Insert your needle up the 'bar.'

Step 3. Then find the bar directly across from the first bar, on the other piece of knitting. Insert the darning needle up this bar.

Step 4. Keep working in this way on every stitch on each side of the piece you are sewing up. After you've sewn up a few bars, pull tightly on both ends of the sewing yarn.

Step 5. Your sewing yarn should virtually disappear.

Step 6. When you have sewn the entire piece (pulling the yarn tight as you go), turn your work to the wrong side and weave in your ends.

CONTINUE...

Garter Mattress Stitch

This stitch will give you an invisible finish if both the pieces you are trying to knit are knitted in garter stitch (knit every row). It can also be used if you are sewing up 'moss' or 'seed' stitch knitted pieces.

Start with the right side of the work facing you.

Step 1. Anchor the sewing yarn to your knitting by stitching up on the first piece and down through the next. You can weave the ends in later.

Step 2. You will notice that garter stitch is made up of 'ridges'. As you look at the image, there is a bottom ridge and a top ridge. We will be climbing these ridges like a ladder. Insert the darning needle up the bottom ridge.

Step 3. Then insert the darning needle up the top ridge on the other piece of knitting.

Step 4. Keep 'climbing' up your work using first the bottom ridge and then the top ridge.

Step 5. After a few stitches have been made, pull tight on both ends of the sewing yarn. Your sewing yarn should virtually disappear.

When you've sewn the entire seam, weave in your ends to the back of your work.

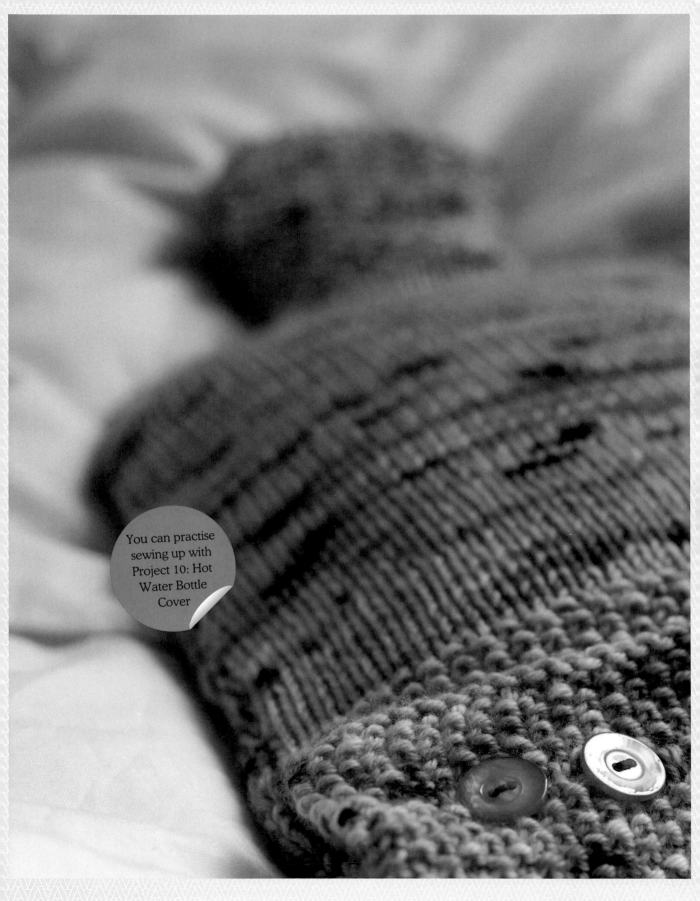

You can practise sewing up with Project 10: Hot Water Bottle Cover

Baby Booties

This is a brilliant second project as it is a good step up from a scarf, but still very simple and quick to finish. Also, who doesn't know someone about to have a baby? The perfect personalised gift!

This is a garter stitch bootie – this means that the stitch used is 'knit' for every row. There is no purl in this pattern.

As this is your first project using a pattern, I have broken it down fully so that you'll have images and help for each stage of the knitting. As you progress through the book, you'll learn more and more so that you'll need less help each time.

Overleaf are instructions written as they would be for a standard knitting pattern. Then I've broken the pattern down using images so you'll know what your knitting should look like at each stage.

YOU WILL NEED

50G DOUBLE-KNIT YARN
I suggest you choose one of the many specialist baby yarns available – Rowan 'Soft Baby' or Debbie Bliss 'Baby Cashmerino'

5MM KNITTING NEEDLES
For a smaller bootie, try using 4mm needles

DARNING NEEDLE
To sew up the bootie

Choosing Yarn

A standard double-knit (DK) weight of yarn is used for this pattern, together with a needle one size bigger than normally used so that the booties are stretchy enough to fit various sizes of baby feet. The needle size should also help you avoid that typical beginners' problem: tight tension.

When choosing yarn, the assistants in the yarn store will help if you want them to; bear in mind that you are knitting for a baby, and choose your yarn accordingly. There are many lanolin-free, organic or cotton yarns available these days, and these are good options if you are worried about allergies. Don't get anything too hot or scratchy – baby skin is very soft. Also, as pretty as they are, it's best to stay away from any yarn too fluffy or with bits or bobbles on it.

Remember Rule Number One

Count your stitches at the end of every row. This is very important to ensure that you are decreasing correctly, and that you end up with identical booties.

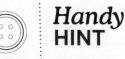

Handy HINT

If you tick off the rows as you knit them, you are more likely to get two booties the same size.

HERE IS THE KNITTING PATTERN

ABBREVIATIONS:

K = Knit

K2tog = Knit two stitches together

St(s) = Stitch(es)

START KNITTING

1 Cast on 38 sts

2 Knit 12 rows

You will now start decreasing:

3 Row 13: K16, K2tog, K2, K2tog, K16.

Count 36 sts.

Row 14: K15, K2tog, K2, K2tog, K15.

Count 34 sts.

Row 15: K14, K2tog, K2, K2tog, K14.

Count 32 sts.

Row 16: K13, K2tog, K2, K2tog, K13.

Count 30 sts.

Row 17: K12, K2tog, K2, K2tog, K12.

Count 28 sts.

Row 18: K11, K2tog, K2, K2tog, K11.

Count 26 sts.

Row 19: K10, K2tog, K2, K2tog, K10. Count 24 sts.

4 Rows 20-27: Knit these next 8 rows.

5 Cast off loosely leaving a long end for sewing up (about 50cm).

6 To finish the bootie, fold it in half and sew up using the long cast-off end of yarn.

HERE IS THE PATTERN WITH PICTURES FOR EACH STAGE

START KNITTING

1

Cast on 38 sts

2

Knit 12 rows

3

Start decreasing

3a

When you have finished the decreasing rows, your bootie should start to take shape

4

Then knit 8 rows

5

Cast off loosely leaving a long end for sewing up (about 50cm)

6a

Hold the bootie right-side out, so that the plait ridge of your cast-off edge is on the inside

6b

Sew from the top of the bootie to the heel using garter mattress stitch

6c

When you get to the heel, turn the bootie inside out – so that the plait cast-off edge is on the outside

6d

Then sew up the bottom of the bootie using backstitch

Weave in all your ends into the inside of the bootie.

Turn the bootie right-side out, then knit another the same!

Handy HINT

If your cast off is too tight, the bootie will be hard to put on the baby's foot. To make your cast off looser, try using a knitting needle 1mm bigger than you used in the rest of your knitting. (See Casting off section, page 21.)

Questions & Answers

My bootie ended up enormous! What happened?
Some beginners knit very tightly and some knit very loosely. This means that your booties might turn out too big or too small or even different sizes each time. Knitting two the same comes with practice, but if your booties are too big, try making another using a 4mm knitting needle rather than the 5mm needle I've suggested.

Variation on the original bootie

The bootie on the left was knitted with 4mm knitting needles and the one on the right with 5mm needles. That is a demonstration of gauge – using different needles will alter the final piece of knitting you make: Bigger needles = bigger knitting. Smaller needles = smaller knitting.

Both my booties are different sizes! What have I done wrong?
Nothing – this is just an example of your beginner's tension acting up. You can't expect to always knit evenly when you are a beginner – so don't worry if you have to knit three or more booties until you get two that match. And if you really have trouble, remember that babies won't complain too much!

Finishing options

These booties are very simple, but you can also add some variation to the last eight rows of the pattern if you want to. Here are just a few finishing options:

Run some ribbon through with a darning needle and tie it in a bow

Instead of just plain garter stitch, try stocking stitch for a pretty rolled edge

1 x 1 rib the last eight rows – see stitch patterns (page 48)

Knit more than 8 rows for a 'boot' look.

Stitch Patterns Workshop

Now that you know how to knit and purl, you can start using these two stitches in different combinations to create all sorts of new patterns.

The most important thing to remember with stitch patterns is that when you knit, you hold the yarn to the back of the work, and when you purl, you hold the yarn to the front of the work.

If you are knitting and purling in the same row, you must move the yarn to the front and back between each knit and purl stitch. If you knit or purl with the yarn in the wrong place, the correct pattern won't appear in your work, and you'll end up with an extra twisted stitch. This will make more sense in practice, so let's move onto the most basic of stitch combinations.

Knit with yarn at back

Purl with yarn at front

Handy HINT

Remember Rule Number One. Counting your stitches when working stitch patterns is essential and will ensure that your pattern stays accurate.

1 x 1 rib

'1 x 1 rib' means that you will be knitting one stitch, then purling one stitch, and repeating the K1, P1 sequence to the end of a row.

Begin with an even number of stitches. You will always start with a knit stitch and end with a purl stitch.

Step 1. Knit one stitch.
Step 2. Bring the yarn towards you to the front of the work, over the top, and through the middle of the needles. YF = Yarn Forward.

Step 3. Purl one stitch. The yarn will automatically be at the front after you purl a stitch.

Step 4. YB = Yarn Back. Pass the yarn to the back of the work, going over and in between the knitting needles.

Repeat steps 1, 2, 3 and 4 to the end of the row: knit one, yarn forward, purl one, yarn back, repeat from the beginning to the end of the row.

When this is written in a knitting pattern, the movement of the yarn forward and back between knit and purl stitches is taken as read, and won't be written in (unless it is in the pattern for a reason – see Eyelet Buttonholes on page 64).

The pattern would be written: K1, P1 rib, repeat to end.

This is what you should expect to see as you knit a 1 x 1 rib stitch. When stretched out, you can see the columns of knit and purl stitches. When the work is allowed to relax, the purl stitches disappear, and you can only see the knit stitches.

1 x 1 rib.
To knit a practice square:
Cast on 20 stitches.
K1, P1 rib, repeat to end. Repeat this row until you have a practice square.

Questions & Answers

Help! I'm in the middle of a row and I've forgotten whether I should be knitting or purling!
This happens. All it takes is a momentary lapse of concentration. Look at the stitches you have already done on your right hand needle. Remember that the first stitch you knitted was a knit stitch, then count up the needle: knit one, purl one, knit one, purl one… oh yes…the next stitch is a knit stitch. Is my yarn at the back? Yes it is. Now keep going.

CONTINUE...

Stitch patterns *continued...*

Stitch patterns *continued...*

Handy HINT

Look closely at your stitches, just where they meet the knitting needle. The purls and knits look different to one another. If you imagine them to be little people, the purls look like they are wearing little polo (turtle) neck sweaters (⌐), and the knits look like they are wearing a 'V'-neck sweater. This is a great little trick to remind you where you are.

Questions & Answers

When will I need to use this stitch?
A rib stitch knits into a narrower and stretchier piece of knitting than garter or stocking stitch. It is often used for the collars and cuffs of knitted garments. Have a look at any sweaters you own – even on machine knitting, you will probably notice that the edges are knitted using a rib stitch.

Now you understand that a knit stitch is made with the yarn held to the back of your work and a purl stitch is made with the yarn held to the front, you can use the stitches in all sorts of beautiful and interesting combinations. Try this one to test your newfound skills.

Now try 2 x 2 rib

To knit a practice square:

Cast on a multiple of four stitches. 20 is a good number for a practice square.

K2, P2 rib, repeat to end.

Moss Stitch

Cast on an odd number of stitches.
K1, P1, repeat to end.

If you start with an odd number of stitches, you will start and end with a knit stitch and your work will appear as one of my favourite stitches – moss (or seed as it's sometimes known) stitch.

Stitch Patterns: Casting Off

If you have been knitting using a stitch pattern, for example, 1 x 1 rib, you must keep working this stitch pattern when you are casting off.

For 1 x 1 rib, this would mean:
K1, P1, cast off, K1, cast off, P1, cast off... and so on, remembering to move the yarn back and forward depending on whether you are knitting or purling the next stitch.

You will find more stitch patterns later in the book.

Knit Hats

After you've knitted a scarf, you will naturally start thinking of hats.

Baby hat with simple flower. See page 74 for flower instructions

Children's and adults' hats

Adult hat is suitable for either a man or woman

This pattern is for a double-knit yarn (perhaps in a yarn to match or complement your scarf). This pattern is for a garter stitch hat with a 1 x 1 rib border, and you have three size options: baby, child and adult. The size of the final hat will depend on your knitting tension, but the patterns below cover the main sizes you might want to knit.

You will have a chance to use your new skills in stitch combinations and decreasing, and also a 'drawstring' finish which is useful for several other patterns in this book (and a pretty nifty way of finishing work as an alternative to casting off).

YOU WILL NEED

DOUBLE-KNIT YARN:
50G FOR BABY AND CHILD SIZES, 100G FOR ADULT HAT
(I have awful childhood memories of itchy hats – I always remember that when knitting a hat now. Rowan 'Pure Wool DK' or Debbie Bliss 'Cashmerino DK' are both warm and soft.)

5MM KNITTING NEEDLES

DARNING NEEDLE

Sizes

This pattern is an additional challenge in that it is written for three different sizes. This is one of the things that beginners can find confusing about knitting patterns, as it means that there is a lot of additional information included for sizes of garments that you don't need. If you have ever done any sewing from sized patterns you may be familiar with this problem.

As this pattern is for three different sizes, there will always be three sets of numbers. The first is for baby size, then child size, then adult size. The first size is written first, with the second two sizes following in brackets: Baby, (Child, Adult).

For example: K10 sts, (12 sts, 0 sts).

Translation:
• for the baby size you knit 10 stitches;
• for the child size you knit 12 stitches; and
• for the adult size you knit no stitches at all.

For consistency, even if no stitches have to be knitted, all three sets of instructions are shown. The pattern will also tell you how many stitches to count at the end of a decrease row.

Before you start knitting...

Use a pencil to lightly circle all the numbers that you will need for the particular size of hat you are making. This way you can simply ignore all the additional information.

ABBREVIATIONS:

K = Knit

K2tog = Knit two stitches together

St(s) = Stitch(es)

Rep = Repeat

1 x 1 Rib = Knit one stitch, purl one stitch

(K1, K2tog) = when a sequence of stitches is bracketed, you have to repeat the entire bracketed section as many times as is written next to the bracketed section. For example: (K1, K2tog) 3 times = K1, K2tog, K1, K2tog, K1, K2tog. You can see why abbreviations are necessary in knitting patterns!

START KNITTING

Cast on 80 sts, (84 sts, 90 sts)
TRANSLATION: 80 sts for baby hat, 84 sts for child hat or 90 sts for adult hat.

1   1 x 1 rib border – Same for all 3 hat sizes:

K1, P1 rib, repeat to end. Repeat this rib row a total of 8 times. Keeping a tally of rows will help you with this.

2   Garter stitch (knit every row) until piece measures 13cm (15cm, 18cm) from beginning.

Start decreasing:

1st Decrease:

(K1, K2tog) rep 26 times, (28 times, 30 times). K2 (K0, K0). Count 54 sts (56, 60).
TRANSLATION: (Knit 1 st, Knit 2 sts together), repeat the bracketed section 26 times for baby, (28 times for child, 30 times for adult). K2 sts (0, 0) – this means that you don't have to knit any stitches for the child and adult sizes. Count 54 sts (56, 60).

K1 row – same for all three sizes.

2nd Decrease:

(K1, K2tog), rep 18 times, (18 times, 20 times). K0, (K2, K0). Count 36 sts, (38 sts, 40 sts).

K1 row – same for all three sizes.

3rd Decrease:

(K1, K2tog), rep 12 times, (12 times, 13 times). K0, (K2, K1). Count 24 sts, (26 sts, 27 sts).

K1 row – same for all three sizes.

4th Decrease:

(K1, K2tog), rep 8 times, (8 times, 9 times). K1, (K2, K0). Count 16 sts, (18 sts, 18 sts).

K1 row – same for all three sizes.

5th Decrease:

(K1, K2tog), rep 5 times, (6 times, 6 times). K1, (K0, K0). Count 11 sts, (12 sts, 12 sts).

K1 row – same for all three sizes.

6th Decrease:

(K1, K2tog), rep 3 times, (4 times, 4 times). K2, (K0, K0). Count 8 sts, (8 sts, 8 sts).

K1 row – same for all three sizes.

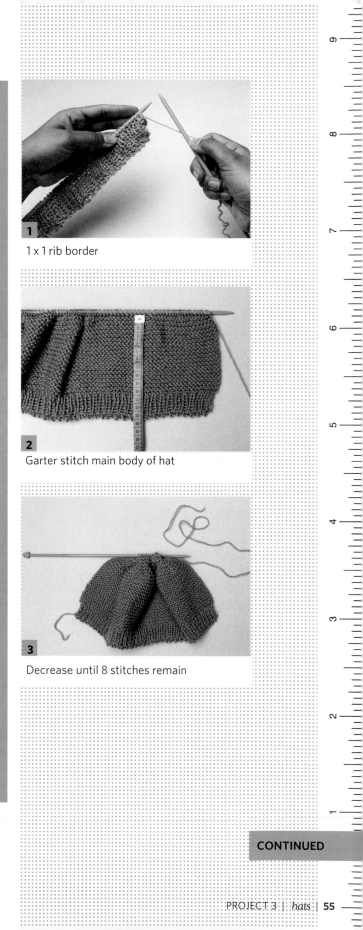

1 1 x 1 rib border

2 Garter stitch main body of hat

3 Decrease until 8 stitches remain

CONTINUED

Drawstring finish (this is the same for all three hat sizes)

When you have finished your decreasing, cut the yarn leaving a long end. This end should measure 50-70cm, depending on which size hat you are making. Pay attention to this method; it will be used again later!

Pom-poms! Pom-poms are a fun addition to hats, scarves, booties and all sorts of knitted work. Most people remember making them at school; here's a quick refresher course.

1 Thread the cut end of the yarn onto a darning needle. Insert the darning needle into the stitches on the knitting needle.

2 Pass the darning needle through the stitches remaining on the knitting needle, one by one, removing them from the knitting needle as they are secured by the yarn on the darning needle.

YOU WILL NEED

CARDBOARD
(from a cereal packet – or any of a similar weight you might have lying around)

. . . .

SCISSORS

. . . .

YARN

. . . .

DARNING NEEDLE
(you can manage without a needle, but it will make the process quicker and easier)

3 Pull the yarn tight.

4 Your piece of knitting should now naturally fall into a hat shape.

5 Sew it up using garter mattress stitch on the main body of the hat, and stocking mattress stitch on the border of the hat.

(See the Sewing-up Workshop on page 38.) There is no right or wrong side to your hat before you start sewing it up, as the rib and garter stitches you've used are both double-sided and there is no cast-off edge.

When you've finished sewing up the hat, weave the ends of the yarn into the inside of the hat.

1 Cut two pieces of cardboard in a circle shape, with a smaller concentric hole cut out of the middle of both pieces. (The size of your pom-pom will depend on the dimensions of the cardboard circles.) Thread a long piece of yarn onto your darning needle.

2 Hold both cardboard circles together and start wrapping them in yarn – using the yarn on the darning needle will make this a bit easier. You'll have to keep re-threading your needle as making a pom-pom takes quite a bit of yarn.

3 Keep wrapping the yarn around the cardboard until the circle of card is completely covered. The more yarn you wrap, the fuller your pom-pom will be.

4 Push the wrapped yarn apart and insert your scissors in between the two circles of cardboard.

5 Start cutting the yarn, keeping your scissors inserted into the gap between the cardboard circles as a guide. This can be fiddly, with a risk of the cut pieces falling off through the hole – I find that laying the work flat on a table and supporting it with your other hand helps.

6 When you've cut all around the circle, slightly separate the cardboard pieces and slide a long piece of yarn into the space and then all the way around the circle.

7 Ease the cardboard circles apart, and tie the long piece of yarn into a tight knot around the 'waist' of the cut pieces.

8 Take the cardboard circles off the wrapped and cut yarn, pull really tight and tie a really, really tight knot so that none of the cut pieces escape your pom-pom.

Increasing Workshop

You have learned how to decrease; now you will learn how to increase. This is a very useful method for creating all sorts of shapes in your work.

As mentioned in previous chapters, there will be more than one way to increase – what I will teach you here is called a 'bar' increase. This is because you will be picking up what looks like a horizontal bar between the stitches. I call it the 'soup and scoop' method – you'll see why in a moment.

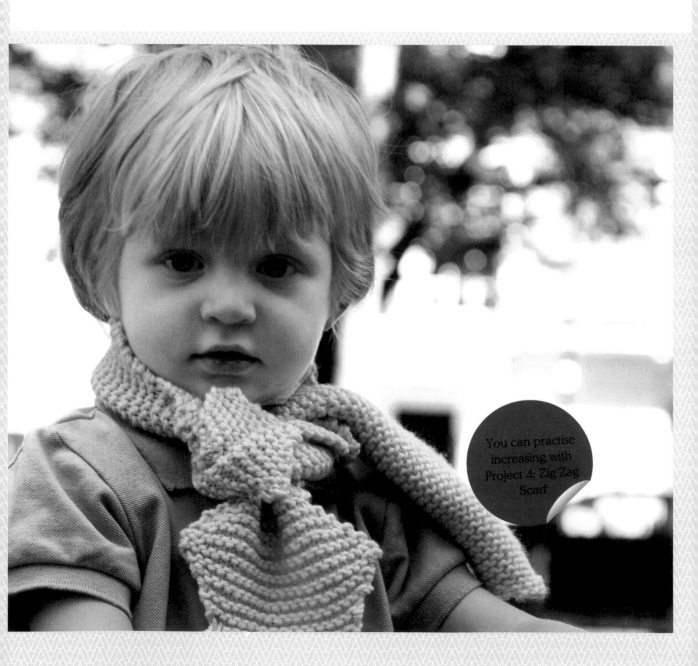

You can practise increasing with Project 4; Zig Zag Scarf

Increasing

In a knitting pattern, when you are asked to increase a stitch, you will read: 'M1'. This abbreviation means 'make one stitch'. The following instructions show how to 'M1' at the beginning of a row; when you have to M1 at the end of a row, you make the stitch just before the last stitch on the row. When you increase in the middle of a row, the pattern will tell you how many stitches to knit before you M1.

Step 1. Knit one stitch.

Step 2. Hold the needles apart and pull down on the work with the thumb and finger of your right hand. You will see a shape that resembles a bowl (of soup).

Step 3. Imagine the tip of the left hand needle to be a spoon. Scoop up the horizontal line of yarn (the soup) from the back to the front (towards your mouth – it is soup after all).

Step 4. Then knit that loop on the left hand needle as if it was a regular stitch. When you count your stitches at the end of this row, you will have one extra.

Handy HINT

When you try to knit the picked up loop, it will feel tight. Don't worry; this is exactly as it should feel. If it's really difficult to pick up and knit, try using your left index finger to 'roll' it towards you. This should loosen it enough to pick it up and knit it.

My 'soup and scoop' method may seem funny, but I find little memory tricks like this make knitting easier for a beginner, especially when you are learning so many new and interesting techniques all at once.

Questions & Answers

How do I increase in a purl row?

Exactly the same way. Remember 'soup and scoop'.

Zig-Zag Scarf

ABBREVIATIONS:

K = Knit

M1 = Make one stitch

St(s) = Stitch(es)

K2tog = Knit two stitches together

START KNITTING

Cast on 3 sts.

Knit 1 row.

1 K1, M1, K to end.

Count 4 sts.

2 Repeat this row until you have 25 sts.

MAIN PATTERN

K2tog, K to end of row. (Count one less stitch.)

Repeat this row until you have 15 sts.

K1, M1, K to end of row. (Count one more stitch.)

Repeat this row until you have 25 sts.

3 Repeat from Main Pattern until your scarf is about 80cm long (for child's size, or longer if it's for an adult).

FINISH ZIG-ZAG SCARF

To finish the scarf with a point (to match the beginning):

K2tog, K to end.

Repeat this row until you have one stitch left. Tie off (same as when you cast off).

Weave in all ends.

This is a twist on the simple scarf. It is an excellent way to practise your increasing and decreasing.

By the time you've finished this scarf, you'll never forget how to increase (M1) and decrease (K2tog).

Handy HINT

Rule Number One: Don't forget to count your stitches at the end of every row! It is very important to keep the pattern looking even in this scarf.

1 Finding the bowl of soup can be harder with so few stitches on your knitting needle, but persevere, it is there

2 Repeat this row until you have 25 sts. Remember that you will be counting one more stitch every row

3 Your scarf is now starting to take zig-zag shape

Finishing Workshop

It is awful to have spent ages knitting something and have it spoilt in the end because the finishing isn't quite right.

You've already learnt how to sew up your pieces of knitting; here are a couple of techniques to add those final touches that will really boost the look and feel of your knitted garments.

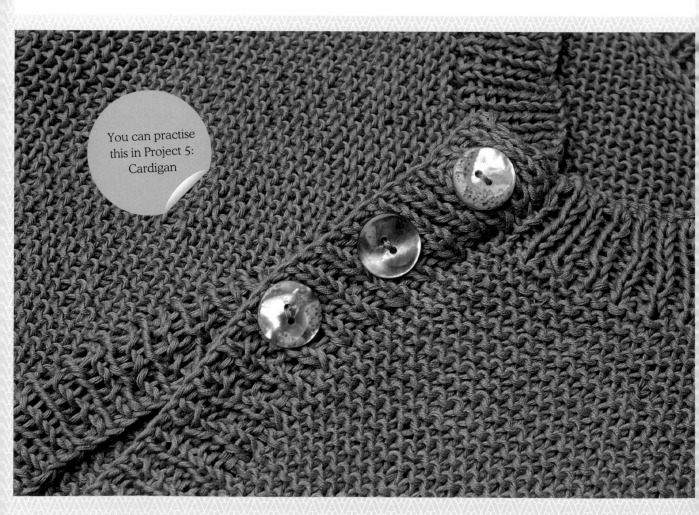

You can practise this in Project 5: Cardigan

Pick Up and Knit

Beginners often complain to me that the edges of their knitting don't look tidy. Pick-Up and Knit is a way of working a border onto your knitting to hide all untidy edges and give an instant professional finish. I love using it on my cardigans. Use 'pick up and knit' to add a rib border to your stocking stitch knitting – it is pretty much the only way I know to stop your stocking stitch from curling up.

You'll need a crochet hook to pick up the stitches – use a size close to that of your knitting needles.

Step 1. Lay out your work so that the knitting needle is facing towards the left, and the right side of the work is facing up. You will be picking up the stitches from the right to the left of your knitting (this seems backwards to how you would usually work), and not from left to right as you might imagine it to be done.

Step 2. Insert the crochet hook into the edge of the work, making sure it slides under two loops of yarn. Face the hooked head of the crochet hook away from you. (The loose end of the yarn at the beginning of this section will be woven in to the back of the work to secure it.)

Step 3. Wrap the yarn over the crochet hook going over and then under the hook, and use the crochet hook to pull that wrapped yarn through the same stitches you inserted the hook into. (Basically this means pulling out the crochet hook; it will bring the yarn with it in a loop.)

Step 4. Place the pulled-through loop of yarn onto the knitting needle.

Repeat this to the end of the pick-up section. Your knitting pattern will tell you how many stitches to pick up.

The pattern will then ask you to knit a border before casting off.

Questions & Answers

How far apart should I be picking up each stitch?

This is hard to explain, but it will come with experience. You roughly pick up one stitch per row of the work. You know how far apart each stitch should look on your knitting needle so remember not to pick up stitches too close or far apart from each other. You don't need to worry too much as this is one of those magic techniques that almost always ends up looking great. Also, patterns may tell you how many stitches to pick up.

Eyelet Buttonholes

Learning how to knit buttonholes into your work can seem daunting, but it's a nifty trick to have up your sleeve – and the method I'm using couldn't be simpler. It'll work if you want to add a small button; for bigger buttonholes there are different methods you can learn at a later date.

I've shown the buttonholes on a piece of knitting that has been made with Pick-up and Knit and a 1 x 1 Rib; this is just as you will do it in the Cardigan pattern, which is the next project.

Start your rib pattern. Then on a right side row, start your buttonholes.

Knit every stitch on your buttonhole row (even if you are working in rib – don't worry, it'll look right in the end) until you get to where you want your buttonhole to sit. Then follow the instructions below.

Step 1. Bring your yarn to the front of your work (YF) as if you were about to purl.

Step 2. Then, instead of purling, knit two stitches together (K2tog). Repeat these steps every time you want a buttonhole until the end of the row. At this stage, it's very important to count your stitches at the end of your row to ensure you have the same number as when you started the row, otherwise your rib stitch won't work.

Step 3. Then continue the rest of your rows in your 1 x 1 rib pattern. The eyelet buttonholes will appear in the next row. Remember to cast off in rib with the wrong side of the work facing you (see the Stitch Patterns Workshop on page 48).

This method of making buttonholes works in the same way on the knit side of stocking stitch and either side of garter stitch.

Knitter's Notes

Remember to count the same number of stitches between each buttonhole, otherwise the buttons will look wonky when the garment is fastened. Plan button-placement before you start knitting the row. Of course, most patterns will tell you how many stitches to count between rows, so you won't need to worry.

Knitting two stitches together with the yarn in the front instead of the back gives you the same number of stitches at the end of your row, and also leaves you with a decorative hole – also used as a buttonhole.

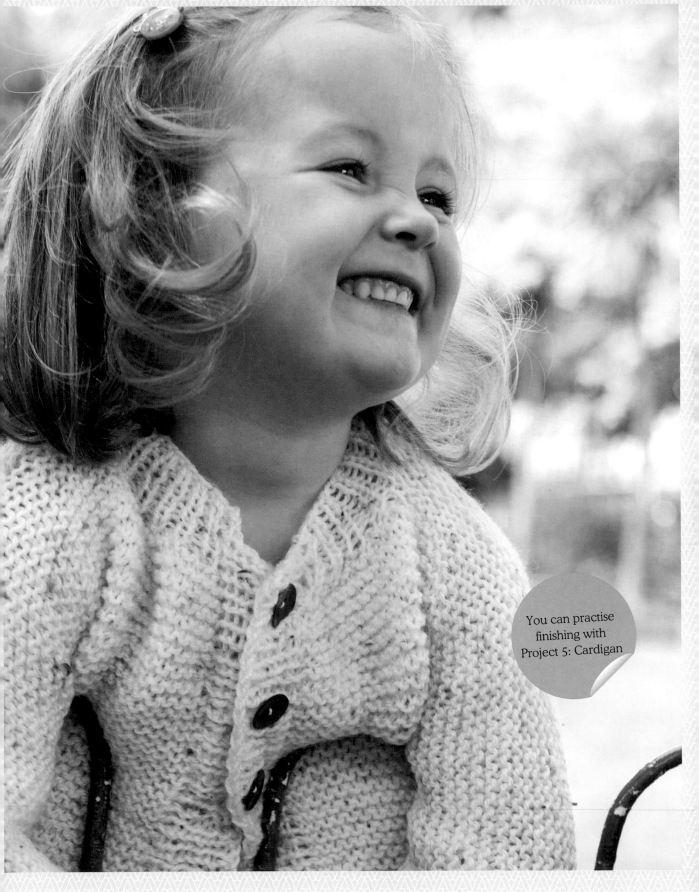

You can practise
finishing with
Project 5: Cardigan

Cardigan (for a baby or child)

This is a pattern for a little cardigan that knits in one piece and is finished using Pick Up and Knit to give it an ultra professional look. If you are sick of cutesy pastel colours, why not try knitting this in bright, stimulating colours or stripes. Then you can have some fun choosing funky buttons as well! Also, as it's knitted in one piece, there's much less sewing (which I find the least fun part of knitting).

Baby clothes need not be pastels!

Classic colours with funky buttons

This pattern includes instructions for two different sizes. Both sets of instructions are incorporated, so you have to remember whether you are knitting for a baby or a child, and follow the numbers accordingly. The numbers for the baby size will be written first, with the child size in brackets immediately after. It may be worth using a pencil to lightly circle all relevant numbers for the size you are knitting before you begin, so that it is clear which instructions you are following throughout.

Sizing: Baby = 3/6 months. Child = 2/3 years.
My sizes are approximate, as they will depend on your unpredictable beginner's tension. If in doubt, choose the bigger size – the child can always grow into it! Also, as you are using a bigger needle than is customary for double-knit yarn, your cardigan will be extra stretchy so it will be wearable by a growing child for longer. It is always better to go bigger with children's garments if you have any doubts at all about sizes.

Use the layout at the start of the pattern to help you get your bearings as you follow this pattern.

YOU WILL NEED

DOUBLE-KNIT YARN. 200G (250G)
(I like Sirdar 'Luxury Soft Cotton DK' which is machine washable – best for tiny sticky fingers. This is an extra long yarn so you need less than you would with most other double-knit yarns – but do shop around for cool yarns.)

5MM KNITTING NEEDLES

CROCHET HOOK FOR PICKING UP AND KNITTING

DARNING NEEDLE

3 SMALL (1CM) BUTTONS

PATTERN LAYOUT

This is the shape of the piece you are knitting. You will start knitting from the back. Then it folds in half along the dashed line. The cardigan sews together along the underarms and sides.

KEY TO DIAGRAM

Fold lines ....

START KNITTING

FOLD LINE

FINISH KNITTING

ABBREVIATIONS:

K =Knit

P = Purl

St(s) = Stitch(es)

M1 = Make one stitch

YF = Yarn forward: bring yarn to the front of work

1 x 1 rib = Knit one stitch, purl one stitch, repeat this sequence to the end of the row

K2tog = Knit two stitches together

START KNITTING

BEGIN WITH THE BACK

Cast on 50 sts (56 sts).

TRANSLATION: Cast on 50 sts for the baby cardigan and 56 sts for the child size cardigan.

1 K1, P1 rib for 8 rows (this is the same for both sizes). Keeping a tally of the rows as you have knitted them will help you with this.

2 Garter stitch (knit every row) until your knitting measures 18cm (23cm) from the beginning.

NOW START THE SLEEVE SECTION OF THE CARDIGAN

3 Turn (swap the needles around in your hands as if to work the next row) and cast on 24 sts (45 sts) using the first stitch on the left needle as if it was the slipknot. This is the first sleeve.

Count 74 sts (101 sts).

Knit across row. Turn and cast on 24 sts (45 sts) for the second sleeve.

4 Count 98 sts (146 sts).

Knit until piece measures 10cm (11cm) from last cast-on edge.

NOW YOU WILL START CREATING THE SPACE FOR THE NECK OPENING OF THE CARDIGAN

5 K 39 sts (58 sts). You will be ignoring these stitches for the time being. Cast off 20 sts (30 sts) for back of neck. (TRANSLATION: K1, K1, cast off the first knitted stitch, K1, cast off, and so on... Keep counting your casting off until you have 38 sts (57 sts) on the left needle and 1 st on the right needle.)

6 Knit the remaining 38 sts (57 sts) on the left needle.

1 1 x 1 rib border

2 This is the back of the cardigan

3 Cast on for sleeve

4 Now you have cast on for both sleeves

5 Knit 39 (58) sts, then cast off 20 (30) sts for back of neck

6 Keep casting off until you have 38 (57) stitches on the left needle and 1 stitch on the right needle (ignoring the first 39 (58) stitches). Knit the remaining 38 (57) stitches.

CONTINUED...

7 You will now be working on this side all the way to the end of the cardigan; then you will go back and work on the 39 sts (58 sts) on the other side, which you will ignore for now.

Knit the 39 sts (58 sts) for 4 rows (6 rows).

Now increase your stitches one at a time – always on the neck side of the cardigan:

K until 1 st remains. M1, K1. Count 40 sts (59 sts).

K1, M1, K to end. Count 41 sts (60 sts).

K until 1 st remains. M1, K1.

There are now 42 sts (61 sts). COUNT!

8 Turn (swap the needles around in your hands as if to work the next row) and cast on 9 sts (12 sts).

Count 51 sts (73 sts).

Knit until sleeve measures 20cm (23cm) from the start of the sleeve section (ending with the point of the needle facing the 'hand-hole' end of the work).

9 Cast off 23 sts (45 sts) (make sure you are casting these off on the sleeve side and not the body side of the cardigan). Knit to end of row.

10 Count 28 sts (this is the same for both sizes of the cardigan).

Knit these 28 sts until piece measures 15cm (20cm) (ending with the point of the needle facing the front opening).

K1, P1 rib for 8 rows.

11 Cast off in rib – remember that you've been working in rib, so you must cast off in rib. See Stitch Patterns (page 48). Always cast off with wrong side of the work facing you.

OTHER SIDE: LEFT

12 Join yarn to sts at neck end: pull the end of yarn from the ball underneath the first stitch on the knitting needle and tie it into a knot with itself. You can weave the end in later.

You will now be working on the 39 sts (58 sts) that you have been ignoring up to this point.

Knit across these 39 sts (58 sts) for 4 rows (6 rows).

K1, M1, knit to end. Count 40 sts (59 sts).

K to last st, M1, K1. Count 41 sts (60 sts).

K1, M1, knit to end.

There are now 42 sts (61 sts). Count!

Knit 1 row.

Turn (swap the needles around in your hands to work the next row).

7

You will now work on the first 39 (58) stitches to the end of the cardigan, ignoring the other 39 (58) stitches

8

Cast on for the front of the neck

9a

Cast off 23 sts (45) sts for the sleeve

9b

10

You will now work this side of the cardigan to the end, then go back to complete the other side

11

Now you will go back to the 39 sts (58 sts) you have been ignoring and finish knitting the other side of the cardigan

12a

Use a crochet hook to attach the new yarn

12b

Secure the new yarn with a knot

CONTINUED...

Cast on 9 sts (12 sts) - ensure this is on neck edge.

Count 51 sts (73 sts).

Knit until sleeve measures 20cm (23cm) making sure the needle is facing the 'hand-hole' end after the last row.

Cast off 23 sts (45 sts) from the hand side of the sleeve. Knit to end of row.

Count 28 sts (same for both sizes).

Knit these 28 sts until piece measures 15cm (20cm) - ending with the point of the needle facing away from the front opening.

K1, P1 rib for 8 rows.

13 Cast off in rib.

NECK BAND

14 Lay out the cardigan with the right side facing up, pick up and knit evenly across right front, back and left front of cardigan. Always pick up an even number of stitches. (For instructions, see the Finishing Workshop on page 62.)

K1, P1 rib for 8 rows.

Cast off in 1 x 1 rib. Always cast off on the wrong side of the work.

Now you will knit the front bands of the cardigan:

RIGHT FRONT - BUTTON SIDE

15 With the right side of the work facing you, pick up and knit evenly across right front opening - start at the bottom of the front opening, and pick up all the way to the top of the neck band. Always pick up an even number of stitches. It's a good idea to make a note of the number of stitches you pick up on the right front so that you can pick up the same number on the left front.

K1, P1 rib for 8 rows.

Cast off in 1 x 1 rib.

LEFT FRONT - BUTTONHOLE SIDE

With the right side of the work facing you, pick up and knit evenly across right front. Always pick up an even number of stitches - try to pick up the same number of stitches as you did on the right front. This time you start at the top of the neck band and work your way down to the bottom of the left front opening.

K1, P1 rib for 3 rows.

Buttonhole row: (Knit 5 sts, YF, K2tog), repeat the bracket sequence twice more (a total of three times for three buttonholes), knit to end of row. See: Eyelet buttonholes (page 64) for further instructions.

16 K1, P1 rib for 4 rows. Your three buttonholes should appear after the first of these four rib rows.

Cast off in 1 x 1 rib.

Securely stitch the three buttons into position, so that they match up with the buttonholes.

Now to sew the cardigan up. As you have knitted the cardigan in one piece, there is a minimal amount of sewing to be done... hooray!

Fold the cardigan in half along the middle - see the Layout diagram (page 68). Be sure to line up the underneath of the sleeves and the sides of the body exactly. You can sew up using backstitch, or using garter mattress stitch along the side of the body, and backstitch on the underneath of the sleeves (remember to hold the knitting right-side out when using mattress stitch, and inside out when using backstitch).

13a

This is what you should be left with. The dotted line is the fold line.

13b

Your cardigan is really starting to take shape: now for the finishing!

14a

Lay work with right side facing up and pick up and knit starting from the right front.

14b

Use crochet hook to pick up and knit the collar.

14c

14d

Pick up an even number of stitches around the whole collar.

14e

This is what the neck band should look like when you have finished picking up and knitting; you are about to start knitting the 1 x 1 rib neck band.

15

Now you will knit the button bands.

16

Button bands.

Flower

This is one of my favourite patterns in the book; it's so easy, and lends itself to infinite lovely variations.

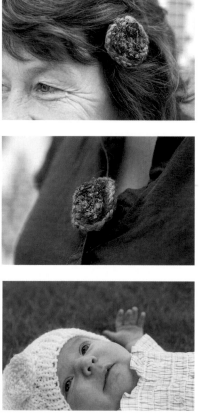

Use your knitted flowers in different ways

You can use any yarn, any needles, any colour. Each different yarn you use will give you a different sized flower (from the same pattern). You can layer the flowers on top of each other to make an elaborate corsage. Sew a pin in the back to turn it into a brooch. Or attach a clip to wear it as a hairpin. Making these gorgeous flowers is a great excuse to use some of the crazy novelty yarns available. I love to sew the flowers to some of the other projects as a decoration. What about a baby cardigan with some mini flowers firmly attached? Or the girly scarf with a flower brooch? The options are endless! Go on – use your imagination and be creative!

YOU WILL NEED

YARN
any that you've got lying around (go wild!)

KNITTING NEEDLES
any that fit the yarn

DARNING NEEDLE

The pattern will give you a different flower depending on the yarn you use

ABBREVIATIONS:

K = Knit

K2tog = Knit two stitches together

START KNITTING

1 Cast on 20 sts.

2 Knit 5 rows.

3 K2tog, repeat to end of row.

4 Count 10 sts.

FINISH

5 Drawstring finish: Cut yarn leaving a long end. Thread this onto a darning needle. Pass the stitches from the knitting needle onto the darning needle. (See Knit Hats on page 52 for further instructions about the drawstring finish.)

6 Pull tight (you should see the flower shape start to emerge) and sew up seam. Weave in all ends.

1

Cast on 20 sts.

2

Knit 5 rows.

3

K2tog, repeat to end of row.

4

Count 10 sts.

5

Drawstring finish: Cut yarn leaving a long end. Thread this onto a darning needle. Pass the stitches from the knitting needle onto the darning needle. (See Knit Hats on page 52 for further instructions about the drawstring finish.)

6a

Pull tight (you should now see the flower shape start to emerge) and sew up seam.

6b

Weave in all ends.

Now go crazy with your imagination – knitted flowers everywhere!

Cable Stitches Workshop

A cable is a pattern in knitting that looks like a twisted section against a plain background.

Once you learn how to create a basic twist, you can experiment and knit all sorts of beautiful patterns. In this section you will learn how to make a simple forward cable and back cable against a garter stitch background.

For cable knitting you will need a cable needle - a small knitting needle with a 'V'- or 'U'-shaped bend in it. This is used to transfer and hold stitches so they can be knitted in different orders.

Forward and back cable stitch

Cable Stitches

I suggest you make a small practice square using the instructions in this workshop before moving on to the next project, which shows you how to knit a cable bag.

Cast on 30 sts (to make a practice piece). You will be repeating a four-row pattern to create this cable practice square.

Row 1: K6, P6, K6, P6, K6.
Row 2: K1 row.
Row 3: K6, P6, K6, P6, K6.

The first three rows in the cabling pattern are quite simple to understand. Remember to bring the yarn forward and back between the knit and purl stitches and remember to count at the end of every row! There's no escaping from Rule Number One.

Then we get to the interesting bit. This is the row where the cable twist is added:

CF = Cable Forward.
CB = Cable Back.
Row 4: K6, CF6, K6, CB6, K6.

CF6 means that six stitches will be used to make the twist. F means that the first three stitches will be in front of the second three stitches. (And vice versa with the CB.)

To work the cable row – Row 4:

Step 1. Knit six stitches.

Step 2. CF6: Pass the next three stitches onto the cable needle – you don't knit these stitches, you simply slip them over from the main needle to the cable needle.

Step 3. Hold this to the front of your knitting (towards your body). Knit the next three stitches (they may feel a little tight).

Step 4. Slip the first three stitches from the cable needle back onto the left-hand needle.

Step 5. Knit these three stitches (they may feel a little tight). Knit six stitches.

Step 6. CB6: Put the next three stitches onto the cable needle. Hold this to the back of your knitting.

Knit the next three stitches (they may feel a little tight).

Slip the first three stitches from the cable needle back onto the left-hand needle.

Knit these three stitches.

Knit six stitches.

This row will put the twist into the stitches to create the cable pattern. The next three rows will put enough space between the cable rows to show off the pattern.

You can practise cable stitches with Project 7: Cable Project Bag (page 81)

Step 7. Repeat the four-row pattern until you have a square (or feel that you have practised enough).

Cable Project Bag

ABBREVIATIONS:

St(s) = Stitch(es)	
K = Knit	
P = Purl	
CF = Cable forward	
CB = Cable back	

START KNITTING

HANDLES (MAKE 2)
Cast on 8 sts.

Stocking stitch until handle measures 25cm.

Cast off.

BAG
Cast on 40 sts.

K1 row.

K12, P4, K8, P4, K12.

K1 row.

K12, P4, K8, P4, K12.

K12, CF4, K8, CB4, K12.

Repeat the last four rows until the piece measures 60cm for the Project Bag (30cm for the Evening Bag).

To finish: K12, P4, K8, P4, K12.

K1 row.

K12, P4, K8, P4, K12.

1 Cast off. Fold the piece in half (right side facing out) and sew up along the long sides using garter mattress stitch. Weave in all ends.

2 Attach the handles firmly – I used an X-shaped stitch – very pretty as well as secure.

My students are always asking me where they can get a good knitting bag – I think that a knitting bag is a useful thing to have if you want to carry projects around, but in my experience, your yarn stash will soon grow so large that you will need something more the size of a suitcase if you want to store everything in one bag! Instead of trying to design a bizarre knitted suitcase, this pattern will help you create your very own Cable Project Bag. Roomy enough to accommodate your current work in progress, it will be an essential piece of kit for holding yarn, needles, patterns and other gadgets so that you can carry your knitting with you wherever you go.

This bag incorporates a simple cable stitch that is easy to knit and exciting enough to impress all your friends! It can be knitted in a variety of sizes and used as a knitting bag, or for books and papers, or even as a little evening bag if you make it smaller.

1 Layout of Cable Project Bag and handles

2 Sew handles on securely

Lacy Wrap

This versatile wrap is a beguilingly simple way to create a gorgeous lacy knit.

Garter eyelet stitch

Using a double-knit yarn, you can choose something utterly luxurious like silk yarn to add glamour to this shawl. It can be worn in a variety of ways, and it is the perfect way to ward off chills on a spring evening. This pattern is also a terrific challenge to the ambitious beginner knitter. You will notice that the needle size I am using is bigger than the size recommended for double-knit yarn; this is because I want to give your shawl an open lacy weave which will make it a beautiful flowing piece of fabric.

YOU WILL NEED

150G DOUBLE-KNIT YARN
(You can choose from the huge variety of double-knit yarns available; I used Debbie Bliss 'Pure Silk' for my wrap – simply lovely silk yarn, and extra long so you would only need two skeins. Debbie Bliss 'Alpaca Silk DK' is a good choice for a bit more warmth – 3 skeins needed in this yarn.)

6MM KNITTING NEEDLES

ABBREVIATIONS:

K = Knit

St(s) = Stitch(es)

YF = Yarn forward: bring your yarn to the front of your knitting over the top of the needles (see Stitch Patterns Workshop, page 48)

M1 = Make one stitch (see Increasing Workshop, page 58)

K2tog = Knit two stitches together

START KNITTING

Cast on 4sts.

Row 1: K1 row. Count 4 sts.

1 Row 2: K1, M1, K until you have 1 stitch left on your left needle. M1, K1. Count 6sts. (Finding where to M1 will be tricky with so few stitches, but persevere as it will become easier the more you knit.)

Row 3: K1 row. Count 6 sts.

2 Row 4: Eyelet row: K1, M1 (YF, K2tog), repeat the bracketed section until 1 stitch remains on the left needle. M1, K1. Count 8 sts. (The stitches will look uneven after this row but will all straighten out after Row 5.)

Row 5: K1 row. Count 8 sts.

3 Repeat these 5 rows until you count 114 sts.

Cast off loosely. When casting off, if you are worried that your cast off is too tight, try casting off using a 7mm needle. This will make the cast off looser.

Weave in your ends.

1 Make one stitch

2a Yarn forward

2b Knit two stitches together

3 Your knitting may look untidy at the start, but persevere and you will see the pretty eyelet pattern emerge once you have repeated the pattern a few times

I find this chart helpful for keeping track of where I am with this pattern. I just cross off the numbers at the end of each row.

ROW	STITCH COUNT													
1	4	8	12	16	20	24	28	32	36	40	44	48	52	56
2 INC	6	10	14	18	22	26	30	34	38	42	46	50	54	58
3	6	10	14	18	22	26	30	34	38	42	46	50	54	58
4 EYELET INC	8	12	16	20	24	28	32	36	40	44	48	52	56	60
5	8	12	16	20	24	28	32	36	40	44	48	52	56	60

ROW	STITCH COUNT													
1	60	64	68	72	76	80	84	88	92	96	100	104	108	112
2 INC	62	66	70	74	78	82	86	90	94	98	102	106	110	114
3	62	66	70	74	78	82	86	90	94	98	102	106	110	
4 EYELET INC	64	68	72	76	80	84	88	92	96	100	104	108	112	
5	64	68	72	76	80	84	88	92	96	100	104	108	112	

Mittens

This is a pattern for a simple, stylish pair of mittens. Knitted in aran yarn (a slightly heavier weight than double-knit), these are warm, fun and quick to make! What more could you ask for in mittens? Also, this pattern provides a real knitting challenge that you will definitely be ready for if you have followed the book this far.

There are three sizes to choose from: Baby Mittens, Child Mittens and the quintessential Lady Mittens. The Baby Mittens pattern is written separately as it is different to the patterns for children's and women's sizes.

Child and Lady Mittens

Any aran-weight yarn will work wonderfully for this pattern. Aran yarn is slightly thicker than double-knit, and knitting it up on 5mm knitting needles will give you a very warm, cosy pair of mittens.

Unlike most mitten and glove patterns, my mitts fit either hand so you can sidestep that annoying mistake everyone seems to do when they first knit mittens – making two mittens for one hand! (It happens to the best of us.) Just make two the same and forget all about left or right or nasty 'reverse shaping.' Don't worry if they look a bit small as you are knitting them, they are meant to fit snugly, and they will have enough stretch to be comfortable.

YOU WILL NEED

CHILD'S MITTENS

50G ARAN-WEIGHT YARN

5MM KNITTING NEEDLES

DARNING NEEDLE

LADIES' MITTENS

100G ARAN-WEIGHT YARN
(I used Debbie Bliss 'Cashmerino' for my pair and they turned out soft and extra warm!)

5MM KNITTING NEEDLES

DARNING NEEDLE

ABBREVIATIONS:

K = Knit

P = Purl

St st = Stocking stitch

St(s) = Stitch(es)

1 x 1 rib = Knit one stitch, purl one stitch

M1 = Make one stitch (See Increasing Workshop)

K2tog = Knit two stitches together

START KNITTING

Cast on 20 sts. Try to make the cast-on stitches looser than you usually might.

1 1 x 1 rib for 10 rows.

START INCREASING FOR THUMB

2 K10, M1, K10. Count 21 sts.

P1 row.

K10, M1, K1, M1, K10. Count 23 sts.

P1 row.

K1 row.

P1 row.

K10, M1, K3, M1, K10. Count 25 sts.

P1 row.

K1 row.

P1 row.

K10, M1, K5, M1, K10. Count 27 sts.

P1 row.

K1 row.

P1 row.

CHILD'S MITTENS

Follow the left-hand page for instructions for Child's Mittens. Please note that the text on the images corresponds with the child-size mittens, but the images will be a useful aid when knitting either size.

Handy HINT

If you are having trouble making your cast-on stitches looser, try casting on with a knitting needle 1mm bigger than that you'll use for the rest of the pattern. Then knit your first row onto the recommended needle size for the pattern (discarding the larger needle), and continue following the pattern with the recommended needles.

1

1 x 1 rib for 10 rows.

Follow the right-hand page for instructions on Ladies' Mittens

ABBREVIATIONS:

K = Knit	
P = Purl	
St st = Stocking stitch	
St(s) = Stitch(es)	
1 x 1 rib = Knit one stitch, purl one stitch	
M1 = Make one stitch (See Increasing Workshop)	
K2tog = Knit two stitches together	

START KNITTING

Cast on 24 sts. Try to make the cast-on stitches looser than you usually might.

1   1 x 1 rib for 15 rows.

START INCREASING FOR THUMB

2   K12, M1, K12. Count 25 sts.

P1 row.

K12, M1, K1, M1, K12. Count 27 sts.

P1 row.

K1 row.

P1 row.

K12, M1, K3, M1, K12. Count 29 sts.

P1 row.

K1 row.

P1 row.

K12, M1, K5, M1, K12. Count 31 sts.

P1 row.

K1 row.

P1 row.

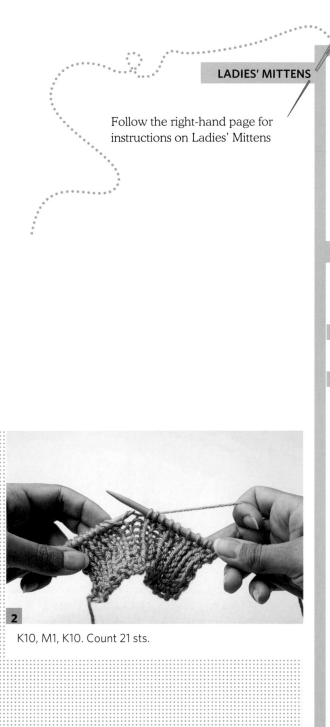

2

K10, M1, K10. Count 21 sts.

CONTINUE...

CHILD'S MITTENS CONTINUED....

K10, M1, K7, M1, K10. Count 29 sts.

P1 row.

K1 row.

P1 row.

K10, M1, K9, M1, K10. Count 31 sts.

P1 row.

K1 row.

P1 row.

3 SEPARATE FOR THUMB

K20 sts. Turn – this means swap the knitting needles around in your hands as if you were about to start knitting the next row. The reason for this is that you are about to knit the thumb to completion before working on the main finger-section of the mitten.

P9. Turn.

K9. Turn.

4 Continuing to 'turn' in this manner, working on these centre 9 sts only, stocking stitch until the thumb section measures 6cm from separation, making sure that the last row you do is a purl row. At this stage, it's a good idea to count your rows as you work them so that you can ensure both hands are the same size.

DECREASE FOR THE TOP OF THE THUMB

(K1, K2tog), repeat 3 times in total. Count 6 sts.

P1 row.

(K1, K2tog), repeat 2 times in total. Count 4 sts.

P1 row.

3

Separate for thumb

5

Drawstring finish for thumb

5 DRAWSTRING FINISH FOR TOP OF THUMB:
Cut the yarn leaving a long end. Thread this end onto a darning needle. Transfer the 4 stitches from the knitting needle onto the darning needle one by one and pull tight.

6 Fold thumb in half and sew up from the top of the thumb to the base of the thumb. Remember: inside-out if you are using backstitch (as I did) or right-side out if you are using mattress stitch. See Sewing-up Workshop on page 38.

4

Work on thumb only

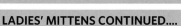

6

Sew up thumb

LADIES' MITTENS CONTINUED....

K12, M1, K7, M1, K12. Count 33 sts.

P1 row.

K1 row.

P1 row.

K12, M1, K9, M1, K12. Count 35 sts.

P1 row.

K1 row.

P1 row.

K12, M1, K11, M1, K12. Count 37 sts.

3 **SEPARATE FOR THUMB**
P24 sts. Turn – this means swap the knitting needles around in your hands as if you were about to start knitting the next row. The reason for this is that you are about to knit the thumb to completion before working on the main finger-section of the mitten.

K11. Turn.

P11. Turn.

4 Continuing to 'turn' in this manner, working on these centre 11 sts only, stocking stitch until the thumb section measures 6cm from separation, making sure that the last row you do is a purl row. At this stage, it is a good idea to count your rows as you work them so that you can ensure both hands are the same size.

DECREASE FOR THE TOP OF THE THUMB
(K1, K2tog), repeat bracketed section 3 times in total, K2. Count 8 sts.

P1 row.

(K1, K2tog), repeat twice, K2. Count 6 sts.

P1 row.

(K1, K2tog), repeat twice. Count 4 sts.

5 **DRAWSTRING FINISH FOR TOP OF THUMB**
Cut the yarn leaving a long end (about 80cm). Thread this end onto a darning needle. Transfer the 4 sts from the knitting needle onto the darning needle one by one and pull tight.

6 Fold thumb in half and sew up from the top of the thumb to the base of the thumb. See Step 6 opposite.

CONTINUE...

CHILD'S MITTENS CONTINUED....

Turn the thumb right-side out.

7 Using the remainder of the long end of the yarn you used to sew up the thumb, and with right side (the knit side) of the work facing you, M1, then knit 11 sts. (With this M1, it's not as easy to find the loop to pick up between the stitches – just persevere.) Count 23 sts.

Purl 1 row.

(At some point soon you will have to join new yarn – in the same way that you would normally.)

Starting with a knit row, stocking stitch these 23 sts until the work measures 6cm from the base of the thumb, making sure that the last row you do is a purl row. At this stage, it's a good idea to count your rows as you work them so that you can ensure both hands are the same size.

DECREASE FOR TOP OF MITTEN:

(K1, K2tog) a total of 7 times, K2. Count 16 sts.

P1 row.

(K1, K2tog) a total of 5 times, K1. Count 11 sts.

P1 row.

8 **DRAWSTRING FINISH FOR TOP OF MITTEN**
Cut the yarn, leaving a long end. Thread this end onto a darning needle. Transfer the remaining 11 sts from the knitting needle onto the darning needle one by one and pull tight.

9 Fold the mitten in half and sew it up all down the side.

Weave in all your ends.

7
Use the remainder of the long end of the yarn

8b
Cut the yarn leaving a long end.

Knit another the same!

8a

Drawstring finish for top of mitten

9

Fold the mitten in half and sew it up all down the side

Turn the thumb right-side out.

7   Using the remainder of the long end of the yarn you used to sew up the thumb, and with right side (the knit side) of the work facing you, M1, then knit 13 sts. Count 27 sts. (With this M1, it's not as easy to find the loop to pick up between the stitches – just persevere).

Purl 1 row.

(At some point soon you will have to join new yarn – in the same way that you would normally.)

Starting with a knit row, stocking stitch these 27 sts until the work measures 11cm from the base of the thumb, making sure that the last row you do is a purl row. At this stage, it's a good idea to count your rows as you work them so that you can ensure both hands are the same size.

DECREASE FOR THE TOP OF THE MITTEN:

(K1, K2tog), repeat a total of 9 times.
Count 18 sts.

P1 row.

(K1, K2tog), repeat 6 times in total. Count 12 sts.

P1 row.

(K1, K2tog), repeat 4 times in total. Count 8 sts.

P1 row.

8   **DRAWSTRING FINISH FOR TOP OF MITTEN**
Cut the yarn leaving a long end. Thread this end onto a darning needle. Transfer the eight stitches from the knitting needle onto the darning needle one by one and pull tight.

9   Fold the mitten in half and sew it up all down the side. Weave in all your ends.

Wear with warmth!

Baby 'Hand-Hat' Mittens

When knitting these baby mittens, you will notice that they have no thumbs. Don't worry, it's not a mistake – there's a good reason for the thumb-free mitten. All the mummies, daddies and baby-sitters amongst you will know that small babies often scratch their faces as they are waving their little hands about. Mittens with thumbs aren't practical in such a tiny size, but these little 'hand-hats' are perfect to protect delicate soft skin.
They are as quick to knit as baby booties, and make an unusual, thoughtful and practical gift for any new baby.

Please note that these are not knitted in the same Aran-weight yarn as the child and adult mittens. Any double knit will do for this pattern, but you should consider a 100% cotton if you are concerned about baby allergies.

YOU WILL NEED

BABY MITTENS

50G DOUBLE KNIT YARN
(This will give you plenty of yarn for a pair of matching booties too. I prefer to choose natural cotton yarns as the mitts are likely to end up in baby-mouths: Sirdar 'Luxury Soft Cotton DK' is a good choice. Cotton yarns spilt easily so be extra careful when knitting or you'll end up with extra stitches.)

4MM KNITTING NEEDLES

DARNING NEEDLE

ABBREVIATIONS:
K = Knit
P = Purl
St(s) = Stitch(es)
K2tog = Knit two stitches together

START KNITTING

Cast on 24 sts.

1 K1, P1 rib for 8 rows.

2 Garter stitch (knit every row) until your knitting measures 7cm from the beginning.

3 START DECREASING FOR MITTEN-TOP:

(K1, K2tog) Repeat the bracketed sequence 8 times. Count 16 sts.

K1 row.

(K1, K2tog.) Repeat 5 times. K1. Count 11 sts.

K1 row.

(K1, K2tog.) Repeat 3 times. K2. Count 8 sts.

K1 row.

4 DRAWSTRING FINISH FOR TOP OF MITT:

Cut the yarn leaving a long end. Thread this end onto a darning needle. Transfer the 8 sts from the knitting needle onto the darning needle one by one and pull tight.

Fold the mitt in half and sew up.

5 Weave in all your ends. Make another exactly the same and... ahh! Tiny baby mittens.

1 K1, P1 rib for 8 rows

2 Garter stitch (knit every row) until your knitting measures 7cm from the beginning

3 Decrease to eight stitches

4 Drawstring finish for top of mitt

5 Fold the mitt in half and sew up.

Hot Water Bottle Cover

This is the ultimate in cosy winter gifts – give it to your mum for Christmas, your granny for her birthday, or keep it for yourself. Your toes need never be cold again!

Any double-knit yarn will work in this pattern; just remember that you will be taking this knitting to bed with you, so choose something extra soft.

A mixture of moss stitch and stocking stitch makes this one-piece knit both pretty and simple. If you need a refresher on your moss stitch, go to the chapter about stitch patterns (see page 51) and knit a practice square – a little bit of practice goes a long way in knitting.

YOU WILL NEED

100G DOUBLE-KNIT YARN
Something suitable for cuddling up to, but still beautiful – there are endless choices in DK yarn.

4MM NEEDLES

DARNING NEEDLE

7 SMALL FLAT BUTTONS (1CM)

SEWING NEEDLE AND THREAD FOR BUTTONS

PATTERN LAYOUT

This is the shape of the piece you will be knitting. The hot water bottle cover is knitted in one piece and folded in the middle and sewn.

KEY TO DIAGRAM

Fold lines ·································
Buttons ⊕ ⊕ ⊕ ⊕ ⊕ ⊕ ⊕

START KNITTING HERE:
← Cast on 41sts
  Moss stitch 7cm

FOLD

← Stocking stitch to 30cm from the beginning

← Cast off 12, K to end
  Cast off 12, P to end

← Moss stitch for 18cm

FOLD

← Cast on 12, K1 row
  Cast on 12, P1 row

← Stocking stitch for 30cm

← Moss stitch 10 rows
← Buttonhole row
← Moss st 8 rows

Cast off
END KNITTING

ABBREVIATIONS:

K = Knit	
P = Purl	
St(s) = Stitch(es)	
St st = Stocking stitch	
YF = Yarn forward	
K2tog = Knit two stitches together	
Rep = Repeat	

START KNITTING

Cast on 41 sts.

K1, P1, rep to end.
(Repeating this row with an odd number of stitches will create moss stitch.)

Moss stitch until piece measures 7cm from the beginning.

K1 row.
P1 row.
This is stocking stitch (st st).
Continue in st st until the entire piece measures 30cm from the beginning – making sure that the last row you do is a purl row (wrong side).

Cast off 12 sts, K to end. Count 29 sts.
Cast off 12 sts, P to end. Count 17 sts.

Moss stitch for 18cm from cast-off edge – making sure that the last row you do is on the wrong side of the work (purl stitch).

With the knitting in your left hand and the empty needle in your right – using the first stitch on the left needle as if it were the slipknot – cast on 12 sts. Count 29 sts.
K1 row.
Turn (swap the needles in your hands). Cast on 12 sts. Count 41 sts.
P1 row.

Buttonholes

Starting with a K row, stocking stitch until the piece from your new cast-on edge measures 30cm – making sure that the last row you do is a purl row (wrong side).

Moss stitch 10 rows.

BUTTONHOLE ROW:
K4, (YF, K2tog, K3), repeat the bracketed section until you have 5 sts left. K5.

Moss stitch 8 rows. (Your buttonholes will appear after the first of these 8 rows of moss stitch.)

Cast off.

SEWING UP:

Using darning needles and yarn, fold in half along the middle of the short moss stitch section (see Layout diagram). Sew up into hot water bottle shape, leaving flap at bottom.

Sew on seven small flat buttons in a matching sewing thread, using a normal sewing needle (the yarn and darning needle will probably be too thick to sew buttons on with).

You will be left with a 7cm flap with buttonholes to fold over and button so that your hot water bottle doesn't fall out of its cosy cover.

Buttons

Colinette hand-painted 'Cadenza' yarn was used for this cover

Necktie

It's pretty difficult to think up good gifts for my dad every year.
He has a huge number of framed photos of me, fancy colognes
he never uses and shirts in all styles and colours!

So how about something any Big-Daddy won't be able to resist wearing?
I've designed a funky yet utterly wearable necktie that will appeal to
his inner Daddy-Cool! Why not make one for each of the men in your
family? Or wear your tie in the same way one stylish girl-knitter I know
does – it looks great on a high powered businesswoman with a pencil
skirt, crisp white shirt and a pair of sexy–librarian spectacles!

The tie is knitted in a fine 4-ply yarn that will not be too bulky for a tie,
but will still hold its shape well. Four-ply yarn is available in a variety
of materials and colours, but I've been using self-striping sock yarn; it
changes colour as if by magic and saves you having to weave in any
ends (and it's pretty exciting not knowing what colour will come next!).
You will notice that the tie is knitted entirely in garter stitch so that it lies
perfectly flat and makes a good tidy knot.

YOU WILL NEED

50G 4-PLY YARN
Self-striping sock yarn is a good choice for this knitted tie. Try Opal, Regia
or Schoeller and Stahl yarn. If you want a one-colour tie, any 4-ply yarn
will work.

2.75MM KNITTING NEEDLES

ABBREVIATIONS:

K = Knit

St(s) = Stitch(es)

M1 = Make one stitch

K2tog = Knit two stitches together

START KNITTING

Cast on 3 sts

K1 row.

1 K1, M1, K1, M1, K1. Count 5 sts.

K1 row.

K1, M1, knit until 1 sts remains on left needle, M1, K1. Count 7 sts.

You will find that the 'make one' is a bit difficult with so few stitches, but persevere – it will be worth it in the end.

2 You will see the 'V'-point of the tie emerging in your knitting. The first few M1s will feel a bit hard to find, but it will get easier the more rows you knit.

Repeat the last two rows until you have 25 sts.

K5 rows

Decrease row: K1, K2tog, K until you have 3 sts left, K2tog, K1. Count 23 sts.

K25 rows

Decrease row: K1, K2tog, K until you have 3 sts left, K2tog, K1. Count 21 sts.

K 25 rows.

Decrease row: K1, K2tog, K until you have 3 sts left, K2tog, K1. Count 19 sts.

K25 rows.

Decrease row: K1, K2tog, K until you have 3 sts left, K2tog, K1. Count 17 sts.

K25 rows.

Decrease row: K1, K2tog, K until you have 3 sts left, K2tog, K1. Count 15 sts.

K25 rows.

Decrease row: K1, K2tog, K until you have 3 sts left, K2tog, K1. Count 13 sts.

1 M1 = Make one stitch

2 'V' of tie

Stylish ladies can wear this tie too!

K25 rows.

Decrease row: K1, K2tog, K until you have 3 sts left, K2tog, K1. Count 11 sts.

Knit every row until the tie measures 140cm from the beginning.

Cast off.

Weave in the ends at the beginning and end of the tie.

I like a Windsor knot myself!

Fingerless Wrist-Warmers

These wrist warmers are perfect for the funky teenager who wants an extra layer, or a sophisticated alternative to gloves for the discerning lady.

You can have some fun with them by sewing on accessories – try buttons, beads, knitted flowers or pom-poms. Try changing the yarn (or using self-striping yarn) to make striped warmers, or play with the length on the wrist before starting the hand increase to turn them into slip-on sleeves… There are lots of options here for personalising and using your creativity. In no time at all you will have something funky, fun and original!

The main stitch used in this pattern is stocking stitch, and I've used an 'eyelet' pattern to create decorative holes. This is the same method you used when making buttonholes, but purely for prettiness without the need for buttons.

I know I'm only giving you a one-size-fits-all option, but I've tried these on a variety of women's hands from skinny teenagers to curvaceous kittens – they will fit!

YOU WILL NEED

DOUBLE-KNIT YARN 100G
Be bold and brave with funky colours for cool teenagers – double-knit yarn comes in endless varieties.

4MM KNITTING NEEDLES

DARNING NEEDLE

ABBREVIATIONS:

K = Knit

P = Purl

St(s) = Stitch(es)

K2tog = Knit two stitches together

YF = Bring the yarn to the front between the two needles

START KNITTING

Cast on 30 sts loosely.

K1 row.

P1 row.

K1 row.

P1 row.

Row 1: K14, YF, K2tog, K14.

Row 2: P1 row.

Row 3: K1 row.

Row 4: P1 row.

Repeat the last 4 rows a further 8 times each. You will count a total of nine eyelets when you are done.

START INCREASING FOR HAND:

K13, YF, K3, YF, K14. Count 32 sts.

P1 row.

K1 row.

P1 row.

K13, YF, K5, YF, K14. Count 34 sts.

P1 row.

K1 row.

P1 row.

K13, YF, K7, YF, K14. Count 36 sts.

Layout of wrist-warmers

Knitter's Notes

YF = Yarn forward. This is the same move you make when you bring the yarn to the front of the work, over the top of your knitting needles, when you are about to purl. But instead of purling, you knit two stitches together. K2tog with the yarn in front creates a decorative 'eyelet' pattern, whilst keeping the same number of stitches that you started with.

Handy HINT

Try and keep your cast-on stitches loose. If you have trouble with this, I suggest using a 5mm knitting needle to cast on with, then starting and continuing the knitting with 4mm needles for the rest of the pattern.

Handy HINT

When doing an eyelet pattern, it's especially important to count your stitches at the end of each row so that you have the correct number and your eyelet pattern is evenly distributed.

P1 row.

K1 row.

P1 row.

K13, YF, K9, YF, K14. Count 38 sts.

P1 row.

K1 row.

P1 row.

K13, YF, K11, YF, K14. Count 40 sts.

P1 row.

K1 row.

P1 row.

K13, YF, K13, YF, K14. Count 42 sts.

P1 row.

K1 row.

P1 row.

K13, YF, K15, YF, K14. Count 44sts.

P1 row.

K1 row.

P1 row.

K13, YF, K17, YF, K14. Count 46 sts.

P1 row.

K1 row.

P1 row.

K13, YF, K19, YF, K14. Count 48 sts.

Questions & Answers

How am I increasing without a M1?
When you knit a stitch with the yarn forward, you create an increase and eyelet at the same time.

Sew up side seam using stocking mattress stitch.
See the Sewing-up Workshop on page 39

Sew up for thumb opening

P1 row.

K1 row.

P1 row.

K1 row.

Cast off leaving a long end for sewing (about 50cm).

Phone Home

The teenage boy is such a difficult creature to knit for. But if you've knitted something for your daughter/niece/younger sister, then you can't leave out your son/nephew/younger brother… But what to make for a grouchy, slouchy teenage boy? Nothing pretty, no accessories…hmm. And then… Eureka!

This mobile phone cover is not too soppy a gift for a lad, and it has the additional use of protecting his mobile phone (or iPod) from getting battered in his school bag! Plus, it can be tailored to suit whichever sports team he supports (or if he's a grungy geek or a would-be rocker, try knitting it all in black and sewing on a pirate patch – yaar!). As a knitter, this project is a great way to use up oddments of yarn as it doesn't take much.

P.S. This is not just for the boys; I quite fancy a pink and purple one with sequins!

YOU WILL NEED

DOUBLE-KNIT YARN
Any small amounts of double-knit you have will do.

4MM KNITTING NEEDLES

DARNING NEEDLE

Handy HINT

In a pattern with so many colour changes, it is a good idea to keep a tally of the rows as you knit them so your stripes change accurately. And remember: colour changes must always sit at the same end of your knitting.

ABBREVIATIONS:
K = Knit
St(s) = Stitch(es)

START KNITTING

Cast on 25 sts in first colour – red.

Knit 16 rows.

Cast off 6 sts, knit to end. Count 19 sts.

Cast off 6 sts, knit to end. Count 13 sts.

Change to second colour – white.

Knit 16 rows.

Change to first colour – red.

Knit 32 rows.

Change to second colour – white.

Knit 14 rows.

Change to first colour – red.

Knit 2 rows.

Turn so that the stitches are in your left hand and an empty needle in your right, cast on 6 sts. Count 19 sts.

Knit 1 row.

Turn so that the stitches are in your left hand and empty needle in right, cast on 6 sts. Count 25 sts.

Continuing in first colour – red, knit 16 rows.

Cast off. Weave in all ends – make sure you weave the ends on the wrong side of the work (where the colour change is not as tidy).

1 Fold the piece in half inside out along the dotted line and sew up the sides, underarms, sleeves and shoulders, leaving a 3 or 4cm gap at the 'neck' to insert the phone into. This gap should be a bit smaller than the width of the phone, so that it will stretch to put the phone in and the phone won't fall out. Then turn it right-side out and pop the phone in.

Remember to use red yarn to sew up the red section and white yarn to sew up the white section (or whatever colours you've chosen).

2 I decorated the phone cover by cutting numbers and letters out of felt and sticking them on with fabric glue. Try using initials, numbers, or your favourite football player's team number.

1 Fold in half and sew up

2 Decorate your phone home with glued on felt pieces

Manly Scarf

This is a variation on the theme of the ordinary scarf. I've added a couple of twists to take it away from the image of the granny-knitted present and given it a direct route to modern-man-chic.

Garthenor Organic yarn and 7mm knitting needles used in this image

It is also fun for the knitter as it uses a 2 x 2 rib which, while it may take a bit longer to knit, makes for great practice in knitting and purling – and it incorporates a funky stripe as well. Choose your colours with care – is the man in mind an avid supporter (or loather) of a football team that sports particular colours? Does he have favourite colours, or colours he strictly avoids? A stripe can say so much about a man.
Decisions, decisions…

YOU WILL NEED

200G CHUNKY-WEIGHT YARN
This will usually require a 7 or 8mm knitting needle. You need 100g each of two different, carefully chosen colours of yarn, to give 200g in total.

7/8MM KNITTING NEEDLES
Look at the yarn label.

Handy HINT

K2, YF, P2, YB will create a 2 x 2 rib. The movements of the yarn are not shown in the pattern, as the knitter will know where the yarn needs to be to keep the pattern and stitch count even.

But as a beginner you should count your stitches at the end of every row, and if you forget where you are in the middle of a row, go to the stitches that you've already knitted (on the right-hand needle) and count what you've already done: e.g. "K2, P2, K2, P2… what's next? Oh yes, K2. Is my yarn at the back? It is? Keep working!"

ABBREVIATIONS:

K = Knit

P = Purl

St(s) = Stitch(es)

YF = Yarn forward

2 x 2 Rib = knit two stitches, purl two stitches

START KNITTING

Cast on 28sts.

Knit 2 sts, Purl 2 sts. Repeat this sequence of K2, P2 to the end of the row.

Repeat this row for a total of 10 rows.

Change to next colour.

K2, P2 rib for 10 rows.

Change to next colour.

K2, P2 rib for 10 rows.

Continue this sequence until the scarf has eleven stripes in each colour.

Cast off in 2 x 2 rib.

1   WEAVE IN ALL YOUR ENDS
Weave your ends in vertically along the edge of the scarf.

1 Weave in your ends vertically on 2 x 2 rib

  Handy **HINT**

Casting off in 2 x 2 rib
K1, K1, cast off 1. (Yarn forward. P1, cast off 1. P1, cast off 1. Yarn back. K1, cast off 1. K1, cast off 1.) Repeat to end of the row remembering to knit and purl in the same places that you have been throughout the scarf.

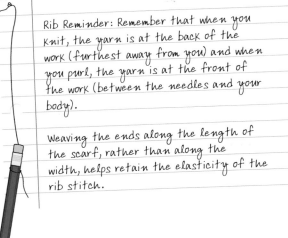

Knitter's Notes

Rib Reminder: Remember that when you knit, the yarn is at the back of the work (furthest away from you) and when you purl, the yarn is at the front of the work (between the needles and your body).

Weaving the ends along the length of the scarf, rather than along the width, helps retain the elasticity of the rib stitch.

Girly Scarf

A variation on a regular scarf, this is a floaty, feminine piece that is more of an adornment than a way to keep warm.

It is also more of a challenge, in that the yarn working for you in this scarf is a definite step up from the standard yarns we've been using so far.

The fact that this piece is so pretty means that all the ladies – from your four-year old princess to your grandmother – will be vying to wear it!

You'll be using a very fine mohair yarn; this looks more like thread than yarn, and feels utterly luxurious. Using needles far larger than recommended gives a faux lace effect and also knits up super quick. Although this yarn is challenging for a beginner knitter (it will be hard to see, let alone undo, mistakes), any little mistakes disappear in the beauty of the yarn and the loose weave.

This scarf works well on a mild spring day, or, as I mostly use it, in the evenings as more of a wrap. It is perfect to jazz up a simple outfit, and so quick to knit that you'll want to make one in every colour!

YOU WILL NEED

25G EXTRA FINE MOHAIR
(I love Colinette's hand painted 'Parisienne' or Rowan 'Kidsilk Haze'.)

8MM KNITTING NEEDLES

Knitter's Notes

With this pattern, you are using knitting needles several sizes bigger than recommended on the yarn label. This gives a very open weave to your work and creates a lacy effect that's very pretty, and satisfying for a beginner to knit.

Handy HINT

A few tricks to remember when knitting this scarf:

• Keep your stitches much looser than you usually would. It will make the knitting easier, and won't affect the pattern.

• If you add new yarn, tie an extra knot – weaving in ends won't be very secure in such an open weave.

• My guinea pigs have preferred bamboo needles as they are less slippery when knitting such loose stitches.

• And don't worry if it looks a bit odd in the beginning – this yarn may be more difficult to get used to working with, but it's very forgiving and hides all mistakes beautifully! Persevere.

ABBREVIATIONS:
St(s) = Stitch(es)

START KNITTING

Cast on 30 sts loosely.

Knit every row until the scarf measures 100cm (or your desired length). This scarf works well in different lengths. Try casting off after 70cm or 150cm.

Cast off very loosely.

Give to your favourite lady (or keep it for yourself!). Original, simple and very beautiful...

Using fine yarn and bigger needles gives a faux lace effect

Little 'n' Large Cushions

You can easily knit all sorts of beautiful items for your home – a knitted cushion adds a lovely original touch to a chic, modern interior, or makes a cosy addition to a traditional room.

This versatile pattern is knitted using a 'basket weave' stitch pattern, and can be used to make a chunky cushion, or a smaller scented knit pillow to fragrance your linen closet. You use the same pattern, just different yarn, needles and filling depending on whether you are knitting the large or little size.

Using the same pattern you can make a scent pillow or a chunky cushion cover

Basket weave stitch

YOU WILL NEED

SMALL SCENTED CUSHION	LARGE CUSHION
50G DOUBLE-KNIT YARN (Any oddments of double-knit yarn will do nicely.)	**200G SUPER BULKY YARN** (Rowan 'Big Wool' is perfect for the large cushion cover.)
4MM KNITTING NEEDLES	**12MM KNITTING NEEDLES**
THREE SMALL (1CM) BUTTONS	**THREE LARGE BUTTONS** (Approx 4cm in diameter.)
DRIED LAVENDER OR POT POURRI	**DARNING NEEDLE**
AN OLD PAIR OF TIGHTS OR SOCKS	
DARNING NEEDLE	**CUSHION PAD** This should be around 5–10cm bigger than your finished cushion cover so that your knitting stretches tight over the pad. This will show off your basket weave to its best advantage.

Enjoy and Experiment

One thing that you mustn't forget is that this learning-to-knit business is fun! Don't get stressed or frustrated. There will always be a more experienced knitter not very far away, who you can ask for help.

Patterns are just a starting point – you should use them as a guide rather than as a set of strict and inflexible rules. The best knitters bring their own style, ideas and creativity to each project they work on.

Mix and match the patterns you have been given in this book in any way you want to. Go wild in your colour choices. Try things even if you aren't sure they'll work. You never know what you'll discover (about knitting and yourself)!

Some ideas to start you off:

• Create the full Baby Combo: get your (or anybody else's) new addition kitted out in matching hat, mitts, cardigan and booties;

• Knit a His 'n' His Manly Scarf set, or Hers 'n' Hers Girly Scarves;

• Try knitted flowers on EVERYTHING!

• Embellishments: sew buttons, sequins, ribbons, patches, or anything else you fancy onto your knitting;

• Play with different-sized needles to create different effects and sizes: large needles = bigger item; small needles = smaller item.

Onwards and Upwards

So now, if you've been following the instructions in this book, you should be able to:

- cast on;
- cast off;
- knit;
- purl;
- increase;
- decrease;
- add stripes or embellishments to your work;
- create stitch patterns;
- sew up your knitting;
- follow a basic pattern; and
- make lots and lots of wonderful knitting!

What's next? Well, you may look at commercial knitting patterns and still feel confused. That's to be expected. At least now though you should be able to approach them knowing that you are knitting perfect stitches, you've got a few decent projects under your belt, and you feel confident in your ability to learn some new techniques.

Remember:

- Count your stitches every row

- Don't abandon your work in the middle of a row – it's very easy to forget where you are

- Remember to tick off your rows as you work them on the pattern so that you don't forget where you are

- If you are unhappy with your work, don't be afraid to start again

- There are loads of brilliant knitters around every corner… ask for help!

What's next for you to learn?

- Tension squares and their importance in creating fitted garments.

- Abbreviations – there are more out there that we haven't covered. Sl1, psso, kfb – don't worry, they all have translations.

- Techniques – for every method of doing something that you've learnt in this book, there are five more out there. You will encounter increasing by knitting into the stitch more than once, decreasing by passing stitches over, and endless methods of casting on. Find your own favourite techniques.

- Knitting patterns – there are millions to choose from. I suggest you start on patterns labelled for beginners; even in those you'll have lots of new exciting things to learn.

Good luck and happy knitting.

Useful Notes:
Conversion Charts and Abbreviations

It would be much less confusing if everyone in the world could agree on just one system of measurement for sizes, lengths and weights, but we might be waiting a while for that to happen. So, until then, here are some useful facts and figures to help you with your knitting wherever in the world you may be.

Conversion Charts

KNITTING NEEDLE SIZES	
UK - mm	USA
2	0
2.5	1
2.75	2
3	2
3.25	3
3.50	4
3.75	5
4	6
4.5	7
5	8
5.5	9
6	10
6.5	10.5
8	11
10	15
12	17
15	19

CENTIMETRE - INCHES	
CENTIMETRE	INCHES
1	0.39
5	1.97
10	3.94
15	5.9
20	7.87
25	9.84
30	11.8

YARN WEIGHT	
GRAMS	OUNCES
25	0.88
50	1.76
75	2.65
100	3.5
150	5.29
200	7.05
250	8.81

YARN	
UK	USA
2 PLY	LACE WEIGHT
4 PLY	FINGERING
DOUBLE KNIT	SPORT/DOUBLE KNIT
ARAN	WORSTED
CHUNKY	BULKY

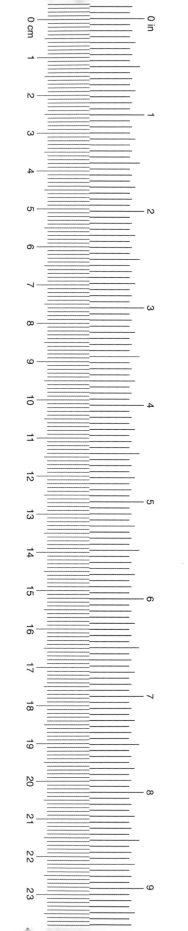

Abbreviations

Beginners often ask me why knitting patterns include such a lot of abbreviations. Well, the short answer is that if they didn't, all the patterns would be pages and pages longer than they are! I've used as few abbreviations in my patterns as I can – I want all my patterns to be beginner-knitter-user-friendly above all else. But if I hadn't included some abbreviations (quite apart from the fact that this book would be 500 pages long!), you as a beginner wouldn't have had the chance to become accustomed to all the abbreviations you will undoubtedly come across in knitting patterns during your knitting career.

To help you, I have explained the abbreviations used in each pattern along the way, but here is a revision list of all the abbreviations used in the book.

K = Knit
P = Purl
St = Stitch
Sts = Stitches
St st = Stocking stitch
Dec = Decrease
Inc = Increase
Rep = Repeat
Tog = Together
K2tog = Knit two stitches together
M = Make a stitch: increase
YF = Yarn forward
YB = Yarn back
CF = Cable forward
CB = Cable back
DK = Double-knit yarn

Stockists

Colinette
www.colinette.com
Beautiful hand-painted luxury yarns

Debbie Bliss
www.debbieblissonline.co.uk
Gorgeous yarns, stylish patterns and more!

Garthenor Organic Yarns
www.organicpurewool.co.uk
Soil Association certified organic knitting yarns

Get Knitted
www.getknitted.com
Terrific shop and online store with some
hard-to-find yarns as well as all the favourites,
and knitting accessories

Hip Knits
www.hipknits.co.uk
Luxurious hand-painted yarns and fibres

I Knit London
www.iknit.org.uk
Shop, groups and sanctuary for knitters

John Lewis
www.johnlewis.com
Good selection of favourite yarns and accessories

Loop
www.loop.gb.com
London yarn boutique with knitting supplies sourced
from all over the world

Rowan
www.knitrowan.com
Yarns, patterns, knitting books, workshops and
much more

Sirdar
www.sirdar.co.uk
A great source for yarn and accessories – look out for
their amazing novelty yarn selection

Knitty gritty

The next steps

Acknowledgements

Invaluable in my work are my fabulous test knitters and students who've tried and tested my patterns and workshops. Guinea pigs – Abi Dove, Alex Mclean, Alison Forsythe, Amelia Healey, A. Goga, Caroline Fenton, Catherine Alaguiry, Catherine Esland, Cetra Coverdale, Charlotte Saunders, Cheryl Williams, David Withington, Dawn Bray, Debbie Coughlin, Ellen Grace, Ellen Parnavelas, Fionne Harrington, Grace Edghill, Giulietta Driver, Harriet Tenenbaum, Hayley Dalton, Helen Wakeley, Jane Freimiller, Jane Wilson, Jayne Morgan, Jennifer Hill, Jill Petty, Karen Blair, Karla Hammond, Kate Bullas, Kate Shurety, Kathryn Matthews, Kaye Archer, Kylie Archer, Linda Hill, Mary Cowin, Megan Kelly, Michelle Ryan, Natalie Billington, Niki Stevens, Owen Pearson, Rhiann Thomson, Rowena Hill, Ruth Ball, Samantha Bell, Sarah Hook, Seb Arnold, Seeta Patel, Sim Burton, Sue Richards, Summer Mughrabi, Sybil Caines, Vicky Cowin and Wendy Meteyard – thank you so much!

Thank you to everyone involved in the photo shoots (it's not that easy modelling knitwear in the summer!): Alexis Larusson, Alix Stredwick, Amelie Blair, Ava James, Beatrice Roberts, Ben Neuville, Caroline Fenton, Carrie Cracknell, Catherine Alaguiry, Chris & Yvonne Abbess, Eva Karkut-Law, Eva Larusson, Jane Freimiller, Jemima Roberts, Jess Schiazza, Jonathan Allen, Karen Blair, Lauren Neuville, Lilia Larusson, Lucy Neuville, Owen Pearson, Peter Brownell, Peter Schiazza, Poppy Blair, Rachel Weatherup, Robin Priestley, Rowena Hill, Summer Mughrabi and her lovely flat, Susan Neuville, Tracy Karkut-Law and the flat I want to live in, Wendy Meteyard and Woody Brownell.

So many people helped make this book possible and coped with my numerous trials, tribulations and tantrums. My grateful thanks go to my parents, for the example they set and for showing me the person I aim to be; all my students, for fuelling my passion for creating; Susan James and Peter Schiazza, for having enough faith to go through it all again; Owen Pearson for the OPMs; everyone within cycling distance, for turning up to help whenever I panicked; and not forgetting me, for being allergic to wool fibres and continuing to be me even when it wasn't a comfortable thing.

Sponsors

Yarn and other materials were kindly donated by the generous people at:

Introduction

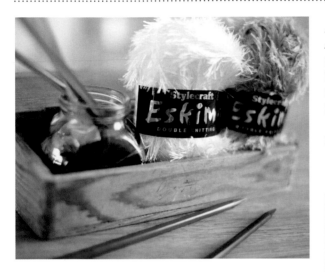

As with my first book, *Knitty Gritty: Knitting for the Absolute Beginner*, everything has been tried and tested by advanced-beginner and intermediate knitters, who have played an essential part in making this a user-friendly guide to the next stage in your knitting know-how.

I hope you enjoy the ride!

So ... you've knitted approximately 111 scarves, a few odds and ends, and been thoroughly baffled by a pattern written in Martian (I mean 'the ancient language of Knit') for a stylish little cardie that would be perfect if it were a little bit longer, had three-quarter-length sleeves and was stripy. Welcome to The Next Step in your knitting career! I'm Aneeta and I will be your guide in this tour of everything from mysterious knitting abbreviations to three-needle bind-offs to short-row shaping. We will be stopping off at the Stitch Library for a group hug and there is an optional detour to Sock City.

I plan to warm you up with some beguilingly simple patterns that will teach you a few essentials of shaping and finishing, and then throw you head-first into the excitement of double-pointed needles, giving patterns a personal touch, and a few other SSKs and SKPOs.

Tension and gauge

Knitting tension (or the gauge of your knitting) can seem like a mathematical minefield when you first learn about it. What it means is ensuring that you knit the same sized piece, with the same number of stitches as in a knitting pattern, to make a garment the same size as the one shown.

Tension is less important for projects like scarves, shawls and bags, as these don't need to have an exact fit. But they are very important to consider if you are knitting a garment with a fitted shape. If your tension isn't accurate, you might do a lot of knitting only to end up with a garment that's too big or too small, which would be very annoying!

This can be tricky, as we all knit tighter or looser than the knitter next to us, and I've found that this often trips up less experienced knitters, but it can be important, so I'll try to explain it.

Most gauges are measured in stocking stitch, but they can also be specific to the stitch used in an individual pattern. I'll explain it for stocking stitch – but the principle is the same for all stitches.

Gauges are usually measured in stitches per 10cm. This means how many stitches (and rows) you need to knit to end up with a square that measures 10 x 10cm. For example, using double knit yarn and 4mm needles, the standard tension is 22sts x 30 rows = 10cm square

of stocking stitch. This means that if you cast on 22sts and knit in stocking stitch for 30 rows, you should end up with a 10cm square of knitting.

Every knitting pattern states the tension required in terms of a small sample square of knitting called a tension square, which you should knit before you start to check that you are working to the correct tension.

It is suggested that every time you use a new yarn to knit a garment that needs to fit precisely, you work a tension square before you start. As I said, although a gauge for the yarn will be shown at the start of most knitting patterns, it's not essential to work a tension square for items like toys, scarves, etc. that don't need a precise fit. If you are knitting a scarf that asks for double knit yarn for example, you can confidently use any double knit yarn available for this non-fitted project.

Learn to read the information on the yarn label. It will tell you the optimum needle size and the gauge, as well as useful stuff such as washing instructions. You might find it useful to start a scrapbook for your knitting projects, and stick in the yarn label and a bit of the yarn for each pattern.

Note to Knitters

The stitch count is more important to get right than the row count. This is because most patterns ask you to work to a certain length rather than to a specific number of rows, so it's easier to rectify any tension issues in the length of your knitting.

However, if you are about to embark on a garment that is shaped, and needs to fit, a tension square is recommended. Here are a few things to remember when knitting a tension square:

1. When you are working a tension square, start by casting on around 10 more stitches than the gauge asks for. This way, you can measure the stitches in the middle of the square and get a more accurate measurement than if measuring right to the ends of a knitted piece.

2. For the same reason, work a few more rows than the gauge specifies, so you aren't measuring right to the edge.

3. If your square works out to be smaller than it should be, you need to work another tension square using bigger needles (start with 1mm bigger).

4. If the square ends up bigger than it should be, your tension is too loose and you need to try again with smaller needles.

How to measure the gauge of a tension square

Step 1: Using the recommended needles for your yarn, knit a practice square about 10sts and 10 rows bigger than the tension square shown on the yarn label. For example, the gauge for the yarn in the photo is 14sts x 22 rows in stocking stitch on 7mm needles = 10cm square. Therefore I knitted my tension square to 24sts and 32 rows.

Step 2: Then pin out a section 10cm square. The area you've measured out should contain 14sts x 22 rows.

Questions & Answers

Help! I've counted the right number of stitches but not the right number of rows.

Getting the stitch count right is more important than getting the right number of rows. This is because most patterns tell you to knit to a certain length, rather than a specific number of rows.

I've counted 18sts within my 10cm square and not 14sts as the yarn label says.

If you have more stitches than you should have, your tension is too tight. If you have fewer stitches than you should have, your tension is too loose. If the tension is too tight, re-knit the square using bigger needles (or smaller needles if the tension is too loose).

Note to Knitters

Some knitting projects, such as scarves, blankets and toys, will not be too badly affected if your tension is slightly off. The time to be concerned is if you are knitting a precisely fitted garment. But as with everything, don't worry too much. Figuring out tension will take a bit of getting used to and you'll need to exercise your maths muscles, but you'll work it out. As I'll tell you again and again in this book, be patient.

A tension square isn't always necessary for children's garments; you can always knit one size bigger for a child if you want to be on the safe side.

The projects

I hope you find the size you're looking to knit in the projects shown in my book. Whilst I've tried to accommodate small, medium and large sizes for most of the garments, this is primarily a book for you to learn some intermediate techniques, and how to understand patterns in general. So if you don't find the size you need here, then hopefully the skills you learn whilst working on my projects will give you the knowledge and confidence to try all of the myriad of patterns to be found in other books and on the Internet.

The techniques and tips you'll learn whilst knitting the projects in this book are designed to give your work personality and finesse, and to give you as a knitter the confidence to be individual and brave in your knitting choices.

Please remember that my aim is to teach you some intermediate knitting skills and give you belief in yourself as a knitter. Then you can go forth and tackle some of the 'trendier' patterns you'll find out there in the wider knitting world!

Choosing your yarn (The Science Bit)

Rather than following the traditional knitting pattern route of saying exactly which brand of yarn you must use for a pattern, I will be giving you options and instructions so you can work within the correct gauge and weight of yarn, but be more creative and flexible with the yarn you choose, to suit you and your budget. The way I've done this is to give an approximate metreage of yarn required, rather than going by weight. Different fibres have different weights. For example, cotton is lighter than wool, so a 50g ball of cotton will have a longer metreage than a 50g ball of pure wool. So rather than tell

 Handy **HINT**

Substituting yarn
If the pattern says to use a specific yarn that you can't find or don't wish to use (for example, I'm allergic to pure wool so always try to find a cotton or man-made alternative), then checking your gauge by knitting a tension square will help you in making the correct choice of yarn for your pattern. Always take the pattern with you when shopping for yarn, as knitting shop staff have lots of practice in yarn substitution.

you to use, say, 100g of a specific yarn, I will state the approximate metreage you'll need to work at a specific gauge. Then you can read the yarn labels, which all describe the metreage as well as the weight, and choose a yarn with the correct gauge to go with the pattern.

For example:

For the Adult booties on p.168, you need 107m yarn, 10mm needles, and a tension of 9sts for a 10cm square knitted in stocking stitch. A yarn that will knit up to that gauge is Rowan Big Wool, and there are 80m in each 100g ball of that wool. Here's the Science Bit:

Total number of metres needed for the project ÷ the number of metres in the ball of yarn = the number of balls of yarn you need.

For the Adult booties, the maths would be:

107m (the amount needed for a pair of booties)
÷ 80m (the metreage in one ball of Rowan Big Wool)
= 1.34

So you need approximately 1.34 balls of Rowan Big Wool to knit a pair of Adult booties. Of course you would need to buy two balls and would have a bit left over at the end.

Well done to you all for sticking with me through the maths part!

My method is not the traditional way of showing yarn quantities for a pattern, but I hope that it will make your knitting choices more fluid and less prescribed, thus adding to the individuality of your knitting. It'll mean a little more maths for you at the start, but in the long run it will mean that you get to make more creative decisions in your knitting.

How to use this book

The main thing to remember is that this book aims to teach you and give you confidence in your knitting. Follow the techniques chapters carefully, and if some practice is suggested, then please do it – it will benefit you in the long run, I promise! When you come to try out the projects, if you are a less confident knitter, follow the patterns as written. If you are more confident or become more confident as you work through the book, feel free to adapt the patterns to suit you. Be brave and you'll learn so much more about

knitting than you can learn from any book! Don't be afraid to experiment: I've learnt more from the mistakes I've made in my knitting than from following every pattern exactly as it is written.

I hope that I've given you enough information to guide you, but not so much that you won't be able to use your initiative to progress further. Once you've mastered the techniques, you can be as creative as you dare!

Techniques

Casting on

There are lots of different ways to cast on, but here are two of the most used methods. Sometimes a pattern will suggest a particular method, and at other times you are free to experiment and find out which method you like the best.

Basic two-needle cast-on

I find this the simplest method for less experienced knitters, as it has many of the same moves as the basic knit stitch.

Step 1: Start with the slip knot on the left-hand needle and pick up the stitch with the right-hand needle, pushing the tip through to the back so that the needles are crossed left over right. Hold both the needles in your left hand.

Step 2: Wrap the yarn back and then middle around the right-hand needle (the one that's crossed at the back).

Step 3: Push the tip of the right-hand needle into the loop on the left-hand needle, under and to the front of the work.

Step 4: Stand the needles up straight and hold the stitches with your thumbs.

Step 5: Insert the tip of the left-hand needle up into the stitch on the right.

Step 6: Release (pull out) the right-hand needle out of the stitch: you have cast on a new stitch.

Continue until you have as many stitches as you need.

Thumb method

You might find that you get a neater edge if you use the thumb method, if you are starting with a ribbed border, or you might just prefer it to the two-needle cast-on. Have a go and start learning about your own preferences.

Handy HINT

It's always hard to tell how much yarn to leave in the long tail of yarn. Be cautious: leave as much as you think you need and then add a bit more! It's very frustrating if you cast on lots of stitches and run out of yarn just before you have the number you need. A good tip is to cast on 10sts and see how much yarn that uses. You can then do a bit of maths to multiply it to the amount you need, and add on a bit for luck. Think more, rather than less!

Step 1: Make a slip knot, leaving a long tail of yarn. This long tail will be needed to make the cast-on stitches, so make sure you leave plenty.

Hold the needle with the slip knot in your right hand. Keep the yarn attached to the ball in your right hand, and the long tail of yarn in your left hand.

Stand your left thumb so it is facing upwards, holding the long tail of yarn behind your thumb.

Step 2: Put your left thumb under and up the long end of the yarn.

Step 3: Put the needle up the yarn you've wrapped around your left thumb.

Step 4: Move the needle to your left hand and wrap the yarn that's attached to the ball back and then middle around the needle, using your right hand.

Step 5: Move the needle back over to your right hand and lift the yarn wrapped around your left thumb over the needle.

Step 6: Release the yarn from your left thumb and pull tightly on both ends of the yarn.

Continue until you have the number of stitches you require.

Basic stitches

Knitting is made up of two basic stitches: knit and purl. Using them in different combinations gives you different effects. Let's brush up on the basics.

How to do knit stitch

Start with the needle with the cast-on stitches in your left hand and the empty needle in your right hand.

Note to Knitters

You will notice that I often talk about the 'back', 'middle' or 'front' in relation to making a stitch. 'Front' is closest to you, 'back' is furthest away from you, and 'middle' is in between the two knitting needles when they are crossed over.

Step 1: Pick it up. Insert the tip of the right-hand needle into the stitch on the left-hand needle – from the bottom to the top. Keep the needles crossed, left over right.

Step 2: Back and then middle. Holding both the needles in your left hand (between the thumb and first two fingers) wrap the long end of the yarn to the back of both needles (away from you) and then through the middle of the needles (back towards you).

Step 3: Underneath and to the front. Bring the tip of the right-hand needle under the first loop on the left-hand needle.

Step 4: Release. Gently push the stitch on the left-hand needle off, using your left thumb. Repeat to the end of the row.

How to do purl stitch

3a

3b

Step 1: Pick it up. Insert the tip of the right-hand needle into the stitch on the left-hand needle – from top to the bottom. Keep the needles crossed, right over left. The yarn should be at the front of the work.

Step 2: Middle and then front. Holding both the needles in your left hand (between thumb and first two fingers), wrap the long end of the yarn through the middle of the needles and then to the front of the needles.

Step 3: Underneath and to the back. Take the tip of the right-hand needle under the first loop on the left-hand needle and to the back of the left-hand needle.

4

Step 4: Release. Gently push the stitch on the left-hand needle off, using your left thumb. Repeat to the end of the row.

Garter stitch = if you knit every row.

Stocking stitch = if you knit one row, then purl one row, and repeat.

Stitch combinations

Handy HINT

Once you can knit and purl in combination, you have hundreds of stitches at your fingertips. Experiment, concentrate and don't forget to count your stitches at the end of every row.

Rib stitch. If you alternate knit and purl stitches on an even number of cast-on stitches, you get 1 x 1 rib.

Moss stitch. If you alternate knit and purl stitches on an odd number of cast-on stitches, you get moss stitch.

Note to Knitters

When you knit, the right-hand needle goes to the back and the yarn is held to the back.

When you purl, the right-hand needle goes to the front and the yarn is held to the front.

When you work with knit and purl stitches, you have to move the yarn to the back, over and between the needles when you are knitting and to the front when you are purling. Pay attention, or you'll end up with a mistake!

Shaping: decreasing and increasing

Note to Knitters

Shaping knitting is essential if you want to do more than knit in straight lines. By learning how to increase and decrease, you can knit any shape you want and this will be invaluable if and when you choose to design your own knitting patterns, or adapt patterns to suit your shape.

Decreasing

There are lots of ways of doing everything in knitting. In my first book, which was for the absolute beginner to knitting, I only showed you one basic way of doing each technique. For example, decreasing was K2tog. Now I want to add to your shaping repertoire and abbreviation know-how.

How you choose to decrease will affect the finished look of your edging. There are different methods depending on which way your knitted edge will slant.

In this picture, the right-hand slope is slanting to the left and the left-hand slope is slanting to the right – this is with the right side of the work facing you (i.e. the knit side on stocking stitch). Please note that this is not a fully fashioned raglan, as the shaping is done right at the edge of the knitting. (A fully fashioned raglan is when the shaping is made one or two stitches in from the edge of the knitting so it shows as a ridge on the edge – you'll see this in the Ladies' raglan jumper on p.172.)

To create a right slant

The simplest way of decreasing is K2tog or P2tog. Both these methods give you a slant to the right – as you look at the knitting from the right side of the work (on stocking stitch).

K2tog = Knit two stitches together.

P2tog = Purl two stitches together.

To create a left slant

On the knit side – this is the right side (RS) of the work – K2tog tbl. This means that you knit two stitches together through the back of the loops – pick up the stitches, wrap the yarn back and middle around the back needle, bring that needle underneath and to the front, and release both stitches.

On the purl side – this is the wrong side of the work (WS) – P2tog tbl. This means that you purl two stitches together through the back of the loops – bring the needle to the front, wrap the yarn middle and front around the front needle, bring that needle underneath and to the back, and release both stitches.

K2tog tbl

K2tog tbl = Knit two stitches together through the back of the loop.

P2tog tbl

P2tog tbl = Purl two stitches together through the back of the loops.

Note to Knitters

'Knitwise' means treat the stitches as if you were about to knit them.

'Purlwise' means treat the stitches as if you were about to purl them.

continue...

SSK = Slip, Slip, Knit

Step 1: Slip two stitches, one by one, knitwise (as if you were about to knit them), from the left needle to the right needle, without knitting them.

Step 2: Insert the left-hand needle into the front of both these stitches: you are now in position to knit the two stitches together.

Step 3: If you look closely at the base of the stitch you've knitted, you can see that it slants to the left. This will become more apparent the more decrease rows you knit.

SKP = Slip, Knit, Pass (or SKPO = Slip, Knit, Pass Over)

Step 1: Slip a stitch knitwise (as if you were about to knit it).

Step 2: Knit the next stitch.

Step 3: Pass the slipped stitch over the knitted stitch by inserting the left-hand needle down into the front of the slipped stitch on the right-hand needle, then lift it over the stitch you have just knitted (as if you were casting it off). There is now one less stitch remaining on the right-hand needle.

Increasing

M1 = Make One
The simplest way of increasing is
M1 = Make one stitch. This is where
you pick up the loop in between two
stitches and knit it.

Step 1: Find the horizontal loop of yarn that runs between two stitches and pick it up towards you with the left-hand needle, from the back to the front.

Step 2: Then knit the loop that you have just picked up. It'll feel tight, but this is normal.

KFB = Knit Front and Back

Another way of increasing you'll often see in patterns is KFB. The result doesn't look very different from an increase made by M1, but it's still a useful trick to have up your knitted sleeve.

Step 1: Pick up the stitch, wrap the yarn around the needle, and work the stitch but do not release it from the left-hand needle.

Step 2: Then pick up the same stitch by going into the back of it.

Step 3: Wrap the yarn around the back needle, back and then middle.

Step 4: Work the stitch by bringing the right-hand needle under and to the front.

Step 5: Now release the stitch. You'll see that you have two stitches on the right-hand needle where you've knitted twice into one stitch, thus increasing!

Handy HINT

Rule Number One:
It's very important that you always have the correct number of stitches, especially after a decrease or increase row. Count your stitches!

Casting off

Basic cast-off

Casting off (or binding off) is what you do when you have completed your knitting, so it can live independently from the needles. It's your first step in achieving a neat finish (this is something I'll talk about a lot in this book!).

Step 1: Knit two stitches.

Step 2: Insert the tip of the left-hand needle down into the first stitch that you knitted on the right-hand needle.

Step 3: Lift the lower stitch over the top stitch and off the right-hand needle. Finally, release the stitch you lifted over the right needle off the left needle. You will then have one stitch on the right-hand needle.

Step 4: Keep casting off in the same way, until you have one stitch left on the right-hand needle and the left-hand needle is empty. Then cut the yarn, leaving a tail, which you will need to weave in later.

Step 5: Pass the cut end of the yarn through the last stitch left on the knitting needle, and pull it tight. This is called fastening off.

Drawstring finish

A drawstring finish is a way of finishing your knitting as an alternative to casting off. It works when you want the knitting to have a rounded edge, for example at the top of a hat or the fingers of gloves.

Note to Knitters

Some patterns will require you to fasten off as a way of finishing. For example, the Christmas tree on p.256 decreases to one stitch, therefore you only need to fasten off as there are no stitches left to cast off.

Step 1: Cut the yarn, leaving a long tail, and thread it onto a darning needle.

Step 2: Pass the darning needle through the stitches remaining on the knitting needle one by one, removing them off the knitting needle as they are secured by the yarn on the darning needle.

Step 3: Pull the yarn tightly: you'll see that it acts like a drawstring on the stitches. You can now use the yarn on the darning needle to sew up your seam as required in your pattern.

Three-needle bind-off

The three-needle bind-off is one of my all-time favourite techniques. It's a hugely satisfying way of finishing your work if you have two edges that need to be sewn together – for example on the top of a hood, as I'll show you in the Versatile kiddies' jumper pattern on p.192. I promise that once you've had a go, you won't tire of showing off the tidy finish on the outside and the inside of your work!

Step 1: You need to start with the same number of stitches on two needles. Hold both the needles in your left hand, with the right sides of the work facing each other and the points of the needles facing to the right. (If all your stitches are on one straight needle, transfer half your stitches onto another needle, with the points of both needles facing the edges of the knitted piece.)

Step 2: Using a third straight knitting needle, the same size as you've been knitting with, and held in your right hand, pick up a stitch from the tips of both needles, as if you were knitting (knitwise). First, you pick up the stitch from the needle closest to you, then from the needle that's further away from you.

Step 3: When you have picked up these two stitches, knit them together (it's a bit fiddly, but persevere!).

You'll be releasing both the stitches on the left-hand needles at the same time as you knit them together. You will now have one stitch knitted on the right-hand needle.

Step 4: Repeat so you have two stitches on the right-hand needle. Then, using the tip of the needle nearest to you in your left hand, lift the first stitch on the right-hand needle over the second stitch, thus casting it off.

Continue along the row. You are now casting off using three needles!

You'll see on the right side of the work that this gives you a really neat finish.

Continue casting off all the stitches in the same way to the end, then fasten off as normal. Weave the end of the yarn into the wrong-side seam of your cast-off. Turn your knitting the right side out and see your neat finish – you'll soon see why this is one of my favourite techniques!

Kitchener stitch

Kitchener stitch gives a similar-looking finish to a three-needle bind-off, but uses a different technique. You'll get a very tidy result, which is useful for finishing the toe of a sock, for example.

To set up, you need the same number of stitches on two needles. Hold the work with the right side facing outwards, and arrange your needles so that they are parallel to each other, and both tips are pointing towards the right. Hold the work in your left hand.

Cut the yarn, leaving a long tail, and thread it onto a darning needle – hold this in your right hand.

To start, insert the darning needle into the front stitch (the one on the knitting needle nearest to you) purlwise (as if to purl) and pull the yarn through.

Then insert the darning needle into the back stitch (the one on the knitting needle furthest away from you) knitwise (as if to knit). Pull the yarn through the stitches, leaving the stitches on the knitting needle.

Please note that you only need to do this at the beginning of your Kitchener stitch.

Note to Knitters

Kitchener stitch is also sometimes called grafting.

Kitchener stitch: now repeat the following instructions until you have one stitch left on each knitting needle:

Step 1: Insert the darning needle into the front stitch knitwise, and slip the stitch off the knitting needle.

Step 2: Then insert the darning needle into the front stitch purlwise, leave the

stitch on the knitting needle and pull the yarn through both stitches.

Step 3: Insert the darning needle into the back stitch purlwise, and slip the stitch off the knitting needle.

Step 4: Then push the darning needle into the back stitch knitwise, leave the

stitch on the knitting needle and pull the yarn through both stitches.

Continue in this way – you'll soon see your tidy finish!

Repeat steps 1–4 until you have one stitch remaining on each of the needles in your left hand.

To finish the last two stitches, slip the front stitch knitwise and slip the back stitch purlwise. Pull the yarn through. Then take the yarn to the inside of the work by pushing the darning needle through to the inside of your sewn-up knitting.

Weave the end into the wrong side of your knitting and enjoy the tidy finish.

Handy HINT

A little phrase that I repeat to myself as I do Kitchener stitch might help you:

Front: knit, slip, purl, leave – pull through.

Back: purl, slip, knit, leave – pull through.

Finishing techniques

I-cord

I-cord is a method for knitting a very small tube. You use two double-pointed needles. This technique is a pretty cute way of finishing off a kiddy's hat (see p.226) or it can be used to knit limbs for your toys (see p.258).

Step 1: Cast on the number of stitches your pattern requires onto a double-pointed needle (dpn).

Step 2: Knit one row.

Step 3: Slide the knitting down to the other end of the double-pointed knitting needle.

Step 4: Hold the knitting in your left hand and pull the yarn to the right.

Step 5: Knit the next row with the yarn pulled from the other side of the

knitting. This will feel strange, but you have to trust me here!

Continue in this way, every time sliding the stitches to the other end of the double-pointed needle and knitting the next row by pulling the yarn to the right.

At the end of every few rows, pull the knitting down from the needle to stretch it a bit. You'll soon see your I-cord forming.

To finish, you can cast off normally or use a drawstring finish and weave the end into the inside of your I-cord.

Pick up and knit

This is a technique whereby you pick up stitches from one edge of a piece of knitting and continue working in that direction. You'll mostly see it used for neckbands on sweaters and button bands on cardigans. I love it, as it makes for such a neat finish. You'll need a crochet hook to pick up the stitches – use one in a size close to, or slightly smaller than that of the knitting needles.

Step 1: Lay out your work with the right side facing upwards. You will be picking up the stitches from the right to the left of the knitting, and not from left to right as you might imagine it to be done. Insert the crochet hook into the edge of the work, making sure that it slides under two loops of yarn.

Step 2: Wrap the yarn around the crochet hook and pull the hook back out from the two loops of yarn.

Step 3: Place this yarn on a knitting needle (which will be pointing to the left).

Continue picking up stitches along the edge of your knitting in this way.

Handy HINT

When picking up stitches from a long length of knitting, I suggest that you mark out sections with dressmaking pins. Divide each section into eight equal parts and work out how many stitches you need to pick up per section. This will ensure that you don't get to the end and discover that you are way out on your numbers.

Buttonholes

You can knit a small buttonhole by following this basic instruction: YF, K2tog (yarn forward, knit two together). The size of your buttonhole will be relative to your yarn and needle size.

Buttonholes are often worked on a ribbed border; the technique for working buttonholes is the same, whatever stitch you are using, but I'll be showing it to you on a rib as it's a useful bit of knowledge to have.

Note to Knitters

Knitting with the yarn forward gives you an extra stitch, and knitting two stitches together gives you one fewer stitch, so you'll have the same number of stitches at the end of the row as you started with.

continue...

Buttonholes *continued*...

Buttonholes in a ribbed border

To get a really tidy finish for buttonholes on a ribbed border, you need to know exactly when to rib. A pattern will often tell you to rib a certain number of stitches in between the buttonholes. To do this, you need to be able to tell whether the next stitch is a knit or a purl simply by looking at it. For a refresher on this, see Recognising rib stitches (p.160).

For example, the pattern could say: '[rib 12, YF, K2tog], repeat a further ten times'. To rib 12, you need to know exactly which stitch to start ribbing with: a knit or a purl. So you would work 12 stitches of rib (starting with a knit or a purl as the pattern demands), then YF, K2tog – that sequence of knitting will give you a buttonhole with 12 stitches of rib in between each buttonhole.

Step 1: Work to where you want the buttonhole to be.

Step 2: YF (bring the yarn to the front of the work, in between the two needles).

Step 3: K2tog (knit the next two stitches together).

Make sure, at the end of the buttonhole row, that you have the same number of stitches as you started with.

In the row after the buttonhole row, you'll continue your rib as you have been doing in previous rows (continue as 'set'). When you get to where you made a buttonhole, it will look a bit like a crossed-over stitch. This isn't a mistake – this is how it should look after you've worked the YF, K2tog.

Continue ribbing over the buttonhole stitch, making sure to follow your stitches accurately.

At the end of the row after the buttonhole row, you should see the buttonholes appear neatly!

Blocking

Blocking is a technique by which you stretch and shape a knitted fabric into specific dimensions. This can be helpful if your work needs to be a certain shape, or if two knitted pieces need to be exactly the same size, or if the holes in lace knitting need to be more opened up to show off the pattern.

This is a tricky subject for me, as my personal opinion conflicts with the traditional view. The traditional view is that all knitting should be blocked if you want to achieve a good finish. Personally, however, I don't always like the look of blocked knitting, as I feel it flattens the texture of the fabric and, for me, spoils the natural look of knitting. This is especially true on raised stitches such as cable work.

However, I do approve of blocking for fine lace patterns. Lacework on delicate yarn does benefit from blocking, as it opens out the weave of the fabric and shows it to its best advantage. I also use blocking on 'whimsies' such as the knitted Christmas tree (see p.256), as it helps to stiffen the shape.

Handy HINT

If you find that a garment you've knitted is coming out a bit smaller than you expected, blocking can put some ease into the fabric, therefore making it a little bigger. But beware, as this isn't an exact science!

Techniques

There are several techniques for blocking:

1. Pin and spray (shown below).

2. Steam blocking. This is where you pin the garment to an ironing board and hold a steam iron over it, very close to the surface but not quite touching, and then press the steam button. Do this all over the fabric, wait a couple of hours until the fabric is completely dry and then unpin it. Repeat a couple of times before unpinning for very fine lace: see the Fir tree lace shawl on p.278.

3. Wet blocking. This is the most drastic method of blocking, which I suggest you use only on very fine lacework. Immerse the knitting in cool water (beware of using water that's too warm, especially with wool fibres). Lay out a sheet of plastic (a bin bag will do) and cover it with towels larger than the piece of knitting. Lay the wet knitting on the towels and pin the work into the shape and dimensions you want it to be. Then you can remove any excess

moisture by laying more towels on top of the work and pressing gently. Leave the work pinned in position until it's completely dry.

4. Weight blocking. This is where you spray the knitting, cover it and weigh it down with heavy books until it is dry. This will stiffen the knitting into shape. See the Christmas tree on p.256.

The pin and spray method

You can see on these squares of Fir tree lace (see p.278), that the square on the left has been blocked and the square on the right has not.

Step 1: Pin the piece into shape on a padded surface (for example an ironing board, a large piece of foam or a specialised knitting board). Your pattern may specify dimensions for the knitted fabric; if so, follow these.

Step 2: Spray the fabric with a mist of water and leave until dry.

Sewing up

For most knitters, sewing up isn't their favourite part of a knitting project. In fact, I know lots of knitters who knit in the round in order to avoid it as much as they can. But I'm different – I really enjoy finishing a project and getting it to look as professional as possible, because it doesn't matter how good a knitter you are, if you bodge something together, it will show!

The tricksy thing about sewing up is that it's a little bit different every time, depending on the stitch you're knitting with and the angle of the edge of your work. I'll try and show you a few different ways of sewing up to add to your repertoire and help you to take a big step towards making your knitting neat and professional, with a touch of class.

Mattress stitch

This stitch will give you an invisible finish if both the pieces to be joined are knitted in stocking stitch (knit one row, purl one row). It can also be used when working with rib stitch.

These two pieces of stocking stitch knitting are side by side

If you look closely at the 'V' of the stitch and dig your darning needle into the 'V', you'll pick up a horizontal bar inside the 'V'.

Pick up the centre bar from one side, then the next and so on, back and forth. After you've picked up about four centre bars, pull tight and you'll see that you've sewn up the pieces with a near-invisible finish. You'll often be using the centre-bar technique for the side and underarm seams of your cardigans and jumpers.

These two pieces of stocking stitch knitting are end to end

Handy HINT

If you feel like you aren't getting a tidy finish, try again; this time working a little further in from the very edge of your knitted piece. You'll find it isn't as neat if you're trying to find your centre bars and sides of the 'V' too near the edge of the knitting.

If your pieces of knitting are end to end, for example a shoulder seam, you need to pick up the two sides of the 'V' of the stitch with your darning needle.

Pick up the two 'V' sides from one piece, then the other, about four times before pulling tight for a neat finish.

These two pieces of stocking stitch knitting have the end and side facing each other

This situation might occur when you are sewing a sleeve into the body of a jumper or cardigan.

If your pieces of knitting face in different directions, as they would if you were sewing a sleeve into the body of a garment, for example, you mix both techniques. On one side, pick up the centre bar, and on the other side, pick up two sides of the 'V'. Pull tight for a neat finish.

Sewing a sleeve into a body

Note to Knitters

I'm showing you how to do this technique as if you were sewing in a sleeve. This is why we start from the middle (by the shoulder seam) and work out towards the underarm. Then you go back and sew the other side, from the shoulder seam to the other underarm. This will help to ensure that the sleeve is evenly placed.

The sleeve is on the right and the body piece with the shoulder seam is on the left. Start sewing up in the centre, by the shoulder seam. Note that you are picking up the centre bar on the body (on the left) and two sides of the 'V' on the sleeve (on the right).

continue...

Sewing a sleeve into a body *continued...*

 Handy HINT

Thread a darning needle with a long piece of yarn when you start sewing in the middle. When you pull the yarn through the first stitch, leave a long enough tail for you to go back and sew the other half of the sleeve with the same piece of yarn.

Here's what the final seam should look like. Another nice, neat finish!

Angled edges (not fully fashioned)

These two pieces of knitting have an angled edge – this could be some shaping around a sleeve or a (not fully fashioned) raglan edge. You can see that I'm picking up the centre bar from each side, then pulling the yarn tight for a tidy finish.

You can see here the finish you'll get if you are sewing up a raglan that is not fully fashioned – this is where the decreases are made right at the edge of the knitting. You'll be using this technique on sections of the Ladies' classic cardigan on p.200.

Angled edges (fully fashioned)

Look out for this technique on the Ladies' raglan jumper on p.172.

You can see that the decreases are more defined on this piece of knitting, as they are made one stitch in from the edge: K1, SSK, K to last 3sts, K2tog, K1.

Once again, you are picking up the centre bar from each side, but you are leaving one fully distinct stitch on the inside of the work. You can see it clearly on the left of the darning needle.

When you pull up the yarn tightly, you'll see one stitch at the edge of the raglan on each side. These come together to make two neat stitches, side by side along the sewn seam.

Here's your tidy finish!

The principle is the same on a fully fashioned finish where the decreases are made two stitches in from the edge, for example in the Men's bulky jumper on p.180.

Sewing up around corners

Here I'm sewing in a right-angled piece (see, for example, the modified drop shoulder in the Versatile kiddies' jumper on p.192). I mix and match my centre bar and two sides of the 'V' techniques as I need to.

You can see that the result took plenty of initiative, but it's worth it for the final look.

These angles are as you might find when sewing up a fitted sleeve, as in the Ladies' classic cardigan (see p.200). I start off with two sides of the 'V' on both pieces.

Pull tight as you go.

What you'll find, as you gain experience in sewing up pieces with different angles, is that you'll have to adjust your sewing from one side to the next. Don't be afraid to undo a few stitches and try them another way until you get a satisfying finish.

Sewing up garter stitch

Look closely at the garter stitch and you'll see ridges. Each ridge has a top and a bottom. With a darning needle and yarn, pick up the bottom ridge on one side.

Then pick up the top ridge on the other side, and work back and forth.

Pull the yarn tight every few stitches.

Whip stitch

This is a very simple stitch for sewing up, in which you pick up a loop from each side of the knitting.

Handy HINT

You won't be tying knots at the beginning and end of your sewing up. Leave a long tail at each end and weave them in along the seam on the inside of your knitting.

Note to Knitters

You'll hear me go on and on about a tidy finish ... I don't want you to spend months knitting something and let yourself down with the sewing up. Be patient and it'll be worth it in the end!

Easing in

This is a technique that you might know if you sew, but it's just as useful for a knitter when making up projects and garments. Sometimes the two pieces of knitted fabric you are sewing together won't be exactly the same length, row for row or stitch for stitch. This is often the case with sleeves, for example. This is when you have to 'ease in' your sewing or, as I call it, 'make it fit'. To make the two sides fit each other, every now and again, at regular intervals, you will need to pick up an extra loop of the fabric on the side that is longer.

Handy HINT

As well as paying attention to the spot you are sewing, also remember to keep an eye on the end point – that's the point in the knitting where the sewing-up should end neatly.

If the centre-bar side is too long, occasionally (and evenly spread out throughout the length of the sewing-up), pick up two centre bars at once.

If the two sides of the 'V' side is too long, occasionally (and evenly spread out throughout the length of the sewing-up), pick up three 'V' sides at once.

Note to Knitters

You have to use your initiative when sewing up – never more so than when you need to 'ease in' – but as you'll hopefully have several projects under your belt by the time you get to a project that requires this technique, I have every confidence in your judgement!

Note to Knitters

You won't need to ease in if you are sewing up two pieces that are the same, for example, the front and back of the body part of a jumper, but it's still very useful to keep checking the end point of your sewing so that you can make sure the pieces will sew together accurately. If you find yourself a stitch or two out, you can use the trick of picking up an extra loop on the side that is longer.

Knitting SOS!

This chapter gives you some handy hints and tips to smooth your knitting journey, and also answers a few niggling questions that never seem to be explained in patterns. It's not an exhaustive list by any means, but is hopefully somewhere for you to turn in those head-scratching moments that all knitters have.

Knitting rules

Here are a few rules to make your knitting journey a smooth one. As you move on to more involved patterns and challenging techniques, I think you'll find them helpful for keeping your stitches in order.

Rule Number One: At the end of every row, count your stitches! There's no getting away from this essential rule of knitting.

Rule Number Two: Never put down your knitting in the middle of a row. It's easy to lose concentration if you do, and you may make a mistake that could be hard to fix.

Rule Number Three: Try to knit at least two rows every day. You want to keep in the swing of knitting – leaving it for days (or worse still, weeks) at a time will make it less easy in the long run. This is especially true if you are working on a more complicated stitch or pattern.

Rule Number Four: This might seem to be a funny one, but you'll learn that it's essential! When knitting in a group with other knitters or crafters (and this is something I've learnt from experience with knitting students), always do your counting silently. There will always be someone else in the room who is counting at the same time, and we all know how annoying it is to lose count!

Handy HINT

Sometimes you will find that you run into something that just doesn't make sense, no matter how many times you try it. I still find this when writing a pattern or working out a new stitch. My tried and tested advice is to keep calm, take a break and come back to it later. There's really no point in flogging yourself when you are tired. I've often found that something I can't get right for hours in the evening can make sense in ten minutes when I'm fresh in the morning. I say again and again that knitting is about the journey as much as the destination.

Frogging: *how to un-knit your knitting*

We're all human ... even the perfectionists! Sometimes even the best knitters in the world will lose concentration and make a mistake. I reckon we all know what it's like to knit when we should have purled! So although I'm an advocate of the 'Keep Calm and Carry On' method of knitting, on occasion you will want or need to undo several stitches or rows.

Undoing your knitting one stitch at a time
This is for when you've made a mistake in a row so just need to backtrack for a few stitches.

In this image you can see that point A is the stitch that is currently on the needle. The hole at point B is the stitch below, which the current stitch is coming out of – this is the previous row to the row on the needle.

Insert the tip of the left needle, away from you, into the previous row.

Then push the stitch from the current row off the right-hand needle. Pull the end of the yarn – this will undo the stitch.

You can continue un-knitting one stitch at a time until you get to the place in your knitting before the mistake. Then, you'll find that you are already in the correct position to keep on knitting – with the knitted stitches on the right-hand needle and the stitches you've undone (to be knitted) on the left-hand needle.

Undoing several rows at a time
This is for use when you're really unhappy with what you've knitted and need to go back several rows. This is also known as 'frogging'.

Pull the stitches off the knitting needle (this can take guts) – but if it has to be done, then be brave! Pull on the yarn to unravel the knitting until you are at the row before the row you want to keep. You will undo this row, one stitch at a time, to get to the row you want to keep and put the stitches back on the knitting needle.

Hold the knitting in your right hand and the empty needle in your left hand. Put your thumb at the base of the first stitch, holding it firmly – this is to stop the stitch laddering any further than you want it to.

Gently pull the yarn out so that you are undoing only the first stitch on your work and follow through by simultaneously pushing the empty needle through the stitch, remembering to push the needle away from you.

On the needle in your left hand, you now have the first stitch of the row you want to start working from. Continue undoing the stitches one at a time and putting them safely back onto the left needle.

Note to Knitters

Frogging is not recommended for lace knitting, as it's really tricky to undo rows when you might have yarn-overs or extra lace loops. For lace, the best way is to use a saver row (see p.161).

Handy HINT
At this point, Rule Number One is invaluable in helping you check that you picked up all the stitches. Count, count, count!

continue…

Frogging *continued…*

What NOT to do!

It's easy to make a mistake when picking up frogged stitches. You may think that you got it right, but then the next row will be very tight to knit and later on you'll see a row that looks a bit odd.

Here you can see a row where the stitches all look twisted. This is because the stitches have been put back on the knitting needle backwards.

If you put the needle through the stitch towards you, you've made a mistake. You'll notice this when you're knitting the next row, as it will feel really tight to knit.

When you put the stitches back on the knitting needle, be sure to push the needle into the stitch AWAY FROM YOU.

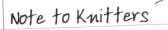

Note to Knitters

Whether you are un-knitting knit or purl stitches, the principle is the same. If you can't easily find the previous row, try moving the yarn forwards or backwards between the needles, as this should make it clearer. And always push the needle away from you into the stitch.

Recognising rib stitches

Rib is where you knit and purl stitches so they appear in columns in your knitting. You'll mostly find ribbing on the cuffs and collars of jumpers and cardigans, and the cuffs of gloves and socks. It creates a stretchier fabric than garter or stocking stitch.

When you knit a stitch, the yarn is at the back.

When you purl a stitch, the yarn is at the front.

A very useful little trick is knowing exactly where you are on a rib row without having to count from the beginning of the row. If you know exactly what knit and purl stitches look like, you'll save a great deal of time and you'll have taken another step in really understanding the structure of your knitting, which will make you a more **confident knitter.**

Handy HINT

I like to describe my stitches as if they were little faces – with the stitch on the needle as the face. You can see that the first 'face' on the left-hand needle is wearing a V-neck jumper, and the stitch to its left is wearing a horizontal line that I call a polo-neck jumper. So you can remember this as: 'P' for polo, 'P' for purl. It may seem funny, but I guarantee that you'll be looking for the V-necks and polo-necks as an easy way of knowing which stitch you are on in a rib pattern!

Note to Knitters

This knowledge will come in especially handy when you are casting off in a rib pattern.

If you look at this piece of I x I rib, you can see the columns of stitches. Look closely and you'll notice that one column looks like a 'V' (the knit stitches); the other column is almost hidden between the Vs and looks like a little horizontal line (the purl stitches).

Saver row

Learning new stitches and knitting lace can be complicated, and a small lapse in concentration can mean you have the wrong number of stitches at the end of your row. Rather than having to undo an entire row, here's a little SOS trick to 'save' your stitches. I'm not a natural lace knitter, but love the effect of lace, so I found this technique really useful when knitting my Fir tree lace (see p.278). You can use this technique on any stitch pattern you like, if you're worried about going wrong.

Take a contrasting coloured yarn (cut a piece that is about three times the width of your knitting) and thread it onto a darning needle. When you are at the end of a repeat for a stitch pattern (about to start Row 1 of a stitch pattern sequence), thread the yarn through all the stitches on the knitting needle.

Thread the contrasting yarn through a couple of stitches at a time, and pull it through as you go, leaving a long tail dangling at each end.

You'll end up with a length of contrasting yarn running through all the stitches on the needle.

continue...

KNITTING SOS! | 161

Saver row continued...

Continue knitting the pattern.

Note to Knitters

Only use a piece of saving yarn after the end of a pattern repeat. This way, you know that if you ever have to undo, you will start knitting again from Row 1 of your repeat.

If you make a mistake, simply pull out the knitting needle and undo the knitting until you get to the row that's on the saver yarn.

You'll see that the stitches won't undo any further than your saver row.

Then you'll easily be able to insert the knitting needle back into the stitches. Make sure you keep the working end of the yarn towards the tip of the knitting needle.

You are now ready to start knitting from Row 1 of the pattern repeat. The saver yarn can be pulled out whenever you want to remove it.

Note to Knitters

This SOS technique will work on all stitches - try it any time you are working on something new and are worried that you might make a mistake.

Turning

A pattern will sometimes instruct you to 'turn' the work in the middle of a row. Turning is what you do at the end of every row you knit, in order to be able to start the next row. It may seem counter-intuitive to turn in the middle of a row, but it will be for a good reason, so trust your pattern.

Here, I've turned in the middle of the row and am now ready to start working in the opposite direction.

Adding yarn

You can add new yarn at the end of a row, but it may be neater to add it in the middle of a row. The technique is the same either way.

When you are ready to add new yarn, tie the new end of the yarn around the end that's currently attached to the work (the end that is running out).

Push the knot of the new yarn down to the needle and simply continue knitting.

Weaving in ends

It's really important to give plenty of time and care to weaving in your ends of yarn. As with all aspects of 'finishing' your work, it'll make all the difference to the final knitted product. You can weave in ends with a crochet hook, but if you leave slightly longer ends, you can get a really tidy finish with a darning needle.

If you've added new yarn in the middle of a row, you'll spot a little hole where you changed yarn. Turn to the wrong side of the knitting and undo the little knot that was holding the new yarn in place.

On the wrong side of the knitting, thread one of the ends through a darning needle. Then weave it in and out of the stitches, first taking the yarn over to the opposite side of the hole.

This crossing-over-the-hole technique makes sure that the hole vanishes neatly.

Weave the end up and down the stitches at the back of the work approximately five times. Pull the yarn

so that it is snug, but take care not to yank it too tightly or it will show on the front of the knitting.

Snip the ends close to the knitting once they have each been woven in about five times on each side.

You can see that the hole is now neatly closed up.

Note to Knitters

If you've added yarn at the end of a row, or have loose ends from sewing up, weave these ends in along the nearest seam. It's very like whip stitch (see p.156) – you are simply sewing in the ends about five times so they are held securely without needing a knot.

Note to Knitters

If you'd prefer to add new yarn at the end of a row rather than in the middle, and when you have loose ends from sewing up, you can use a darning needle or crochet hook to weave ends in along a seam.

How to tell the right side from the wrong side

A pattern will often indicate whether you are knitting on the right side or wrong side of the work. This is usually just for your information. You don't have to do anything except make sure you are on the correct side of your knitting.

RS = Right side. On stocking stitch, the RS is the knit side.

WS = Wrong side. On stocking stitch, the WS is the purl side.

Working a two-row colour change

If you'd like to change the colours of your yarn in short bursts, here's how to do it without leaving hundreds of ends to weave in. This technique only works if you change colour every two rows, and use only two colours in your knitting.

This simple technique for working with two-row stripes can quickly transform any of the basic patterns in this book into something more colourful. I think it's especially effective to knit long, vertical stripes like those on the scarf on long circular needles (see p.241).

This works well on both stocking and garter stitch. The technique is the same on both. I've used it here on garter stitch to create a fine blue and pink striped pattern.

When you are ready to start your two-row stripe, join in the second colour (the blue in these photos) WITHOUT cutting off the first colour (the pink).

Work two rows using the second colour (knit two rows if you are using garter stitch; or knit one row, purl one row if you are using stocking stitch).

continue...

Working a two-row colour change *continued…*

Once you've worked these two rows, you'll find yourself back on the side of the knitting where you initially joined the second colour of yarn. Let go of the end of the second colour (blue), pick up the first colour (pink) and work two rows. The pink yarn will be carried up the side of the work to where you want to start knitting with it. The blue can simply wait at that end until you've worked two rows and are back at the end with the blue.

When you have worked two rows using the pink, you'll be back to the end with the blue yarn and can work the next two rows in blue.

Continue in this way, alternating two rows of each colour. The yarn not currently in use waits at the edge of the work, and the yarn in use is worked for two rows at a time. The yarn is carried up the side of the work and makes a neat edge all by itself. You'll only need to weave in the ends at the beginning and end of the two-colour striped knitting.

You'll soon see a very tidy, fine stripe appear in your knitting.

You can see how this technique has been used to great effect on the Ladies' raglan jumper (see p.172), Girls' pinafore dress (see p.186), Versatile kiddies' jumper (see p.192) and Lengthways-striped scarf (see p.241).

How to count rows

= 1 stitch

= 2 rows

If you are counting stitches on stocking stitch, look for the V-shapes. Each 'V' is one row if you count up the column.

In garter stitch, you can see that there are ridges, each with a top and bottom part. Each ridge is two rows.

Markers

Sometimes a knitting pattern will ask you to place a marker – this is to help you with your pattern in upcoming rows.

PM = Place marker.
PM/SM = Pass marker/slip marker.
When you get to the marker in the next row, pass it from the left-hand needle to the right-hand needle without knitting it.

Tips for following knitting patterns

Sometimes a knitting pattern can seem as though it's written in Martian, but here are a few tips to help you on your way:

- Make a photocopy of the pattern so that you can scribble all your notes on it as you go.

- Then decide which size you want to knit.

- Go through your pattern with a highlighter pen, marking the instructions for your size throughout. (Knitting patterns print the instruction for the smallest size, followed by brackets that contain the instructions for the other sizes.) That way you'll cut out all the information you don't need, so you don't end up following the wrong instructions.

- Remember to knit a tension square if you're knitting an adult garment.

- Tick off rows as you go. That way, when you pick up your knitting you'll always know exactly where you are.

Adult booties

This is a pattern that I've been asked to design again and again by knitters who loved the baby bootie pattern in my first book.

It's a slightly more sophisticated version, which is still very easy to knit, but with an added sole. Perfect for padding around the house on cold winter days… just add pyjamas and a hot-water bottle for a perfect outfit to knit in.

GAUGE

An exact gauge isn't necessary for this project. Approximately 9sts in stocking stitch, using 10mm needles should give a 10cm square.

SIZE

One size (this should fit all adults)

ABBREVIATIONS

K = Knit

P = Purl

St(s) = Stitch(es)

St st = Stocking stitch

K2tog = Knit two stitches together

K2tog tbl = Knit two stitches together through the back of the loops

P2tog = Purl two stitches together

P2tog tbl = Purl two stitches together through the back of the loops

PM = Place marker

SM = Slip marker (slip the marker from the left-hand needle to the right-hand needle without knitting it)

1 x 1 rib = K1, P1 rib to end

Rep = Repeat

RS = Right side

WS = Wrong side

YOU WILL NEED

SUPER-BULKY YARN
such as Rowan Big Wool, Sirdar Bigga or Debbie Bliss Como. If you were using Rowan Big Wool, as shown in the photos here, you would need approximately 1.4 balls (so buy 2 balls and you'd have a bit left over).

107M YARN
(this is approximate, depending on the foot size you are knitting for)

10MM KNITTING NEEDLES

DARNING NEEDLE

START KNITTING

FOOT

Cast on 46sts.

K 1 row.

P23, PM, P to end.

K to 2sts before the marker, K2tog tbl, SM, K2tog, K to end. Count 44sts.

P to 2sts before the marker, P2tog, SM, P2tog tbl, P to end. Count 42sts.

Rep the last two rows until 22sts remain, ending with a purl row.

Work 1 x 1 rib for 10cm (you can remove the marker on the first rib row) ending with a RS row.

Cast off on WS (so the purl side of the foot is facing you) in pattern, leaving a long tail of yarn about 70cm long for sewing up with.

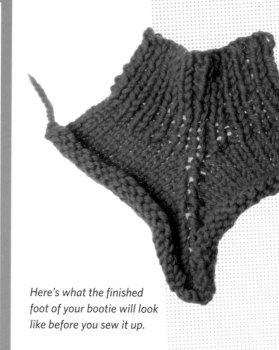

Here's what the finished foot of your bootie will look like before you sew it up.

SOLE

Cast on 10sts.

Work 1 x 1 rib to end.

Rep the last row until the piece measures 2cm less than the length of the sole of your foot – you can adjust this to your foot size; the main body of the slipper will stretch to fit the sole when you come to sewing it up.

Cast off in pattern, leaving a long tail of yarn about 100cm for sewing up.

The bootie's sole.

Note to Knitters

Casting off in pattern means that you cast off in the normal way, but you knit the knit stitches and purl the purl stitches. This gives a subtle, neat finish.

Knit the sole so it measures 2cm less than the length of your foot.

Making up

Fold the foot in half and sew up the back using mattress stitch. You can now see the slipper shape emerging.

To sew on the sole, turn the bootie inside out and use whip stitch to sew the sole to the foot. (See p.156 for how to do whip stitch.)

Handy HINT

The size of the sole will vary according to the length of your foot, but you can still make different sized soles fit into the foot by easing in as you sew (see p.157).

Handy HINT

If you want a little more padding between your foot and the floor, simply slip an inner sole for a shoe into your bootie.

Ladies' raglan jumper

This is a pattern for a classic, simple ladies' jumper with a slightly fitted waist and fully fashioned raglan sleeves. A raglan sleeve is joined onto the body of a garment with a diagonal seam.

'Fully fashioned' means that the decreases are made a stitch or two in from the edge of the knitting, which gives a very tidy edge to your seams and makes the sewing-up process much more straightforward than it would be on non-fully fashioned seams.

Don't let the classic lines of this jumper fool you – you can jazz it up with colours, stripes, yarn choices and embellishments. It's the sort of garment you'll not only learn lots of neat knitting tricks on, but one that you'll wish you owned in lots of different colours, as its simple design looks good with everything! I hope that you will find this knitting project satisfying both to make and wear.

The fully fashioned raglan finish makes for a really neat seam. The size 12 jumper in this photo was knitted using 14 ½ balls of Debbie Bliss Alpaca Silk Aran. It's soooo soft and cosy!

YOU WILL NEED

ARAN-WEIGHT YARN
such as Debbie Bliss Alpaca Silk Aran or Sublime Cashmere Merino Silk Aran
Size 8–10: 729m
Size 12: 940m
Size 14–16: 1,162m
Size 18–20: 1,328m

5MM KNITTING NEEDLES

4.5MM KNITTING NEEDLES

4.5MM CIRCULAR NEEDLE, 40CM LONG

CROCHET HOOK
(I always suggest you use a hook one size smaller than the knitting needles)

DARNING NEEDLE

STITCH HOLDER

GAUGE

18sts and 24 rows in stocking stitch, using 5mm needles = 10cm square.

SIZE

8–10 (12, 14–16, 18–20)

ABBREVIATIONS

K = Knit

P = Purl

St(s) = Stitch(es)

St st = Stocking stitch

K2tog = Knit two stitches together

M1 = Make one stitch by picking up the loop in between two stitches

SSK = Slip, slip, knit

Cont = Continue

Rep = Repeat

Rem = Remaining

1 x 1 rib = K1, P1 rib to end

START KNITTING

BACK AND FRONT (the same until ***)

Using 4.5mm needles, cast on 78 (90, 98, 106)sts.

Work 1 x 1 rib until work measures 4 (4, 5, 6)cm.

Change to 5mm needles and starting with a knit row, work st st until work measures 6 (8, 10, 10)cm from beginning, ending with a purl row.

Handy HINT

When changing needle sizes on the first knit row of the stocking stitch, the stitches will be on 4.5mm needles. Work that first knit row on to a 5mm needle, then discard the 4.5mm needles and continue with the 5mm needles.

WAIST SHAPING

Decrease row: K1, SSK, K to last 3sts, K2tog, K1. Count 76 (88, 96, 104)sts.

St st for 7 rows (P 1 row, K 1 row, P 1 row, K 1 row, P 1 row, K 1 row, P 1 row).

Decrease row: K1, SSK, K to last 3sts, K2tog, K1. Count 74 (86, 94, 102)sts.

St st for 7 rows (P 1 row, K 1 row, P 1 row, K 1 row, P 1 row, K 1 row, P 1 row).

Decrease row: K1, SSK, K to last 3sts, K2tog, K1. Count 72 (84, 92, 100)sts.

St st for 7 rows (P 1 row, K 1 row, P 1 row, K 1 row, P 1 row, K 1 row, P 1 row).

Decrease row: K1, SSK, K to last 3sts, K2tog, K1. Count 70 (82, 90, 98)sts.

St st for 7 rows (P 1 row, K 1 row, P 1 row, K 1 row, P 1 row, K 1 row, P 1 row).

Increase row: K1, M1, K to last st, M1, K1. Count 72 (84, 92, 100)sts.

St st for 7 rows (P 1 row, K 1 row, P 1 row, K 1 row, P 1 row, K 1 row, P 1 row).

Increase row: K1, M1, K to last st, M1, K1. Count 74 (86, 94, 102)sts.

St st for 7 rows (P 1 row, K 1 row, P 1 row, K 1 row, P 1 row, K 1 row, P 1 row).

Increase row: K1, M1, K to last st, M1, K1. Count 76 (88, 96. 104)sts.

St st for 7 rows (P 1 row, K 1 row, P 1 row, K 1 row, P 1 row, K 1 row, P 1 row).

Increase row: K1, M1, K to last st, M1, K1. Count 78 (90, 98, 106)sts.

Starting with a purl row, continue in st st until piece measures 39 (43, 47, 50)cm from beginning, ending with a purl row – this is the length of your jumper from the underarm.

Note to Knitters

If you wish to shorten or lengthen the jumper to suit your body length, this is where to do it – I suggest that you alter the pattern by no more than 5cm, or the jumper will be too out of shape for the pattern. Don't forget to make the same alteration on both the front and the back of the jumper!

RAGLAN SHAPING

Cast off 2 (5, 7, 7)sts, K to end.
Count 76 (85, 91, 99)sts.

Cast off 2 (5, 7, 7)sts, P to end.
Count 74 (80, 84, 92)sts.

Decrease row: K1, SSK, K to last 3sts, K2tog, K1.
Count 72 (78, 82, 90)sts.

P 1 row.

***

BACK ONLY

Rep the last 2 rows until 32 (34, 34, 36)sts remain, ending with a purl row.

Transfer these stitches to a holder and set aside for now.

FRONT ONLY

Rep the last 2 rows until 54 (56, 60, 60)sts remain, ending with a purl row.

NECK SHAPING

(Please note that you will now be shaping the front for the neck AND continuing with the raglan shaping.)

K1, SSK, K17 (18, 19, 19). Cast off 14 (14, 16, 16)sts, K to last 3sts, K2tog, K1.

(To cast off in the middle of a row: knit the initial 17 (18, 19, 19)sts, THEN K1, K1, cast off the first knitted stitch and count 1, K1, cast off and count 2, and so on ... keep counting until you have counted 14 (14, 16, 16) cast-off stitches. Remember to count accurately!)

You now have 19 (20, 21, 21)sts on each side.

Working on the right side of the neck only (leaving the left side on the needle):

P 1 row.

Decrease row: SSK, K to last 3sts, K2tog, K1.

Rep the last 2 rows until 5 (4, 7, 5)sts remain, ending with a decrease row.

P 1 row.

K to last 3sts, K2tog, K1.

Rep the last 2 rows until 3sts remain, ending with a purl row.

K3tog.

Fasten off.

LEFT FRONT:

With WS of work facing you, rejoin yarn.

P 1 row.

K1, SSK, K to last 2sts, K2tog.

Rep the last 2 rows until 5 (4, 7, 5)sts remain, ending with a decrease row.

P 1 row.

K1, SSK, K to end.

Rep the last 2 rows until 3sts remain, ending with a purl row.

K3tog.

Fasten off.

Note to Knitters

HOW TO REJOIN YARN

STEP 1: Using a crochet hook, pull a strand of yarn through the nearest space below the first stitch on the needle.

STEP 2: Tie that into a knot with itself.

STEP 3: Use the long tail of the yarn to continue knitting.

STEP 4: When you've finished the knitting, weave the short tail of the yarn into the back of the work.

SLEEVES (make two the same)

Using 4.5mm needles, cast on 38 (42, 46, 48)sts.

Work in 1 x 1 rib until the work measures 4cm.

Changing to 5mm needles and starting with a knit row, begin st st.

Increase row: K1, M1, K to last st, M1, K1. Count 40 (44, 48, 50)sts.

St st for 7 rows (P 1 row, K 1 row, P 1 row, K 1 row, P 1 row, K 1 row, P 1 row).

Increase row: K1, M1, K to last st, M1, K1. Count 42 (46, 50, 52)sts.

Rep the last 8 rows until you have 54 (54, 54, 54) sts, ENDING WITH AN INCREASE ROW.

St st for 5 rows (P 1 row, K 1 row, P 1 row, K 1 row, P 1 row).

Increase row: K1, M1, K to last st, M1, K1. Count 56 (56, 56, 56)sts.

Rep the last 6 rows until you have 56 (66, 74, 80) sts, ending with an increase row (please note that you'll already have the correct number of stitches for the smallest size).

Continue in st st until sleeve measures 46 (50, 52, 52)cm, ending with a purl row.

RAGLAN SHAPING

Cast off 2 (5, 7, 7)sts, K to end. Count 54 (61, 67, 73)sts.

Cast off 2 (5, 7, 7)sts, P to end. Count 52 (56, 60, 66)sts.

Decrease row: K1, SSK, K to last 3sts, K2tog, K1. Count 50 (54, 58, 64)sts.

P 1 row.

Rep the last 2 rows until you have 10 (10, 10, 10) sts, ending with a knit row.

Cast off.

Making up

Sew the back raglan to the back of the sleeves using mattress stitch. Start from the underarm section, picking up the two 'V's of the stocking stitch, and work your way towards the neck. You'll pick up the centre bar along the diagonal edges.

See p.34 for instructions on fully fashioned angled edges.

Note to Knitters

Make sure you follow the line of the decrease - by this I mean that if you look closely, you can see a neat row of 'V's running up the edge you are sewing. Keep one full line of 'V's to the inside of your sewing line - this way, the lines on both sides of the seam will join together to make a flawless finished seam.

Handy HINT

I always suggest that you sew the sleeves to the back first, then the front. This way, you can get used to the technique on the back and you'll be an expert on it by the time you get to the front of the jumper!

Then sew the front raglans to the fronts of the sleeves.

Pick up and knit for the neckband

With the RS facing, transfer the centre back stitches to a straight 4.5mm needle. The point of the knitting needle will be facing the right-hand side of the back of the neck.

Work these stitches in 1 x 1 rib onto the circular needle.

Using the crochet hook, pick up and knit 8sts from the top of the left sleeve.

Pick up and knit 20 (21, 23, 23)sts down the left front.

Then 14 (14, 16, 18)sts across the cast-off stitches of the centre front.

Then 20 (21, 23, 23)sts up the right front.

Finally, pick up and knit 8sts across the top of the right sleeve.

Count 104 (108, 114, 116)sts in total.

Join and work 1 x 1 rib until the neckband measures 4 (4, 5, 6)cm, ending the last round at the centre of the back of the neck.

Turn – so that the WS of the work is facing you, and cast off in pattern.

(To cast off in pattern: K1, P1, cast off, K1, cast off, P1, cast off ... and so on, remembering to move the yarn back and forward depending on whether you are knitting or purling the next stitch. Fiddly, but worth it for extra neatness.)

You'll be left with a small gap where you end the cast-off of the neckband. Simply thread the tail of yarn onto a darning needle and sew up the gap with a couple of stitches before weaving the end into the inside of your knitting.

Side and underarm seams

Using mattress stitch, sew up the side and underarm seams. Always start from the underarm and sew towards the wrist, then go back to the underarm and sew down towards the waist. You'll be using a simple centre bar mattress stitch. This is the easiest way of ensuring that the underarm seams join up neatly.

Now for the dull bit ... sit yourself in front of a good film and spend a rainy afternoon weaving in all those pesky ends! A tidy finish is worth its weight in gold and can really add that professional edge to your knitting.

Want an instant change of neckline? Cast on 100sts using 4.5mm needles and work in 1 x 1 rib for around 15–20cm. Cast off. Sew your knitting into a tube and you have a slip-on polo-neck! You can also knit this in the round (see p.220).

This knitter personalised her jumper by knitting the body and sleeves using two-row colour changes with solid-colour ribbed borders (see p.165).

Men's bulky jumper

This jumper will knit up in no time using super-bulky yarn.

If you are just learning about shaping and sewing up, I think you'll like seeing it grow quickly, and the big yarn and needles will make the sewing-up process much easier as you'll really be able to see into the nooks and crannies of the fabric.

This is a great project for building up your confidence with knitting adult garments.

This jumper isn't just for the boys; I can see it being cosy winter wear for girls, too!

YOU WILL NEED

SUPER-BULKY YARN such as Rowan Big Wool, Sirdar Bigga or Debbie Bliss Como
36 inch chest: 571m
38 inch chest: 583m
40 inch chest: 611m

10MM KNITTING NEEDLES

12MM KNITTING NEEDLES

CROCHET HOOK
(I always suggest using a hook one size smaller than the knitting needles)

DARNING NEEDLE

Sewing up is easier on 'big' knitting as you can really see the stitches. The size 38 jumper in the photo was knitted using just under 8 balls of Rowan Big Wool.

GAUGE

9sts in stocking stitch, using 10mm needles = 10cm square.

SIZE

Chest size (inches) 36 (38, 40)

ABBREVIATIONS

K = Knit	
P = Purl	
St(s) = Stitch(es)	
St st = Stocking stitch	
2 x 2 rib = K2, P2 rib to end	
K2tog = Knit two stitches together	
M1 = Make one stitch by picking up the loop in between two stitches	
SSK = Slip, slip, knit	
Cont = Continue	
Rep = Repeat	
Rem = Remaining	

START KNITTING

BACK AND FRONT (the same until ***)

Using 10mm needles, cast on 44 (44, 48)sts.

Work 2 x 2 rib until work measures 7 (7, 8)cm.

Size 38 only: Changing to 12mm needles, K1, M1, K to last st, M1, K1.

All other sizes: Changing to 12mm needles, K 1 row.

Count 44 (46, 48)sts.

Starting with a purl row, work st st until piece measures 41 (42, 43)cm from beginning, ending with a purl row.

***

BACK ONLY

SHAPE ARMHOLES

Cast off 3sts, K to end. Count 41 (43, 45)sts.

Cast off 3sts, P to end. Count 38 (40, 42)sts.

K2, SSK, K to last 4sts, K2tog, K2. Count 36 (38, 40)sts.

P 1 row.

K2, SSK, K to last 4sts, K2tog, K2. Count 34 (36, 38)sts.

Rep the last 2 rows until you have 6 (8, 8)sts, ending with a knit row.

Cast off on the WS of your work.

FRONT ONLY

SHAPE ARMHOLES

Cast off 3sts, K to end. Count 41 (43, 45)sts.

Cast off 3sts, P to end. Count 38 (40, 42)sts.

K2, SSK, K to last 4sts, K2tog, K2. Count 36 (38, 40)sts.

P 1 row.

Rep the last 2 rows until you have 24 (26, 26) sts, ending with a purl row.

SHAPE NECK OPENING

K2, SSK, K6 (6, 6), cast off 4 (6, 6) sts, K to last 4sts, K2tog, K2.

(To cast off in the middle of a row: knit the initial 6 (6, 6)sts, THEN K1, K1, cast off the first knitted stitch and count 1, K1, cast off and count 2, and so on … keep counting until you have counted 4 (6, 6) cast-off stitches. Remember to count accurately!)

You will now work on each side of the neck separately.

Handy HINT

When changing needle sizes, on the first knit row of the stocking stitch, you'll have the stitches on 10mm needles. Work that first knit row onto 12mm needles, then discard the 10mm needles and continue with the 12mm needles.

RIGHT SIDE

P 1 row.

K2tog, K to last 4sts, K2tog, K2.

P 1 row.

K2tog, K to last 2sts, K2tog.

P 1 row.

K to last 2sts, K2tog.

Rep last 2 rows until 2sts remain.

K2tog, fasten off.

LEFT SIDE

With WS facing, rejoin yarn and P 1 row.

K2, SSK, K to last 2sts, K2tog.

P 1 row.

K2tog, K to last 2sts, K2tog.

P 1 row.

K2tog, K to end.

Rep last 2 rows until 2sts remain.

K2tog, fasten off.

Handy HINT

I find it really helpful to tick off rows as I've knitted them, so I always know where I am when I pick up my knitting.

SLEEVES (the same until ***)

Using 10mm needles, cast on 24 (24, 24)sts.

Work 2 x 2 rib for 7 (7, 8)cm.

Changing to 12mm needles, K1, M1, K to last st, M1, K1. Count 26 (26, 26)sts.

St st for 5 rows (P 1 row, K 1 row, P 1 row, K 1 row, P 1 row).

K1, M1, K to last st, M1, K1. Count 28 (28, 28)sts.

St st for 5 rows (P 1 row, K 1 row, P 1 row, K 1 row, P 1 row).

K1, M1, K to last st, M1, K1. Count 30 (30, 30)sts.

St st for 7 rows (P 1 row, K 1 row, P 1 row, K 1 row, P 1 row, K 1 row, P 1 row).

Rep last 8 rows until you have 36 (38, 38)sts.

Cont in st st until piece measures 47 (48, 49)cm from beginning, ending with a purl row.

ARMHOLE SHAPING

Cast off 3sts, K to end. Count 33 (35, 35)sts.

Cast off 3sts, P to end. Count 30 (32, 32)sts.

K2, SSK, K to last 4sts, K2tog, K2. Count 28 (30, 30)sts.

P 1 row.

K 1 row.

P 1 row.

K2, SSK, K to last 4sts, K2tog, K2. Count 26 (28, 28)sts.

P 1 row.

K 1 row.

P 1 row.

K2, SSK, K to last 4sts, K2tog, K2. Count 24 (26, 26) sts.

P 1 row.

***

RIGHT SLEEVE ONLY

Rep the last 2 rows until you have 10 (10, 10)sts, ending with a purl row.

Cast off 2sts, K to last 4sts, K2tog, K2. Count 7 (7, 7)sts.

P 1 row

K2tog, K to last 4sts, K2tog, K2. Count 5 (5, 5)sts.

P to last 2sts, P2tog. Count 4 (4, 4)sts.

K2tog, K to end. Count 3 (3, 3)sts.

Cast off.

LEFT SLEEVE ONLY

Rep the last 2 rows until you have 10 (10, 10)sts, ending with a knit row.

Cast off 2sts, P to end. Count 8 (8, 8)sts.

K2, SSK, K to end. Count 7 (7, 7)sts.

P2tog, P to end. Count 6 (6, 6)sts.

K2, SSK, K to end. Count 5 (5, 5)sts.

P2tog, P to end. Count 4 (4, 4)sts.

K2, SSK, K to end. Count 3 (3, 3)sts.

Cast off.

Making up

Note to Knitters

When sewing up this type of raglan seam (where the shaping is done two stitches in from the edge), look for two complete stitches ('V's) before picking up the centre bar towards the edge of the knitted piece.

See p.154-155 for how to do fully fashioned angled edges.

Step 1: Using mattress stitch, sew the right back raglan to the back of the right sleeve.

Step 2: Sew the left back raglan to the back of the left sleeve.

Step 3: Sew the front of the left sleeve to the left front raglan.

Step 4: Sew the right front raglan to the back of the right sleeve.

Neckband

You will now pick up and knit the neckband. This is done in two parts: first the back, then the front.

Note to Knitters

The picked-up stitches around the neck will be close together at the back neckband and further apart from each other at the front. Just make sure that you space the stitches as equally as possible.

Back neckband

With RS facing, using 10mm needles and starting at the centre of the right sleeve, pick up 18 (18, 22)sts, working across the back of the jumper and ending at the centre of the left sleeve.

WS: P2, K2, rep to end.
RS: K2, P2, rep to end.
Rep last 2 rows until the neckband measures 7 (7, 8)cm, ending with a RS row. Cast off loosely on the WS in pattern. Leave a long tail of yarn for sewing up (about 30cm).

Front neckband

With RS facing, using 10mm needles and starting at the centre of the left sleeve, pick up 22 (22, 22)sts, working across the front of the jumper and ending at the centre of the right sleeve.

WS: P2, K2, rep to end.

RS: K2, P2, rep to end.

Repeat the last 2 rows until the neckband measures 7 (7, 8)cm, ending with a RS row. Cast off loosely on the WS in pattern. Leave a long tail of yarn for sewing up (about 30cm).

Note to Knitters

Be sure to use mattress stitch for sewing up to get a really tidy finish on your jumper.

Sew up the side seams of the neck-band.

Sew up the underarm and side seams. Start sewing from the underarm and work towards the wrist, then go back and start from the underarm and sew up towards the waist.

This is the easiest way of ensuring that the underarms join up neatly.

Weave in all ends.

Girls' pinafore dress

Here's a pattern that I really enjoyed designing. It appeared nearly fully formed in my head, and I had instant visions of it being worn everywhere from the beach, to a winter party or a wedding.

This dress combines unfussy lines with a pretty frill; you can choose colour combinations to suit your little lady and accessorise the pattern with anything from knitted flowers to buttons and sequins.

The frill at the bottom produces a really tidy edge, and gives a weight to the skirt that makes it hang elegantly. The straps can be adjusted to suit, so that you can fit it to your girl as she grows taller (if it starts to look too short, you could extend its life by pairing it with trousers underneath, or with bright tights and wellies).

You can knit the dress in any double knit yarn – the most widely available of weights. I love it in cotton for summer, warm wool for winter, and what about a silk or bamboo yarn for a special occasion? Perfect!

You can knit the dress using a two-row colour stripe for a pretty effect. 5½ balls of the luxurious Debbie Bliss Amalfi makes this dress for a girl aged 4–5 years. I think it's elegant enough to be a bridesmaid's dress!

YOU WILL NEED

ANY STANDARD DOUBLE KNIT YARN, so you have lots of choice. I suggest a lovely, drapey cotton for summer dresses (I like Sublime Soya Cotton, Debbie Bliss Amalfi or Rowan Purelife), or a warm wool for a winter dress, worn with a long-sleeved T-shirt underneath (I suggest Rowan Handknit Wool or Debbie Bliss Cashmerino DK).
Age 1–2 years: 306m
Age 3–4 years: 477m
Age 4–5 years: 524m

4MM KNITTING NEEDLES

4MM CIRCULAR NEEDLE 80CM LONG, for the frill (optional)

CROCHET HOOK

DARNING NEEDLE

4 SMALL BUTTONS, approx. 1cm in diameter

NEEDLE AND THREAD

GAUGE

22sts and 30 rows in stocking stitch, using 4mm needles = 10 cm square.

SIZE

1–2 years (3–4 years, 4–5 years)

ABBREVIATIONS

K = Knit

P = Purl

St(s) = Stitch(es)

St st = Stocking stitch

2 x 2 rib = K2, P2 rib to end

K2tog = Knit two stitches together

KFB = Knit into the front and back of a stitch

SSK = Slip, slip, knit

YF = Yarn forward

Cont = Continue

Rep = Repeat

RS = Right side

WS = Wrong side

I've written the pattern to be knitted in two colours, like the example below: the first colour is indigo for the frill and bodice, and the second colour is turquoise for the skirt and straps, but you can use whichever colour combination appeals. If you like, you can make the dress in a single colour, or stripe in two or as many colours as you like. Use this pattern as a template to design your own dress!

START KNITTING

BACK AND FRONT (the same until ***)

FRILL

Using 4mm needles and the first colour, cast on 76 (94, 102)sts.

Starting with a knit row, work in st st for 7 rows, ending with a knit row.

WS: K 1 row – this is your first fold line.

RS: KFB, rep to end. Count 152 (188, 204)sts.

Note to Knitters

You might find the stitches are getting a bit squished on a normal straight needle at this point. If so, you can use the circular needle (see p.240 for a workshop on how to knit straight on circular knitting needles).

Starting with a purl row, work in st st for 7 rows, ending with a purl row.

RS: K2tog, rep to end. Count 76 (94, 102)sts.

WS: K 1 row – this is the sewing guideline.

Have fun with your buttons! You'll need about 4½ balls of the lovely Soya Cotton DK by Sublime and ladybird buttons for a summer play-dress in size 3–4 years.

SKIRT

Changing to your second colour of yarn, and starting with a knit row, work in st st for 4 rows, ending with a purl row.

Decrease row: K1, SSK, knit to last 3sts, K2tog, K1. Count 74 (92, 100)sts.

Starting and ending with a purl row, work in st st for 3 rows.

Decrease row: K1, SSK, knit to last 3sts, K2tog, K1. Count 72 (90, 98)sts.

Rep last 4 rows until 50 (58, 62)sts remain.

Cont in st st until piece measures 26 (34, 38)cm from first fold line, ending with a purl row.

Change back to first colour and K 1 row, then P 1 row.

BODICE

RS: K2, P2, rep to last 2sts – start and finish this row with K2.

WS: P2, K2, rep to last 2sts – start and finish this row with P2.

★★★

BACK ONLY

Rep the last 2 rows until you have 4 (6, 7)cm of rib, ending with a RS row.

Cast off in pattern on the WS of the work. Casting off in pattern means that you cast off in the normal way, but you knit the knit stitches and purl the purl stitches. This gives a subtle, neater finish.

FRONT ONLY

Rep the last 2 rows until you have 4 (6, 7)cm, ending with a WS row.

UNDERARM CAST-OFF

Cast off 4sts in pattern, rib to end. Count 46 (54, 58)sts.

Cast off 4sts in pattern, rib to end. Count 42 (50, 54)sts.

RS: K2, P2, rep to last 2sts – start and finish this row with K2.

WS: P2, K2, rep to last 2sts – start and finish this row with P2.

Rep the last 2 rows until you have 12 (13, 14)cm of rib in total, ending with a RS row.

Cast off on the WS of the work in pattern.

STRAPS

Using 4mm needles and the second colour (same as the skirt), cast on 12sts.

RS: K5, P2, K5.

WS: P5, K2, P5.

Buttonhole row: K2, YF, K2tog, K1, P1, K2, YF, K2tog, K2. Count 12sts.

WS: P5, K2, P5.

RS: K5, P2, K5.

Rep the last 2 rows until the strap is approximately 20 (23, 26)cm long, ending with a RS row. Cast off on the WS of the work in pattern, leaving a long tail of yarn for sewing up (about 30cm).

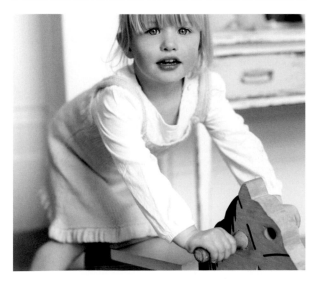

This dress works for all seasons and occasions, depending on how you dress it up or down.

Making up

Using mattress stitch, sew up the side seams of the dress.

Note to Knitters

When you sew up the bodice, make sure the top of the back lines up with the underarm of the front.

Hem

To make the frill, you need to fold it under at the first fold line and sew up using whip stitch.

The frill will fold up easily where it's supposed to. Uncurl it, and sew it up using whip stitch by simply taking a loop from the line where the frill joins the skirt – the sewing guide line – and a loop from the cast-on edge of the frill. See p.156 for whip stitch.

Weave in all your ends neatly.

Sew on buttons so that they are extra-secure. I don't want to hear stories of little girls pulling off their buttons and stuffing them up their noses!

Sew strap

Sew the strap securely to the back bodice.

The weight of the frill adds a pretty detail to this simple pinafore dress. This size 1–2 years dress uses just under 3 balls of Debbie Bliss Cashmerino DK.

Handy HINT

It's a good idea to knit the strap a little longer than you need and sew the excess into the back of the dress. Then, as the girl grows taller, the straps can be unsewn and re-sewn to the dress at a longer length so you can get more wear out of it. My experience is that small children generally grow taller more quickly than they grow wider, and the width of the dress will fit for a longer time than the length.

Variations

Feel free to personalise the dress to suit your little lady:

- Knit flowers to sew on
- Sew sequins or coloured buttons scattered across the skirt
- Knit colour stripes
- Knit a matching headband or handbag for a complete outfit.

Handy HINT

If the straps are too long, you can cross them at the back before buttoning them at the front. This will also help keep the straps on her shoulders.

Handy HINT

If you find that the buttonhole is too big or loose for the button you've chosen, you can tighten it up by sewing some small stitches around it using sewing thread.

Versatile kiddies' jumper

OK … are you paying attention? There's a lot of information coming your way in this versatile jumper-hoodie-or-not-which-different-shoulder-style-are-you-knitting?

'Versatile' is the operative word here. Depending on which size of garment you knit, you will learn how to knit a drop shoulder, modified drop shoulder, hood, simple slashed neckline, long sleeves and short sleeves.

The sizes on offer fit children aged 0–3 months, 1–2 years, 3–4 years and 4–5 years. As with all children's clothing, if you aren't sure, opt for a bigger size – the child in question will definitely grow, and we don't want him or her to grow faster than your knitting!

Size	Neck	Shoulder
0–6 months	slash neck	drop shoulder
1–2 years	hood	drop shoulder
3–4 years	hood	modified drop shoulder
4–5 years	hood	modified drop shoulder

The smallest size, 0–3 months, is the simplest to make. Essentially, it consists of two rectangles for the body. The basic skills involved are ribbing, increasing and sewing up. This would make a great first foray into knitting garments if you'd like to knit something for a new baby that's not too taxing, where you can add personality with embroidery, colour, stripes, combinations, etc.

The next size up, 1–2 years, is slightly higher on the complication rating, as it has a hood. You'll need to learn how to pick up and knit, and you'll use a three-needle bind-off for the hood – one of my favourite techniques for a tidy finish.

The bigger sizes have a hood and a modified drop shoulder for a slightly more fitted look. This is essentially a big and baggy jumper, but the indented sleeve means that the fit around the shoulder has a more compact shape.

Drop shoulder.

Modified drop shoulder.

Questions & Answers

What's she talking about? Modified, drop a whatchamacallit?

A drop shoulder is the simplest sort of shape when knitting a jumper or cardigan. It basically means that the body and the top of the sleeve are simple rectangles with no shaping to make them fit together. You'll never get a sleek, fitted look with this technique, but I love it for making comfortable kids' clothing as it gives them room to move and grow.

A modified drop shoulder is a slightly more fitted version, in that the sleeve is set into the body by means of a simple 'notch' cast off into the body where the sleeve is sewn in.

Personalise your hoodie with different sleeve options or even a bit of freestyle embroidery on the front.

The self-patterning yarn Artesano Hummingbird DK gives a unique look to this jumper. The size 1–2 years size only requires 1½ skeins of this extra-long yarn.

YOU WILL NEED

LOOK FOR DOUBLE KNIT YARN, which comes in limitless options of colours and fibres. My test knitters enjoyed the smooth comfort of Debbie Bliss Cashmerino DK, the funky, self-patterning colours of Artesano Hummingbird DK, stripes in Sirdar Click, and Debbie Bliss Amalfi for a cotton jumper for a summer baby.
0–6 months: 315m
1–2 years: 583m
3–4 years: 611m
4–5 years: 700m

4MM KNITTING NEEDLES

4MM CIRCULAR NEEDLES, any length (you won't be knitting in the round in this pattern)

DARNING NEEDLE

CROCHET HOOK: try using a 3mm or 3.5mm hook, as it will make the picking up a bit easier

Note to Knitters

The quantities given above are for garments with long sleeves. You'll need less yarn if you are knitting the short-sleeved version.

GAUGE

22sts and 30 rows in stocking stitch, using 4mm needles = 10cm square.

SIZES

0–6 months (1–2 years, 3–4 years, 4–5 years).

Please note that these garments are unisex and there will be a difference in size between, for example, a girl aged three and a boy of the same age. The best rule, when knitting for children, is that if you aren't sure, work bigger.

ABBREVIATIONS

K = Knit

P = Purl

St(s) = Stitch(es)

St st = Stocking stitch

1 x 1 rib = K1, P1 rib to end

K2tog = Knit two stitches together

M1 = Make one stitch by picking up the loop in between two stitches

Cont = Continue

Rep = Repeat

RS = Right side

WS = Wrong side

START KNITTING

BACK AND FRONT (the same to ***)

Cast on 58 (68, 74, 86)sts.

Work in 1 x 1 rib until piece measures 3 (4, 4, 5)cm.

***

BACK ONLY

Starting with a knit row, work in st st until piece measures 30 (32, 26, 29)cm from beginning, ending with a knit row.

Sizes 0–6 months and 1–2 years

Cast off.

> **Note to Knitters**
>
> The instructions for the first two sizes: 0-6 months and 1-2 years, are included in knitting patterns as '-' because they have been cast off already and you don't have to take any action.

Sizes 3–4 and 4–5 years

UNDERARM FOR MODIFIED DROP SHOULDER

Cast off - (-, 6, 8)sts, P to end. Count - (-, 68, 78) sts.

Cast off - (-, 6, 8)sts, K to end. Count - (-, 62, 70) sts.

Starting with a purl row, cont in st st until piece measures - (-, 39, 43)cm from beginning, ending with a knit row.

Cast off on the WS.

> **Note to Knitters**
>
> The armhole will measure approximately - (-, 13, 14)cm.

> **Note to Knitters**
>
> The measurements for the body piece might seem a bit odd, with the bigger sizes having less length than the smaller sizes, but that's because they have decreases at the underarm for the modified drop shoulder.

FRONT ONLY

Jumper for age 0–6 months only: the front and back are the same. This size has a slash neck opening and no hood.

All other sizes

Starting with a knit row, work in st st until piece measures – (26, 26, 29)cm from beginning, ending with a purl row.

Sizes 3-4, 4-5

UNDERARM FOR MODIFIED DROP SHOULDER

Cast off – (–, 6, 8)sts, K to end. Count – (–, 68, 78) sts.

Cast off – (–, 6, 8)sts, P to end. Count – (–, 62, 70) sts.

All sizes except 0–6 months

Starting with a knit row, cont in st st until piece measures – (26, 31, 36)cm from beginning, ending with a purl row.

SHAPE NECK OPENING

Separate for neck opening.

K – (26, 24, 26)sts, cast off – (16, 14, 18)sts, K to end. You will now have – (26, 24, 26)sts on either side of the neck.

(To cast off in the middle of a row: knit the initial – (26, 24, 26)sts, THEN K1, K1, cast off the first knitted stitch and count 1, K1, cast off and count 2, and so on … keep counting until you have counted – (16, 14, 18) cast-off stitches. Remember to count accurately!)

Now work the stitches on the right front of the neck, ignoring the left front for now – leave the stitches for the left front on the needle but don't knit them.

RIGHT FRONT

P – (26, 24, 26)sts (on the right front), turn.

K2tog, K to end. Count – (25, 23, 25)sts.

P 1 row.

Rep last 2 rows until – (21, 21, 21)sts remain on the right front.

Cont in st st until piece measures – (32, 39, 43)cm from beginning, ending with a knit row.

Cast off.

LEFT FRONT

Rejoin yarn with WS of work facing you and P 1 row.

K to last 2sts, K2tog.

P 1 row.

Rep last 2 rows until – (21, 21, 21)sts remain on the left front.

Cont in st st until piece measures – (32, 39, 43)cm from beginning, ending with a knit row.

Cast off.

Note to Knitters

Many traditional knitting patterns will tell you to put the stitches you are 'ignoring' on a holder. I find this fiddly and unnecessary most of the time, hence the 'ignoring'!

Making up

Using mattress stitch (and picking up the two sides of the 'V' – see p.153), sew up the shoulder seams. Start at the arm edge and sew your way in towards the neck edge.

On the slash neck jumper, sew the shoulder seams for approximately 6cm from the armhole edge towards the neck opening.

Hood

With right side facing, using the 4mm circular needles, and starting at the right-hand (as it's worn) edge of the cast-off stitches on the front of the neck opening, pick up and knit – (15, 19, 20)sts up the right front of the jumper, – (22, 24, 28)sts across the back of the neck, and – (15, 19, 20)sts down the left front (to the edge of the cast-off stitches). Please note that you will not be picking up stitches at the front cast-off edge of the neck opening.

Start picking up and knitting at the slope of the right front.

Please note that you will not be picking up stitches at the front cast-off edge of the neck opening.

Count – (52, 62, 68)sts.

Work back and forth on the circular needle (without joining into a round – you use the needles as if they were normal straight needles – just ignore the fact that the stitches are all on one needle… trust me… it'll make sense when you do it!).

P 1 row.

Increase row: K – (16, 21, 22)sts, [M1, K2] – (10, 10, 12) times, K to end. Count – (62, 72, 80)sts.

Starting with a purl row, cont in st st until the hood measures – (23, 24, 25)cm from the neck, ending with a knit row.

Finish using the three-needle bind-off (see p.145).

Hood border

With right side facing, starting at the right neck front of the hood and using the 4mm circular needles, pick up and knit – (65, 67, 69)sts up the right front edge of the hood, and – (66, 68, 70)sts down the left front edge of the hood.

Count – (131, 135, 139)sts.

Row 1 (WS): P1, K1, repeat to end (start and end this row with a P1).

Row 2 (RS): K1, P1, repeat to end (start and end this row with a K1).

Repeat the last 2 rows a further – (2, 2, 3) times each; that is – (6, 6, 8) rows of rib in total, ending with a RS row.

Cast off in pattern on the wrong side of the work (remember to knit the knit stitches and purl the purl stitches as you cast off).

Sew the edges of the hood border to the open cast-off edge of the front of the neck opening. To be sure to get a neat finish, sew further away from the edge of the work rather than too near the cast-off edge on the front of the neck.

Sleeves

You'll notice you have to 'turn a corner' to pick up and knit for the short sleeves on the modified drop. Don't let this faze you!

SHORT SLEEVES (FOR A VEST TOP)

Sizes 0–6 months and 1–2 years have a drop shoulder rather than the modified drop shoulder of the other sizes, so are slightly different:

With RS facing, starting on the front of your jumper, pick up and knit 58 (66, –, –)sts for the short sleeve. Half of these will be on one side of the shoulder seam and half on the other.

Sizes 3–4, 4–5, years (for the modified drop shoulder):

With RS facing, and starting on the front, pick up and knit – (–, 6, 8)sts along the armhole cast-off, – (–, 35, 40)sts up the sleeve opening to the shoulder seam, – (–, 35, 40)sts down the sleeve opening on the other side of the shoulder seam and – (–, 6, 8)sts along the armhole cast-off on the back of the jumper.

Count 58 (66, 82, 96)sts in total.

Work in 1 x 1 rib for 2 (3, 3, 4)cm, ending with a RS row.

Cast off on WS in pattern.

Sew the underarm and side seams using mattress stitch.

LONG SLEEVES (KNIT TWO THE SAME)

Cast on 30 (34, 40, 46)sts.

Work in 1 x 1 rib until piece measures 3 (4, 4, 5)cm.

K1, M1, K to last st, M1, K1. Count 32 (36, 42, 48)sts.

P 1 row.

K 1 row.

P 1 row.

K1, M1, K to last st, M1, K1. Count 34 (38, 44, 50)sts.

Rep last 4 rows until you have 58 (66, 70, 80)sts.

Cont in st st until sleeve measures 23 (24, 28, 30)cm from the beginning, ending with a knit row.

Cast off on the WS of the work.

Sew the sleeve into the armhole

Fold the sleeve in half and find the centre of the top of the sleeve.

Using a long piece of yarn (about 80cm) on a darning needle, pick up the two sides of the 'V' of the knitting on the centre of the sleeve. Then, on the stitch nearest the shoulder seam on the body of the jumper, pick up the centre bar of the 'V'.

Sewing from the centre of the shoulder seam on the body and the centre top of the sleeve, working your way towards the underarm, sew the body and sleeve together using mattress stitch. Pick up the centre bar on the body and the two lines of the 'V' on the sleeve.

Continue until you reach the cast-off stitches at the underarm – this is if you are knitting the size with the modified drop sleeve. If you're not knitting the modified drop pattern, continue sewing up until you reach the underarm.

For the modified drop sleeve only, continue sewing around the 'corner' of the underarm – you will swap to picking up the 'V's on the body and the centre bar on the sleeve.

This gives a neat finish at the underarm.

Then sew up the sleeve and body seams. Start from the underarm and sew the seam towards the cuff end of the sleeve. Then start sewing from the underarm and sew the seam towards the waist of the jumper. This ensures that the underarm seam has a tidy and accurate finish.

Weave in all the ends.

Ladies' classic cardigan

I'm a huge fan of The Cardigan. I own endless variations of this versatile layer and rarely leave the house without one.

I know that knitting in 4-ply yarn is a labour of love that some of you may run from, but I couldn't resist adding this pattern to the book for those of you who, like me, enjoy the commitment of a project that might take a bit longer to make, but ends up being just that little bit more satisfying. Students often ask me for a 'simple' cardigan pattern for beginners or intermediate knitters. I think that this pattern is the answer, and it comes with options to really make it something special and individual.

Personally, I plan to knit one of these in every colour and sleeve length combination that I can! I hope you'll take advantage of the options I've given to personalise this pattern.

Handy HINT

I suggest you always buy one more ball of yarn than you think you'll need when knitting a big project. Amounts needed can vary, and it's very disheartening to run out of yarn towards the end of a project and find it's no longer available.

Choose the sleeve length to suit you. In the photo, the pink cardigan is a size 8–10 with three-quarter-length sleeves and was knitted using just over 8 balls of Classic Yarns Siena. This is a mercerised cotton yarn, so it weighs a bit more than other yarns, but is still lovely and cool for summer. The long-sleeved cardigan is a size 18–20 and used 10 balls of Sublime Baby Cashmere Merino 4-ply Silk.

YOU WILL NEED

4-PLY YARN
You can choose the fibre to suit the season and experiment with colour; for example you could try a self-patterning sock yarn.

Size 8–10: short sleeves 975m, three-quarter sleeves 1,195m, long sleeves 1,590m
Size 12: short sleeves 1,075m, three-quarter sleeves 1,300m, long sleeves 1,725m
Size 14: short sleeves 1,190m, three-quarter sleeves 1,410m, long sleeves 1,850m
Size 16: short sleeves 1,400m, three-quarter sleeves 1,610m, long sleeves 2,050m
Size 18–20: short sleeves 1,645m, three-quarter sleeves 1,890m, long sleeves 2,330m

2.75MM KNITTING NEEDLES

3.25MM KNITTING NEEDLES

CROCHET HOOK – 3mm is a good size for this fine yarn

DARNING NEEDLE

11 (12, 12, 13, 14) BUTTONS approx. 1cm in diameter

MATCHING SEWING THREAD AND NEEDLE

Handy HINT

You can alter this cardigan pattern by varying the following:
- Sleeve length
- Self-striping yarn (such as sock yarn) will give an extra zing of colour
- Buttons ... one of the perks of knitting is the fun of choosing buttons!

GAUGE

28sts and 36 rows in stocking stitch, using 3.25cm needles = 10cm square.

SIZE

8-10 (12, 14, 16, 18-20)

ABBREVIATIONS

K = Knit

P = Purl

St(s) = Stitch(es)

St st = Stocking stitch

1 x 1 rib = K1, P1 rib to end

K2tog = Knit two stitches together

K2tog tbl = Knit two stitches together through the back of the loops

M1 = Make one stitch by picking up the loop in between two stitches

P2tog = Purl two stitches together

P2tog tbl = Purl two stitches together through the back of the loops

YF = Yarn forward

Rem = Remaining

Cont = Continue

RS = Right side

WS = Wrong side

START KNITTING

BACK

Using 2.75mm needles, cast on 120 (128, 136, 150, 156)sts.

Work in 1 x 1 rib for 10 rows.

Change to 3.25mm needles and starting with a knit row, work in st st until piece measures 35 (36, 37, 38, 39)cm from beginning, ending with a purl row.

ARMHOLES

Cast off 4 (5, 5, 6, 6)sts, K to end. Count 116 (123, 131, 144, 150)sts.

Cast off 4 (5, 5, 6, 6)sts, P to end. Count 112 (118, 126, 138, 144)sts.

Decrease row 1 (RS): K2tog tbl, K to last 2sts, K2tog. Count 110 (116, 124, 136, 142)sts.

Decrease row 2 (WS): P2tog, P to last 2sts, P2tog tbl. Count 108 (114, 122, 134, 140)sts.

Rep the last 2 rows until 104 (110, 118, 126, 132)sts remain, ending with a WS row.

Decrease row 1 (RS): K2tog tbl, K to last 2sts, K2tog. Count 102 (108, 116, 124, 130)sts.

Purl 1 row.

Rep the last 2 rows until 92 (96, 100, 108, 112)sts remain.

Cont in st st until armhole measures 19 (20, 21, 23, 24)cm, ending with a knit row.

Cast off on the WS of your work.

Note to Knitters

Remember that when you measure your armhole, you are measuring in a straight line going from the armhole cast-off upwards to the base of the knitting needle, and not in a diagonal line.

Note to Knitters

This part of the cardigan may seem like a long, dull, samey expanse of stocking stitch ... well, it is! To combat the boredom, I suggest that you relax in front of a film and enjoy this part of the project as something you can knit with less concentration. I find that relaxing, rather than dull!

Handy HINT

Whilst working on this project, I suggest that you knit a few small or easy projects at the same time. That will stop you getting bored or bogged down with your big project, ensure you don't get pains in your hands from working with fine yarn for long periods, and give you the added satisfaction of finishing small projects in the meantime.

LEFT FRONT

Using 2.75mm needles, cast on 56 (60, 64, 72, 74) sts.

Work 1 x 1 rib for 10 rows.

Change to 3.25mm needles and starting with a knit row, work in st st until piece measures 35 (36, 37, 38, 39)cm from beginning, ending with a purl row.

ARMHOLE

Cast off 4 (5, 5, 7, 6)sts, K to end. Count 52 (55, 59, 65, 68)sts.

Purl 1 row.

Decrease row 1 (RS): K2tog tbl, K to end. Count 51 (54, 58, 64, 67)sts.

Decrease row 2 (WS): P to last 2sts, P2tog tbl. Count 50 (53, 57, 63, 66)sts.

Rep the last 2 rows until 48 (51, 55, 59, 62)sts remain, ending with a purl (WS) row.

K2tog tbl, K to end. Count 47 (50, 54, 58, 61)sts.

Purl 1 row.

Rep the last 2 rows until 42 (44, 46, 50, 52)sts remain, ending with a purl (WS) row.

Starting with a knit row, work in st st for 5 (7, 7, 11, 13) rows, ending with a knit (RS) row.

NECK

Cast off 7 (8, 9, 10, 11)sts, P to end. Count 35 (36, 37, 40, 41)sts.

Decrease row 1 (RS): K to last 2sts, K2tog. Count 34 (35, 36, 39, 40)sts.

Decrease row 2 (WS): P2tog, P to end. Count 33 (34, 35, 38, 39)sts.

Decrease row 1 (RS): K to last 2sts, K2tog. Count 32 (33, 34, 37, 38)sts.

Decrease row 2 (WS): P2tog, P to end. Count 31 (32, 33, 36, 37)sts.

Decrease row 1 (RS): K to last 2sts, K2tog. Count 30 (31, 32, 35, 36)sts.

P 1 row.

Rep the last 2 rows until 27 (28, 29, 32, 33) sts remain, ending with a purl row.

Decrease row 1 (RS): K to last 2sts, K2tog. Count 26 (27, 28, 31, 32) sts.

P 1 row.

K 1 row.

P 1 row.

Rep the last 4 rows until 22 (23, 24, 27, 28)sts remain.

Cont in st st until armhole measures 19 (20, 21, 23, 24)cm, ending with a knit row.

Cast off on WS of your work.

Handy HINT

Don't skimp on the length of your cardigan, as this will affect the button bands and buttonholes. Lay your work out flat to measure it, and if you aren't quite sure, work an extra couple of rows.

You can have fun and spend hours choosing your buttons! The short-sleeved cardigan in the photo is a size 16 and was knitted using just over 5 balls of the gorgeous Artesano Alpaca 4-ply.

RIGHT FRONT

Using 2.75mm needles, cast on 56 (60, 64, 72, 74) sts.

Work 1 x 1 rib for 10 rows.

Change to 3.25mm needles and starting with a knit row, work in st st until piece measures 35 (36, 37, 38, 39)cm from beginning, ending with a knit row.

ARMHOLE

Cast off 4 (5, 5, 7, 6)sts, P to end. Count 52 (55, 59, 65, 68)sts.

Decrease row 1 (RS): K to last 2sts, K2tog. Count 51 (54, 58, 64, 67)sts.

Decrease row 2 (WS): P2tog, P to end. Count 50 (53, 57, 63, 66)sts.

Rep the last 2 rows until 48 (51, 55, 59, 62)sts remain, ending with a purl (WS) row.

K to last 2sts, K2tog. Count 47 (50, 54, 58, 61)sts.

Purl 1 row.

Rep the last 2 rows until 42 (44, 46, 50, 52)sts remain, ending with a purl (WS) row.

Starting with a knit row, st st for 4 (6, 6, 10, 12) rows, ending with a purl (WS) row.

NECK

Cast off 7 (8, 9, 10, 11)sts, K to end. Count 35 (36, 37, 40, 41)sts.

P 1 row.

Decrease row 1 (RS): K2tog tbl, K to end. Count 34 (35, 36, 39, 40)sts.

Decrease row 2 (WS): P to last 2sts, P2tog, tbl. Count 33 (34, 35, 38, 39)sts.

Decrease row 1 (RS): K2tog tbl, K to end. Count 32 (33, 34, 37, 38)sts.

Decrease row 2 (WS): P to last 2sts, P2tog tbl. Count 31 (32, 33, 36, 37)sts.

Decrease row 1 (RS): K2tog tbl, K to end. Count 30 (31, 32, 35, 36)sts.

P 1 row.

Rep the last 2 rows until 27 (28, 29, 32, 33)sts remain, ending with a purl row.

Decrease row 1 (RS): K2tog tbl, K to end. Count 26 (27, 28, 31, 32)sts.

P 1 row.

K 1 row.

P 1 row.

Rep the last 4 rows until 22 (23, 24, 27, 28)sts remain.

Cont in st st until armhole measures 19 (20, 21, 23, 24)cm, ending with a knit row.

Cast off on WS of your work.

SLEEVES

The sleeves for the right and left arms are the same, but the start of the pattern varies, depending on the sleeve length that you choose.

SHORT SLEEVE (MAKE TWO THE SAME)

Using 2.75mm needles, cast on 72 (76, 80, 84, 88) sts.

Work 1 x 1 rib for 10 rows.

Changing to 3.25mm needles:

K 1 row.

P 1 row.

K1, M1, K to last st, M1, K1. Count 74 (78, 82, 86, 90)sts.

P 1 row.

K 1 row.

P1, M1, K to last st, M1, P1. Count 76 (80, 84, 88, 92)sts.

Rep the last 6 rows, stopping when you have 84 (90, 96, 106, 112)sts and ending on a P (K, P, K, P) row.

Work in st st for a further 6 (5, 6, 5, 4) rows, ending with a purl row.

Now move on to the armhole shaping instructions, which are the same for all sleeve lengths.

Note to Knitters

On a purl row, M1 is the same method as an increase on a knit row (see p.143).

THREE-QUARTER SLEEVE (MAKE TWO THE SAME)

Using 2.75mm needles, cast on 56 (58, 62, 68, 72) sts.

Work 1 x 1 rib for 10 rows.

Changing to 3.25mm needles:

K1, M1, K to last st, M1, K1. Count 58 (60, 64, 70, 74)sts.

P 1 row.

K 1 row.

P 1 row.

K1, M1, K to last st, M1, K1. Count 60 (62, 66, 72, 76)sts.

Rep the last 4 rows until you have 84 (90, 96, 106, 112)sts.

Cont in st st until sleeve measures 26 (27, 27, 28, 29)cm from the beginning, ending with a purl row.

Now move on to the armhole shaping instructions, which are the same for all sleeve lengths.

LONG SLEEVE (MAKE TWO THE SAME)

Using 2.75mm needles, cast on 68 (68, 72, 76, 76) sts.

Work 1 x 1 rib for 10 rows.

Changing to 3.25mm needles:

K1, M1, K to last st, M1, K1. Count 70 (70, 74, 78, 78)sts.

P 1 row.

K 1 row.

P 1 row.

K 1 row.

P 1 row.

K1, M1, K to last st, M1, K1. Count 72 (72, 76, 80, 80)sts.

Rep the last 6 rows until you have 84 (90, 96, 106, 112)sts.

Cont in st st until sleeve measures 43 (46, 46, 47, 48)cm from the beginning, ending with a purl row
Now move on to the armhole shaping instructions, which are the same for all sleeve lengths.

ARMHOLE SHAPING (THIS IS THE SAME FOR ALL SLEEVE LENGTHS)

Cast off 4 (5, 5, 6, 6)sts, K to end. Count 80 (85, 91, 100, 106)sts.

Cast off 4 (5, 5, 6, 6)sts, P to end. Count 76 (80, 86, 94, 100)sts.

Decrease row 1 (RS): K2tog tbl, K to last 2sts, K2tog. Count 74 (78, 84, 92, 98)sts.

Decrease row 2 (WS): P2tog, P to last 2sts, P2tog tbl. Count 72 (76, 82, 90, 96)sts.

Rep the last 2 rows until 68 (72, 78, 82, 88)sts remain.

Decrease row 1 (RS): K2tog tbl, K to last 2sts, K2tog. Count 66 (70, 76, 80, 86)sts.

P 1 row.

Rep last 2 rows until 56 (58, 60, 64, 68)sts remain.

Decrease row 1 (RS): K2tog tbl, K to last 2sts, K2tog. Count 54 (56, 58, 62, 66)sts.

Decrease row 2 (WS): P2tog, P to last 2sts, P2tog tbl. Count 52 (54, 56, 60, 64)sts.

Rep the last 2 rows until 20 (22, 20, 24, 24)sts remain.

Cast off 3sts, K to end. Count 17 (19, 17, 21, 21)sts.

Cast off 3sts, P to end. Count 14 (16, 14, 18, 18)sts.

Cast off 3sts, K to end. Count 11 (13, 11, 15, 15)sts.

Cast off 3sts, P to end. Count 8 (10, 8, 12, 12)sts.

Cast off remaining stitches.

Note to Knitters

As with most knitting patterns, it's important that you follow the making-up instructions in the order they are written.

Making up

Using mattress stitch, join the shoulder seams of the back to the left and right fronts. Start sewing at the armhole edge and work towards the direction of the neck opening to ensure that pieces fit together correctly.

Handy HINT

This project will have taken you a while to knit, so be patient during the sewing up. Take your time and if you aren't happy with a particular seam, don't be afraid to pull it out and have another go. Remember to refer to the Sewing-up workshop on p.152 as you go.

Neckband

Handy HINT

When picking up stitches from a long length of knitting, I suggest that you mark out sections with dressmaking pins. Divide the section into eight equal parts and work out how many stitches you need to pick up in each section. This will ensure that you don't get to the end and discover you are way out on your numbers.

Using 2.75mm needles and with RS facing, pick up and knit:

50 (52, 54, 56, 58)sts up the right front of the neck,

49 (51, 53, 55, 57)sts along the back of the neck,

50 (52, 54, 56, 58)sts down the left front of the neck.

Count 149 (155, 161, 167, 173)sts.

> ### Note to Knitters
>
> If the neck and button bands seem to have too many stitches to squash onto a normal straight needle, you can knit them back and forth on 2.75mm circular needles. See p.240 for how to work straight on circular needles.

Row 1 (WS): P1, K1, rib to end (you'll start and end this row with a P1).

Row 2 (RS): K1, P1, rib to end (you'll start and end this row with a K1).

Rep the last 2 rows to a total of 10 rows, ending with a Row 2.

Cast off on WS of cardigan in pattern (remember to knit the knit stitches and purl the purl stitches when casting off in rib).

Left front button band

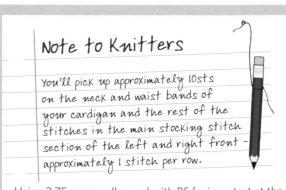

> ### Note to Knitters
>
> You'll pick up approximately 10sts on the neck and waist bands of your cardigan and the rest of the stitches in the main stocking stitch section of the left and right front – approximately 1 stitch per row.

Using 2.75mm needles and with RS facing, start at the top of the neck and pick up and knit 153 (165, 171, 183, 195)sts.

Row 1 (WS): P1, K1 rib to end (you'll start and end this row with a purl stitch).

Row 2 (RS): K1, P1 rib to end (you'll start and end this row with a knit stitch).

Repeat last 2 rows to a total of 10 rows, ending with a Row 2.

Cast off on WS of cardigan in pattern.

Right front button band

Using 2.75mm needles and with RS facing, starting at the waist of the cardigan, pick up and knit 153 (165, 171, 183, 195)sts.

Row 1 (WS): P1, K1 rib to end (you'll start and end this row with a purl stitch).

Row 2 (RS): K1, P1 rib to end (you'll start and end this row with a knit stitch).

Row 3 (WS): As Row 1.

Row 4 (RS): As Row 2.

Row 5 (WS): P1, K1, P1, K1, YF, K2tog, [rib 12, YF, K2tog], repeat a further ten (11, 11, 12, 13) times, rib to end. You'll have a total of 11 (12, 12, 13, 14) buttonholes, which will appear after the next row of knitting.

Row 6 (RS): As Row 2 – look to see the buttonholes appearing and don't forget to count the stitches at the end of the row to make sure you still have the correct number.

Row 7 (WS): As Row 1.

Row 8 (RS): As Row 2.

Row 9 (WS): As Row 1.

Row 10 (RS): As Row 2.

Cast off on WS of cardigan in pattern.

Questions & Answers

What do you mean by 'rib 12'?

Before you work the buttonhole row, have a look at the Recognising rib workshop on p.160. 'Rib 12' means 'continue working 12sts in rib' – to do this you have to know which are the knit stitches and which are the purl stitches are simply by looking at them. Remember your V-necks and polo necks!

See p.160 for instructions on recognising rib.

Note to Knitters

Your buttonholes might seem a bit small, but don't worry. Knitted buttonholes can stretch with use, so I've purposely made them small. Your 1cm buttons will squeeze in, and a tight fit means that they won't pop open (which I find a huge pain on some cardigans I own).

Handy HINT

Be patient with your finishing. On such a big project using fine yarn, a little extra care will really pay off. Consider the effort you put into making up your cardigan as a quarter of the total work you put into this project.

Sew sleeves

See how to sew a sleeve onto a body on p.153.

Sew the sleeves into the armhole opening. To get the best fit, fold the top of the sleeve in half to find the centre.

Start by sewing that to the shoulder seam. On the body, begin by finding the centre bar, and on the top of the sleeve you'll be looking for two sides of the 'V' (see p.153). Don't forget to ease in!

Work your way towards the underarm.

Note to Knitters

Due to the fine yarn and fitted shape, remember to ease in the sleeves carefully (see p.157). You may find you have to take two of the centre bars at a time on the body side instead of the usual one, and just two 'V' sides on the sleeve. Remember to start sewing at the centre of the shoulder seam and work towards the underarm. Then sew up the other side of the sleeve, working again from the shoulder to the underarm.

See Sewing-up workshop on p.152.

Sewing up something so finely knit and shaped means that you'll have to use your initiative – sometimes you'll

be picking up two sides of the 'V' and sometimes you'll be picking up the centre bar.

Once you've sewn one side of the sleeve to the body, you can go back to the middle, where you started sewing the sleeve to the body, and work your way down the other side.

See Sewing up around corners on p.155.

Handy HINT

Don't forget to keep an eye on the underarm – the start of the underarm decreasing is the point where the sleeve and the body must join up. You'll have to ease the sleeve in to make sure this happens.

Side and sleeve seams

Starting from the underarm, using 'centre-bar' mattress stitch, sew up from the underarm to the wrist, then

from the underarm to the waist of the cardigan.

Handy HINT

By starting the side and sleeve seams at the point of the underarm and working towards the wrist, then back from the point of the underarm to the waist of the cardigan, it ensures that you have an exact join between the sleeves and the body.

Buttons

Sew on the buttons securely – lay the cardigan flat, so you can match up the buttons with the buttonholes. When sewing on buttons, first sew the buttons at the top and the bottom of the cardigan, then the button in the middle, and then fill in the gaps. If you

start sewing the buttons from one end and work your way along the button band, it's easy to make a mistake and run out of room for your buttons.

Weave in all your ends neatly.

Gloves

Gloves may seem fiddly little things to knit, but they make a perfect project if you'd like a knitting challenge but don't fancy a 'big' project.

You can add your own touches, using colours in any combination that strikes your fancy – maybe each finger in a different colour? Knitting gloves might seem like a project that needs a lot of coordination on your part, but once you get the hang of it, I reckon you'll be churning them out to make presents for everyone in no time. Don't forget to look at p.218 and knit a matching hat!

YOU WILL NEED

ANY STANDARD DOUBLE KNIT YARN, so you have lots of options when choosing
Ladies' gloves: 139m
Men's gloves: 154m

3MM KNITTING NEEDLES

3.75MM KNITTING NEEDLES

CROCHET HOOK   3mm is a good size for this project

DARNING NEEDLE

Note to Knitters

Although the gauge is calculated using 4mm knitting needles, this pattern uses smaller needles than usual with double knit yarn. This is to create a tighter weave, so that the knitted fabric is warmer and denser. It will make nice, cosy gloves that will fend off winter wind chill.

GAUGE

22sts and 30 rows in stocking stitch, using 4mm needles = 10cm square.

SIZE

Ladies' gloves (men's gloves)

ABBREVIATIONS

K = Knit

P = Purl

St(s) = Stitch(es)

St st = Stocking stitch

1 x 1 rib = K1, P1 rib to end

K2tog = Knit two stitches together

M1 = Make one stitch by picking up the loop in between two stitches

Cont = Continue

Rep = Repeat

Rem = Remaining

START KNITTING

RIGHT HAND

Using 3mm needles, cast on 46 (52)sts.

Work 1 x 1 rib until piece measures 8 (6)cm from beginning.

Handy HINT

I suggest that if you alter the depth of the ribbed cuff, you also make a note of the number of rows you've knitted, using a tally. This means that when you knit the glove for the other hand, you can make sure it is exactly the same length.

Changing to 3.75mm needles and starting with a knit row, st st for 4 rows.

SHAPE THUMB GUSSET

K23 (25), M1, K3, M1, K to end. Count 48 (54) sts.
P 1 row.
K 1 row.
P 1 row.
K23 (25), M1, K5, M1, K to end. Count 50 (56)sts.
P 1 row.
K23 (25), M1, K7, M1, K to end. Count 52 (58)sts.
P 1 row.
K23 (25), M1, K9, M1, K to end. Count 54 (60)sts.
P 1 row.
K23 (25), M1, K11, M1, K to end. Count 56 (62)sts.
P 1 row.
K23 (25), M1, K13, M1, K to end. Count 58 (64)sts.
P 1 row.

Note to Knitters

Gloves that are too short are a pet hate of mine, as I get cold wrists. That's why I've knitted a longer cuff for the ladies' gloves than the men's, as I don't think gentlemen care as much about cold wrists as I do. However, if you want longer or shorter cuffs on the gloves, feel free to adjust the pattern with more or fewer rows of ribbing. Just remember that you'll need more yarn if you are increasing the ribbing.

Note to Knitters

If the man in question is a particularly burly specimen, you might like to add extra rows to each digit. This must be an even number – I suggest 2 or 4 rows. It's unlikely that you'll need more than that.

You'll see your thumb gusset appearing.

DIVIDE FOR THUMB

K38 (42)sts, turn (turning in the middle of a row means swapping the needles around in your hands, ready to start working in the other direction).

P15 (17)sts, turn.

Working on these 15 (17)sts only, st st a further 14 (18) rows on the thumb.

K2tog, rep to last stitch, K1. Count 8 (9)sts.

DRAWSTRING FINISH

Step 1: Cut the yarn leaving a tail of around 40cm, and thread the cut end onto a darning needle.

Step 2: Pass the darning needle through the stitches remaining on the knitting needle, one by one, removing them from the knitting needle as they are secured by the yarn on the darning needle.

Step 3: Pull the yarn tight. The piece of knitting should now fall naturally into a thumb shape.

Sew up from the top of the thumb to the base, using mattress stitch.

HAND

Join new yarn to the tail of yarn you've just sewn the thumb with, and with RS facing, knit to end.

Starting with a purl row, st st 11 (13) rows, ending with a purl row.

DIVIDE FOR FINGERS

FIRST FINGER

K28 (30), turn.

P13 (13), turn and cast on 2sts. Count 15 (15)sts.

Working on these 15 (15)sts only, st st a further 22 (24) rows, ending with a purl row.

K2tog, rep to last stitch, K1. Count 8 (8)sts.

Cut the yarn leaving a long tail (about 40cm), do a drawstring finish and sew up the finger from the tip to the base.

SECOND FINGER

With RS facing, rejoin yarn to the yarn tail you've just sewn the first finger with, pick up and knit 2sts from the cast-on sts at the base of the first finger. K5 (6), turn.

P12 (14), turn and cast on 2sts. Count 14 (16)sts.

Working on these 14 (16)sts only, st st a further 24 (26) rows, ending with a purl row.

K2tog, rep to end. Count 7 (8)sts.

Cut the yarn, leaving a long tail (about 40cm), do a drawstring finish and sew up the finger from the tip to the base.

THIRD FINGER

With RS facing, rejoin yarn to the yarn tail you've just sewn the second finger with, pick up and knit 2sts from the cast-on sts at the base of the second finger.

K5 (6), turn.

P12 (14), turn and cast on 2sts. Count 14 (16)sts.

Working on these 14 (16)sts only, st st a further 20 (22) rows, ending with a purl row.

K2tog, rep to end. Count 7 (8)sts.

Cut the yarn leaving a long tail (about 40cm), do a drawstring finish and sew up the finger from the tip to the base.

LITTLE FINGER

With RS facing, rejoin yarn to the yarn tail you've just sewn the third finger with, pick up and knit 2sts from the cast-on sts at the base of the third finger.

K5 (5), turn.

P to end. Count 12 (12)sts.

Working on these 12 (12)sts only, st st a further 12 (14) rows, ending with a purl row.

K2tog, rep to end. Count 6 (6)sts.

Cut the yarn leaving a long tail (about 60cm), do a drawstring finish and sew up the finger and hand from the tip of the little finger to the beginning of the wrist.

Weave in all your ends – remembering to use the weaving-in yarn on a darning needle to sew up, from the inside of the glove, any little holes you might find at the base of the digits. This is a fiddly job, but be patient (and have a snack before starting)! Take it from me that a tidy finish on a pair of gloves might take a bit of time, but will add much more in the way of 'oohs' and 'aahs' from your impressed friends.

Handy HINT

It is common to end up with little holes at the base of the thumb and fingers.

When you are weaving in the ends, you can use the tails of yarn at the base of the digits to sew up these holes from the inside of the glove.

Or if you find yarn is a bit bulky, you could use matching coloured sewing thread.

LEFT HAND

Using 3mm needles, cast on 46 (52)sts.

Work in 1 x 1 rib until piece measures 8 (6)cm from beginning.

Handy HINT

If you changed the depth of the ribbing on the right glove, remember to refer to your note of the number of rows you knitted, to make sure that you get exactly the same length on the left hand.

Changing to 3.75mm needles and starting with a knit row, st st for 4 rows.

SHAPE THUMB GUSSET

K20 (22), M1, K3, M1, K to end. Count 48 (54)sts.

P 1 row.

K 1 row.

P 1 row.

K20 (22), M1, K5, M1, K to end. Count 50 (56)sts.

P 1 row.

K20 (22), M1, K7, M1, K to end. Count 52 (58)sts.

P 1 row.

K20 (22), M1, K9, M1, K to end. Count 54 (60)sts.

P 1 row.

K20 (22), M1, K11, M1, K to end. Count 56 (62)sts.

P 1 row.

K20 (22), M1, K13, M1, K to end. Count 58 (64)sts.

P 1 row.

DIVIDE FOR THUMB

K33 (39)sts, turn.

P15 (17)sts, turn.

Working on these 15 (17)sts only, st st a further 14 (18) rows on the thumb.

K2tog, rep to last stitch, K1. Count 8 (9)sts.

Cut yarn leaving a long tail of about 40cm and do a drawstring finish.

Sew up the thumb from the tip to the base.

Join new yarn to the yarn tail you've just sewn the thumb with, and with RS facing, knit to end.

HAND

Starting with a purl row, st st 11 (13) rows, ending with a purl row.

DIVIDE FOR FINGERS

FIRST FINGER

K28 (30), turn.

P13 (13), turn and cast on 2sts. Count 15 (15)sts.

Working on these 15 (15)sts only, st st a further 22 (24) rows, ending with a purl row.

K2tog, rep to last stitch, K1. Count 8 (8)sts.

Cut the yarn leaving a long tail (about 40cm), do a drawstring finish and sew up the finger from the tip to the base.

SECOND FINGER

With RS facing, rejoin yarn to the yarn tail you've just sewn the first finger with, pick up and knit 2sts from the cast-on sts at the base of the first finger.

K5 (6), turn.

P12 (14), turn and cast on 2sts. Count 14 (16)sts.

Working on these 14 (16)sts only, st st a further 24 (26) rows, ending with a purl row.

K2tog, rep to end. Count 7 (8)sts.

Cut the yarn leaving a long tail (about 40cm), do a drawstring finish and sew up the finger from the tip to the base.

THIRD FINGER

With RS facing, rejoin yarn to the yarn tail you've just sewn the second finger with, pick up and knit 2sts from the cast-on sts at the base of the second finger.

K5 (6), turn.

P12 (14), turn and cast on 2sts. Count 14 (16)sts.

Working on these 14 (16)sts only, st st a further 20 (22) rows, ending with a purl row.

K2tog, rep to end. Count 7 (8)sts.

Cut the yarn leaving a long tail (about 40cm), do a drawstring finish and sew up the finger from the tip to the base.

LITTLE FINGER

With RS facing, rejoin yarn to the yarn tail you've just sewn the third finger with, pick up and knit 2sts from the cast-on sts at the base of the third finger.

K5 (5), turn.

P to end. Count 12 (12)sts.

Working on these 12 (12)sts only, st st a further 12 (14) rows, ending with a purl row.

K2tog, rep to end. Count 6 (6)sts.

Cut the yarn leaving a long tail (about 60cm), do a drawstring finish and sew up the finger and hand from the tip of the little finger to the beginning of the wrist.

Weave in all the ends – remembering to use the weaving-in yarn on a darning needle to sew up any little holes you might find at the base of the digits, from the inside of the glove.

Variations

You can personalise these gloves in many ways:

- Colour changes – you could even knit every digit in a different colour!

- Fingerless mitts – knit each digit to the length you want before casting off on the WS of the work and sewing up.

- Sew pretty things to the fingers or the back of the gloves, such as buttons or sequins, or embroidery.

- Adjust the length of the cuff – you could even lengthen it to reach nearly as far as your elbow.

Hats: learn to knit in the round

Working in the round may seem like a very advanced knitting technique, but if you follow my few tips and tricks, I hope you'll soon be a convert to circular knitting.

Knitting in the round is traditionally used to knit socks on double-pointed needles, but these days, many knitters and designers take advantage of this seamless technique for all sorts of projects, including hats and even jumpers.

Circular knitting needles come in different lengths as well as needle sizes. The needle sizes are the same as with straight needles, it's the lengths that you'll need to think about in relation to your project. The length refers to the length of the needles taking into account the flexible part. For example, a 40cm circular needle is perfect for a hat. Any longer than that and the flexible part of the needle will be too long for the circumference of the knitting. If you want to knit anything smaller than a hat, for example where the crown of a hat narrows at the top of the head, or socks, you'll need to use double-pointed needles.

I'll start you off on circular needles for a hat and we'll move on to the instructions for double-pointed needles to finish the hat and then later to knit socks.

YOU WILL NEED

ANY STANDARD DOUBLE KNIT YARN
so you have lots of options when choosing. I hate an itchy hat on my forehead – bear in mind the person you are knitting for when you chose your yarn. For example, it's lovely to have the option of cotton when knitting for baby's sensitive skin – I love Debbie Bliss Eco Baby, which is an organic Fairtrade yarn in 100% cotton. Note that it's a little finer than a standard double knit yarn, so the hat may turn out to be a little bit smaller.
Baby: 51m
Child: 60m
Adult small: 84m
Adult large: 108m

4MM KNITTING NEEDLES

4MM CIRCULAR NEEDLES, 40CM LONG

4MM DOUBLE-POINTED NEEDLES, 20CM LONG

DARNING NEEDLE

Handy HINT

If you would like a slightly bigger hat, or if your tension is quite tight, try using 5mm needles instead.

Note to Knitters

These yarn requirements are approximate since your tension may vary as you are learning to knit in the round.

GAUGE

22sts and 30 rows in stocking stitch, using 4mm
needles = 10cm square.

SIZE

Baby (child, adult small, adult large)
The hat can be knitted in four sizes, approximate
to the age/size of the wearer. The fit of the child
size will depend on the age of the child; you can
make the 'adult small' size for an older child. The
main pattern instructions are for a hat with a rolled
brim; instructions for a hat with a ribbed border
are given separately.

ABBREVIATIONS

K = Knit

P = Purl

St(s) = Stitch(es)

St st = Stocking stitch (remember that this is K 1
row, P 1 row on straight needles, and K every round
if you are working in the round)

1 x 1 rib = K1, P1 rib to end

K2tog = Knit two stitches together

Dpn(s) = Double-pointed needle(s)

Rep = Repeat

START KNITTING

Using 4mm straight needles and leaving a long tail
of yarn (about 20cm), cast on 66 (77, 88, 99)sts.

Note to Knitters

Using straight needles to start a piece of
knitting in the round isn't the most traditional
way of working, but if you don't have an expert to
help you, it is a way of guaranteeing that your
work will not get twisted when you join (which is
a huge pain). I still sometimes use this technique
myself - there's never any harm in making life
a little easier. When you get to the end of your
work, the little gap at the beginning that you
knitted on straight needles can be sewn up easily
for a tidy finish.

Starting with a knit row, work in st st for 4 rows,
ending on a purl row.

Knit the stitches from the straight needles on to the
4mm circular needle.

Ribbed border variation

The main pattern shown with the images will
produce a hat with a rolled stocking stitch brim. For
a ribbed border, you'll have to follow the slightly
different pattern – shown here – but the technique
for joining into the round is the same.

**Baby and adult small sizes (an even number
of cast-on stitches):**

- Using straight 4mm needles and leaving a long
  tail of yarn (about 20cm), cast on 66 (88)sts.

- Work 1 x 1 rib to end.

- Rep the last row a further three times to make a
  total of 4 rows of rib.

- In the next row, 1 x 1 rib your stitches onto a
  circular needle.

Once the stitches are all on the circular needles, you'll notice that the knitting is probably twisted along the flexible part of the needle.

Carefully spread out the stitches so that they are untwisted. Keep the working end of the yarn on the right-hand side.

Next you'll need a stitch marker. You can buy these, or (as I prefer to do) use a piece of contrasting coloured yarn tied in a slip knot, which works just as well.

Place the marker on the tip of the right-hand needle, just on top of the last worked stitch. The working yarn is now on the right-hand needle.

Taking care that you haven't twisted the knitting – so it remains a true circle – knit the first stitch from the left part of the circular needle on to the right part of the circular needle. Keep knitting until you get back round to the stitch marker. You have now knitted one round.

- Place marker and join into the round taking care not to twist (follow the instructions with the images for how to do this).

- Note: the first stitch after the marker is a knit stitch. Therefore you'll start every round with a knit and end with a purl just before the marker.

- When you have a total of 4cm of rib, knit every round (this will create stocking stitch in the round) and follow the main pattern to the end.

Hat with ribbed border for child and adult large (an odd number of cast-on stitches):

- Using straight 4mm needles and leaving a long tail of yarn (about 20cm), cast on 77 (99)sts.

- Row 1: K1, P1 rib to end (you'll start and end this row with a knit stitch).

- Row 2: P1, K1 rib to end (you'll start and end this row with a purl stitch).

- Row 3: As Row 1.

- Starting and ending with a purl stitch, 1 x 1 rib your stitches onto a circular needle.

- Place marker and join into the round taking care not to twist (follow the instructions with images on how to do this) – when you join into a round, the first joining stitch will be a purl stitch.

- Note that the stitch either side of the marker will be a purl stitch. That means you'll have two purls next to each other on the rib. Don't worry, as this won't stand out on the rib, and will make it much easier to follow the rest of the pattern after the ribbed border.

- When you have a total of 4cm of rib, knit every round (this will create stocking stitch in the round) and follow the main pattern to the end.

Note to Knitters

Working back and forth on straight needles is called making ROWS. When working on circular or double-pointed needles, you are making ROUNDS. In the round, you create stocking stitch by knitting every round. There is no need to purl. This is because you are essentially always on the right side of your work. Clever, eh?!

Handy HINT

The most important rule when working in the round is that the yarn should always be in your right hand, even when you pick up your knitting. If you find that the yarn is in your left hand, STOP and turn your work!

At the end of the round, you'll reach the marker. Slip this without knitting it.

At the end of your first round, you may see a short line of yarn where you made the initial join into the round. Keep knitting, pulling a little tighter at the join for the first couple of rounds, and that will disappear.

After knitting the first round, check again to be sure that the knitting hasn't twisted.

If you check carefully for the first 3 or 4 rounds that there is no twisting, you're home and dry, as the shape of the hat will be set and unable to twist.

After a few rounds, you'll see that the knitting is joining together seamlessly. There will be a small gap where you knitted on straight needles in the beginning, but you can easily sew this up later, using the length of yarn you left at the cast-on edge for this purpose.

One of the joys of knitting in the round is seeing your work magically appear fully formed, with very little sewing up to do.

Knitting every round, continue in st st until the piece measures 13 (15, 17, 19)cm from the beginning.

Handy HINT

Pull tighter for the first couple of stitches at the beginning of every round. This will ensure a seamless join. And don't worry if you can see the join – this can take a bit of practice to get right. Also, remember to slip the marker every time.

Handy HINT

When putting away your knitting in the round, push the stitches away from the tips to the flexible part of the needle. This will prevent the stitches from falling off the needles when you aren't knitting.

DECREASE FOR TOP OF HAT (changing over to double-pointed needles as the circumference of your hat gets smaller)

BABY

[K4, K2tog], repeat to end. Count 55sts.

[K3, K2tog], repeat to end. Count 44sts.

[K2, K2tog], repeat to end. Count 33sts.

[K1, K2tog], repeat to end. Count 22sts.

[K2tog], repeat to end. Count 11sts.

CHILD

[K5, K2tog], repeat to end. Count 66sts.

– then follow instructions for baby.

ADULT SMALL

[K6, K2tog], repeat to end. Count 77sts.

[K5, K2tog], repeat to end. Count 66sts.

– then follow instructions for baby.

ADULT LARGE

[K7, K2tog], repeat to end. Count 88sts.

[K6, K2tog], repeat to end. Count 77sts.

[K5, K2tog], repeat to end. Count 66sts.

– then follow instructions for baby.

Note to Knitters

As you get fewer and fewer stitches, you will need to work the stitches equally onto three double-pointed needles. This is so that you have enough room to work as the stitches get closer together and the circular needle becomes too long. I suggest that you change to double-pointed needles after the first decrease round on the baby's hat and the second decrease round on the bigger sizes.

Changing over to double-pointed needles

You'll notice, as you work these decreases, that eventually the circular needle becomes too long as the stitches get fewer and fewer. When this happens, work the next round (continuing the decreases as shown on the pattern) by knitting approximately one-third of the stitches on to one of the double-pointed needles (dpns). You'll need to do this after the first or second set of decreases.

Then push the stitches you've just knitted to the centre of the dpn (they'll stay there quite happily for now) and work the next third of the stitches on to another dpn.

You now have two-thirds of the stitches on two dpns and one-third still on the circular needle.

Knit the remaining stitches from the circular needle on to a third dpn (remembering to work the decreases at the same time). Well done! I know this part is fiddly!

Handy HINT

If the marker falls off once you start knitting on double-pointed needles, don't worry. It's the join where you can see the cast-on tail of yarn that's the start and finish of each round.

To work in the round on double-pointed needles, you start knitting on to a fourth double-pointed needle. When you've worked the stitches from one needle, you'll be left with an empty needle. You then use that to work the stitches on the next needle. Each time you work a needle, you'll be left with an empty needle on which to knit the next stitches. Don't panic – this will make sense when you do it!

Now continue working the pattern in the round on the dpns. This will seem strange at first, but persevere! A student once described it as knitting into a bird's nest, and you will get poked by the needles a few times, but my advice is to simply squash the stitches on the needles you aren't using to the middle of the needles and ignore them. They won't slip off: they'll just hang in there, waiting for their turn.

As the stitches get fewer and fewer as you decrease towards the crown of the hat, the double-pointed needles move closer and closer together to make a smaller triangle. Circular needles wouldn't be able to do this, which is why we need to transfer the hat stitches to double-pointed needles.

Finishing

There are a couple of ways to do this. The simplest way is to work a drawstring finish.

Cut the yarn, leaving a long tail. Thread the end onto a darning needle, and pass

the stitches from the dpns on to the darning needle.

Pull the drawstring tightly to close the opening at the top of the hat.

On the inside of the hat, weave this end in using small stitches sewn around the hole at the top of the hat.

Handy HINT

This is a pretty simple hat pattern, but you can think creatively and add a different border, use colourwork (see p.284), Swiss darning (see p.290), or simply sew on buttons or sequins to create any unique look you like.

Making up

Sew up the small opening at the beginning of the hat where you worked on straight needles. You'll have left a 20cm length of yarn for this.

Weave in all your ends.

Handy HINT

If you are making one of the smaller sizes (or indeed any size you like), I-cord (see p.148) makes an adorable alternative finish. When you've completed the decreases, transfer the final 11sts onto a double-pointed needle and work your I-cord. This looks particularly cute on the baby size – you could even sew a pompom onto the end of your I-cord.

Workshop: *Using double-pointed needles*

For circular knitting projects, you can knit in the round directly on double-pointed needles (dpns) without using circular needles at all.

You need this technique for socks, but it works just as well on hats if you find you prefer dpns to circular needles.

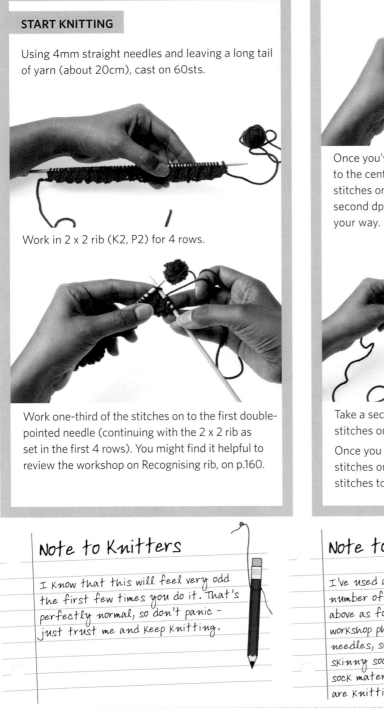

START KNITTING

Using 4mm straight needles and leaving a long tail of yarn (about 20cm), cast on 60sts.

Work in 2 x 2 rib (K2, P2) for 4 rows.

Work one-third of the stitches on to the first double-pointed needle (continuing with the 2 x 2 rib as set in the first 4 rows). You might find it helpful to review the workshop on Recognising rib, on p.160.

Once you've done that, squash those stitches to the centre of the first dpn – this will hold the stitches on the needle as you start using the second dpn, keeping the first lot of stitches out of your way.

Take a second dpn and work the next third of the stitches on to it.

Once you have worked the next third of the stitches on to the second dpn, squash those stitches to the middle as well.

Note to Knitters

I know that this will feel very odd the first few times you do it. That's perfectly normal, so don't panic – just trust me and keep knitting.

Note to Knitters

I've used a 2 x 2 rib border and the same number of cast-on stitches in the images above as for the Ladies' sock, but I've done the workshop photos on double knit yarn and 4mm needles, so you can see it more clearly than on skinny sock yarn. Use this workshop with the sock materials and cast-on numbers when you are knitting your socks.

Finally, work the remaining stitches from the straight needle onto a third dpn.

Now to join!

Once all the stitches are on the three dpns, you'll notice that the stitches are all twisted about the needles.

Your first job is to lay the needles out flat and straighten up the stitches. Keep the working end of the yarn on the right-hand side. Take extra care to ensure that the stitches aren't twisted around the needles, especially at the point where the needles meet. It's here that it's easy to make a mistake, so really take your time.

Fold the needles closed so they form a triangle.

Work a couple of stitches to close the triangle.

Next, take a fourth (new) double-pointed needle and work the stitches from the first dpn on to the empty needle.

Handy HINT

Once again, I know this feels odd, but keep the stitches on the needles you aren't currently working from squished to the middle of each needle, so they are out of your way, and simply ignore them. Easier said than done, you might say, as they can poke you, but persevere!

Keep knitting your ribbed border. Each time you work the stitches on to an empty double-pointed needle, you'll end up with a new empty needle. Put that empty dpn into your right hand and work the stitches from the next needle on to it.

What you are doing now is working in ROUNDS.

As with the instructions for starting on a circular needle, when you finish the first round, lay out the work to check you haven't twisted it. These twists can easily happen in the first few rounds – the place to check is where each needle meets the one next to it. After you've worked a few rounds, the work will be set in its round and you won't need to keep checking it. Don't worry if there's a strand of yarn at the join after the first round: it will disappear after you've worked a couple more rounds.

Handy HINT

The most important rule, when working in the round, is that the yarn should always be in your right hand, even when you pick up your knitting. If you find that the yarn is in your left hand, STOP and turn your work.

Questions & Answers

Panic! I've worked my first round and it looks like the work has twisted!

If this happens in the first round, you can untwist your work by rearranging the needles at the point where they meet the next needle. You can only correct this in the first couple of rounds, which is why it's so important to check.

This technique of using double-pointed needles works on most knitting in the round; you'll definitely need it for knitting socks. If you are a bit nervous, I suggest that you knit the hat before attempting socks, as the socks use much finer yarn and needles, so everything's just that little bit more fiddly. It's not essential of course – feel free to be brave and dive into sock knitting straight away: you can always undo your work and try again if you aren't happy. That's one of the joys of knitting!

Socks

Socks can seem like the holy grail of knitting. My students often tell me that their long-term knitting goal is to knit socks and the main question I hear is: 'Aren't socks *reeeally* difficult?'

My answer is always the same – nothing is difficult if you approach it at the right time and if it's explained in bite-sized pieces. By the 'right time', I mean that you'll enjoy knitting socks more if you are confident with the core skills of knitting. It is a good idea to have several small and large projects under your belt first, so that the basics of casting on, knitting and ribbing will already be second nature and you can concentrate on learning the new skills required for socks.

You might also like to knit a basic hat in the round (see p.218) to hone your circular knitting skills before you start working on tiny double-pointed needles for 4-ply socks. As for the 'bite-sized pieces', I've broken the pattern right down into simple stages with images, so sock knitting won't feel like a risky adventure, but rather an achievable challenge. You'll find plenty of support, hints and tips in my step-by-step instructions.

Before you embark on knitting socks, ask yourself:

1. Can I recognise rib stitches? (See p.160.)
2. Have I knitted the hat pattern in the round? (See p.218.)
3. Can I pick up and knit? (See p.149.)

If the answer to all the above is yes, then you are ready for socks!

Socks can be knitted in any weight of yarn, but my favourite socks, and the ones I find the most satisfying to make, are fine-knit socks in 4-ply sock yarn. These are lightweight enough to wear with shoes (as opposed to chunky slipper socks), and make a great little project to take with you when you travel, as you don't have to carry huge amounts of materials.

I suggest that you always use proper sock yarn (for the adults' sizes), as the yarn includes a small amount of man-made fibre to add strength. Remember that socks are subjected to a lot more wear and tear than most knitted garments, especially around the heel, and you don't want to spend ages knitting something that will end up in tatters after a few wears. That would be very disheartening! For babies' socks, you can use any 4-ply yarn, as these will get less wear than adults' socks.

All in all, sock knitting is a nifty skill for a knitter to have; it's very hard not to get addicted, and socks make lovely gifts to impress your friends and family with … and for yourself, of course!

Handy HINT

If you've never knitted in the round or on double-pointed needles, I suggest that you have a go at knitting a hat in the round first, as that uses 4mm needles and double knit yarn, which is less fiddly when you're learning a new technique than the fine needles and yarn used in this sock pattern.

Note to Knitters

Beware of succumbing to the one-sock syndrome! It's easy to knit one sock and forget about knitting another. Unless you are a one-legged pirate, get knitting that second sock as soon as you finish the first one. Alternatively, you could get a second set of double-pointed needles and knit both socks at the same time.

GAUGE

Approximately 28sts and 40 rows in stocking stitch, using 2.25mm needles = 10cm square.

SIZE

Babies/toddlers (ladies, men)
This pattern is for an average-sized foot. Don't worry, as you can adjust the length later in the pattern depending on your shoe size. Please note that all the images relate to the ladies' size, but the techniques are the same for all sizes.

ABBREVIATIONS

K = Knit

P = Purl

2 x 2 rib = K2, P2 rib to end

St(s) = Stitch(es)

Sl = Slip a stitch from one needle to the next without knitting it

K2tog = Knit two stitches together

SSK = Slip, slip, knit

Dpn(s) = Double-pointed needle(s)

Knitwise = Treat stitches as if you were about to knit them

Purlwise = Treat stitches as if you were about to purl them

RS = Right side

WS = Wrong side

YOU WILL NEED

LOOK FOR SPECIALIST SOCK YARNS, for example Regia, Opal, Araucania Ranco and Mini Mochi. Using a sock-specific yarn will ensure that the socks wear well.
Babies'/toddlers' socks: 72m
Ladies' socks: 300m
Men's socks: 335m

2.5MM DOUBLE-POINTED KNITTING NEEDLES, 15–20CM LONG

3.5MM STRAIGHT KNITTING NEEDLES

CROCHET HOOK
I suggest using a tiny 2mm hook for the pick-up and knit at the heel

DARNING NEEDLE

Handy HINT

If you are using a self-patterning yarn, try to make sure that you start knitting the second sock at the same point in the colour repeat as the first sock. It'll make a subtle difference and give your socks a more professional look.

Note to Knitters

Of course, if you are knitting for larger than average feet, you'll need more yarn. I always think it's best to buy more yarn rather than less, and you can always knit a couple of pairs of the children's socks if you have any yarn left over.

Note to Knitters

This pattern features my easy technique of using straight needles for the cast-on and then moving on to double-pointed needles. Alternatively, feel free to cast on directly to the double-pointed needles if you are experienced at using them – but do take care not to twist when you join into the round.

START KNITTING

CUFF

Using the straight 3.5mm knitting needles, and leaving a long tail of yarn about 30cm long, cast on 36 (60, 72)sts.

Work in 2 x 2 rib for 4 rows.

2 x 2 rib the sts as equally as possible onto three 2.5mm dpns.

Join into a round with the first 2sts, BEING VERY CAREFUL NOT TO TWIST THE STITCHES. See Workshop: Using double-pointed needles (p.227) if you need a reminder.

The cast-on tail of yarn shows the beginning of the round.

Work in 2 x 2 rib until piece measures 3 (7, 8)cm from the beginning.

Note to Knitters

Don't forget that you are now knitting ROUNDS as opposed to ROWS. This is important to remember later in the pattern, when you start knitting the heel.

Remember to check your knitting for twisting at the end of every round for the first few rounds.

Handy HINT

This can seem fiddly, working on such fine yarn and double-pointed needles, but many intermediate knitters have tested these instructions for me and most think that if you take your time, persevere and don't give up, knitting socks on double-pointed needles is achievable!

Handy HINT

See p.160 for how to recognise rib stitches – it will make your life much easier when ribbing in the round on such fine yarn.

Note to Knitters

After you've worked a few rounds, you'll need to shuffle the stitches from one needle to another – you want to make sure that you have an equal number of stitches on each of the three needles.

Note to Knitters

Needle one is the first needle after the cast-on tail; this makes the next one needle two, and the needle just before the cast-on tail needle three.

Questions & Answers

I seem to have a ladder running down my socks where the double-pointed needles meet, but I haven't dropped a stitch. What's going on?

That's a standard feature of a beginner's sock. It's where you've pulled too tightly on the first stitch between the needles, and it's unlikely to disappear when wearing the sock. I find that if I'm too tense when knitting on dpns, I get that 'ladder' on the side, too. In your next sock, try to relax a bit and don't pull too tightly when you move from one needle to the next. I know that's counter-intuitive, but trust me! After a bit more experience with double-pointed needles, this will stop happening.

LEG

Knit every round (on dpns this creates stocking stitch without needing to purl) until the piece measures 7 (21, 22)cm from the beginning. Be sure to work until the end of the round – the cast-on yarn tail will show you where this is.

Handy HINT

Slip knit stitches knitwise, and slip purl stitches purlwise.

Note to Knitters

So far, you've been knitting in the round. For the heel flap, you will be knitting and purling in ROWS, because you are now working as for straight knitting rather than knitting in the round.

Handy HINT

At this stage, check again to make sure you have 12 (20, 24)sts on each needle.

HEEL FLAP

Using a new (empty) needle, knit 9 (15, 18)sts, turn.

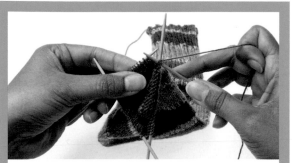

Slip one st, P17 (29, 35)sts – 8 (14, 17) from the first needle and 9 (15, 18) from the second needle. When you start knitting the stitches from the second needle, you'll be working with only three needles (knitting on to the new needle), so it might feel a bit awkward.

Most of the stitches are now on one needle. Turn.

Using another new needle:

Row 1: Slip one st, K17 (29, 35), turn.

The stitches are now on four needles.

The 18 (30, 36) heel-flap stitches are now all on the same needle.

At this stage, it makes it easier to work if you transfer (without knitting) the non-heel stitches equally on to two needles, discarding the fourth needle so the sock is once again on three needles.

You now have 9 (15, 18) stitches on two needles, and 18 (30, 36) stitches on the heel-flap needle.

You will now ignore the non-heel stitches and work only on the 18 (30, 36) heel-flap stitches.

Row 2: Slip 1, P17 (29, 35), turn.

Work the last 2 rows a further 8 (14, 17) times EACH.

This is what the heel flap will look like.

The following charts might help you knit your heel flap – cross off the rows as you work them.

Babies'/toddlers' socks	
Row 1	Row 2
Sl1, K15.	Sl1, P15.
Sl1, K15.	Sl1, P15.
Sl1, K15.	Sl1, P15.
Sl1, K15.	Sl1, P15.
Sl1, K15.	Sl1, P15.
Sl1, K15.	Sl1, P15.
Sl1, K15.	Sl1, P15.
Sl1, K15.	Sl1, P15.

Ladies' socks	
Row 1	Row 2
Sl1, K29.	Sl1, P29.
Sl1, K29.	Sl1, P29.
Sl1, K29.	Sl1, P29.
Sl1, K29.	Sl1, P29.
Sl1, K29.	Sl1, P29.
Sl1, K29.	Sl1, P29.
Sl1, K29.	Sl1, P29.
Sl1, K29.	Sl1, P29.
Sl1, K29.	Sl1, P29.
Sl1, K29.	Sl1, P29.
Sl1, K29.	Sl1, P29.
Sl1, K29.	Sl1, P29.
Sl1, K29.	Sl1, P29.
Sl1, K29.	

Men's socks	
Row 1	Row 2
Sl1, K35.	Sl1, P35.
Sl1, K35.	Sl1, P35.
Sl1, K35.	Sl1, P35.
Sl1, K35.	Sl1, P35.
Sl1, K35.	Sl1, P35.
Sl1, K35.	Sl1, P35.
Sl1, K35.	Sl1, P35.
Sl1, K35.	Sl1, P35.
Sl1, K35.	Sl1, P35.
Sl1, K35.	Sl1, P35.
Sl1, K35.	Sl1, P35.
Sl1, K35.	Sl1, P35.
Sl1, K35.	Sl1, P35.
Sl1, K35.	Sl1, P35.
Sl1, K35.	Sl1, P35.
Sl1, K35.	Sl1, P35.
Sl1, K35.	Sl1, P35.

HEEL

You will now turn the heel (this decreases the stitches on the heel flap).

With the RS of the work facing you and working on the 18 (30, 36) heel sts:

K11 (17, 20), SSK, K1, turn.

P6 (6, 5), P2tog, P1, turn.
Knit to last stitch before the gap – i.e. K7 (7, 6)sts, SSK (slip one st from either side of the gap for this SSK), K1, turn.

Note to Knitters

Where you turned, you'll see there is a gap in the stitches. You SSK or P2tog either side of this gap.

Purl to last stitch before the gap – i.e. P8 (8, 7)sts, P2tog (P2tog from either side of the gap for this P2tog), P1, turn.

Babies'/toddlers' socks	Men's socks
K9, SSK, K1, turn.	K8, SSK, K1, turn.
P9, P2tog, P1, turn.	P9, P2tog, P1, turn.
	K10, SSK, K1, turn.
Ladies' socks	P11, P2tog, P1, turn.
K9, SSK, K1, turn.	K12, SSK, K1, turn.
P10, P2tog, P1, turn.	P13, P2tog, P1, turn.
K11, SSK, K1, turn.	K14, SSK, K1, turn.
P12, P2tog, P1, turn.	P15, P2tog, P1, turn.
K13, SSK, K1, turn.	K16, SSK, K1, turn.
P14, P2tog, P1, turn.	P17, P2tog, P1, turn.
K15, SSK, K1, turn.	K18, SSK, turn.
P16, P2tog, P1, turn.	P19, P2tog, turn.

You'll see the heel start to emerge as you work the shaping rows.

Repeat the last 2 rows until 12 (18, 20)sts remain on the heel section.

Use the chart (right) to tick off the rows as you work them.

Count 12 (18, 20)sts. This is needle one.

K 1 row.

Now you will pick up and knit the heel – you will be picking up and knitting the stitches you slipped when you were knitting and purling the heel-flap rows.

Hold the sock so that the knit side of the work is facing you.

Needle one: Using needle one (the needle that the heel stitches are on) and your crochet hook, pick up and knit 9 (15, 18)sts.

Use the slipped stitches as a guide – they will look like long stitches at the very edge of the heel flap. If you slipped correctly when knitting the heel flap, you should have the exact number of stitches to pick up.

See p.149 for instructions on pick up and knit.

Count 21 (33, 38)sts on needle one – these are the stitches you just picked up plus the stitches you already had on that needle at the end of the heel-turning.

Needle two: Using a new needle (needle two), knit the 18 (30, 36) held non-heel sts – 9 (15, 18)

from first needle and 9 (15, 18) from the next needle. All the stitches are now on two needles.

Needle three: Using a new needle (needle three), pick up and knit 9 (15, 18) sts along the heel flap edge (use the slipped sts as a guide).

Count 48 (78, 92) sts.

Count:

Needle 1: 15 (24, 28) sts.

Needle 2: 18 (30, 36) sts (front of sock).

Needle 3: 15 (24, 28) sts.

Total 48 (78, 92) sts.

Knit 6 (9, 10) sts on to needle three from needle one.

Please note that the start of the round is now at the centre of the heel.

Note to Knitters

Don't worry if it looks like there is a gap at the beginning and end of the pick-up-and-knit stitches – simply pull a little tighter the next time you knit a complete round and these will close up. If you find there is still a little hole, you can sew it up from the inside of the sock later on.

Now for the foot! You will notice that you are now working in the round again.

FOOT
ROUND 1
Needle one: K to last 3sts, K2tog, K1.
Needle two: K all sts.
Needle three: K1, SSK, K to end.
Count 46 (76, 90) sts.
ROUND 2
KNIT THE WHOLE ROUND
Repeat Rounds 1 and 2 until 36 (60, 72) sts remain, ending with a knit round.

Cross off numbers from the following chart to help you keep tally of this stage:

Babies/toddlers	Count				
Round 1	44	42	40	38	36
Round 2	K	K	K	K	K

Ladies	Count							
Round 1	74	72	70	68	66	64	62	60
Round 2	K	K	K	K	K	K	K	K

Men	Count								
Round 1	88	86	84	82	80	78	76	74	72
Round 2	K	K	K	K	K	K	K	K	K

Work in stocking stitch (knit every round) until the piece measures 9cm for the babies'/ toddlers' socks. For the ladies' and men's socks, you will need to measure the foot you are knitting for to get an exact fit. Measure from the end of the heel to the tip of the big toe and subtract 5cm. For example, a size 4 foot is 23cm from heel to toe, therefore you would work to 17cm. Be sure to end at the centre of the heel, as this marks the end of the round.

Measure from the tip of your big toe to the end of your heel – the entire length of the base of your foot, then subtract 5cm.

Once you have worked in stocking stitch until the foot of the sock reaches the appropriate length, decrease for the toe.

TOE

ROUND 1

Needle one: K to last 3sts, K2tog, K1.

Needle two: K1, SSK, K to last 3sts, K2tog, K1.

Needle three: K1, SSK, K to end.

Count 32 (56, 68)sts.

ROUND 2

Knit the whole round.

Repeat the last 2 rounds until 16 (28, 36)sts remain.

Use the following chart:

Babies/toddlers	Count			
Round 1	28	24	20	16
Round 2	K	K	K	K

Ladies	Count						
Round 1	52	48	44	40	36	32	28
Round 2	K	K	K	K	K	K	K

Men	Count							
Round 1	64	60	56	52	48	44	40	36
Round 2	K	K	K	K	K	K	K	K

Repeat Round 1 until 8 (8, 12)sts remain:

Babies/toddlers	12	8			
Ladies	24	20	16	12	8
Men	32	28	24	20	16	12

Knit the stitches from needle one onto needle three – there will now be the same number of stitches on the two remaining needles.

Cut the yarn, leaving a long tail for sewing up. Sew up the toe using Kitchener stitch (see p.146).

To finish, using the long tail of yarn you left when casting on, sew up the small opening at the top of the sock on the ribbed border. You don't have to worry too much about this; a few whip stitches (see p.156) will do the job nicely.

Weave in all ends.

Workshop: *Knitting straight on circular knitting needles*

Circular knitting needles come in different lengths as well as needle sizes. While the needle sizes are the same as for straight needles, it's the length that you'll need to think about in relation to your project, and the way you use your needles.

The length of a pair of circular needles includes the loose 'wire' section in between the needles.

Circular needles need not only be used for knitting in the round: they are a great way to work on a really wide piece of knitting that you wouldn't be able to fit on ordinary straight needles. As well as giving you more room for the stitches, the circular part of the needle will carry all the weight of the knitting, so that you don't have the strain of keeping the weight of a large piece of knitting on your wrists – as you would if you used straight needles.

When working straight on circular needles you simply use the circular needles as if they were straight needles. Push the stitches towards the tip of the needle on the end you are knitting on (the end with the working yarn) and push the stitches away from the needle at the end of your working row.

So, almost as if you are ignoring the circular wire of your needle, you can knit back and forth on the rows of your knitting.

This baby's blanket, knitted using 8 balls of the gorgeous Sublime Baby Cashmere Merino 4-ply Silk, was 310 stitches across. That number of stitches, combined with the weight of the knitting as it gets longer, means that it is much easier to use circular needles than straight ones.

Lengthways-striped scarf

YOU WILL NEED

DOUBLE KNIT YARN:
2 balls in colour A
and 2 balls in colour B

4.5MM CIRCULAR NEEDLE, 80/100CM LONG

START KNITTING

Cast on 250sts using colour A.

Knit 2 rows.

Join colour B without cutting colour A (see p.165 for two-colour stripes).

Knit 2 rows in colour B.

Pick up colour A again and continue in this way, knitting 2 rows in each colour, until your scarf is as wide as you want it to be (this one has about 60 rows in total).

Cast off and weave in the ends.

Handy HINT

You'll be hard pushed to follow Rule Number Two of knitting here (don't stop in the middle of a row), as each row is soooo long. What you need to remember, if you pick up your knitting in the middle of a row, is that the yarn should be on the right-hand side of the knitting. Pick up your knitting with the needles in each hand as if to start working: if the yarn you are knitting with is on the right-hand needle, you are good to go. If the yarn is on the left-hand needle, turn the work around in your hands so it's on the right-hand needle.

This scarf was knitted using Debbie Bliss Cashmerino DK. It has a cast-on of 250 stitches, so it makes sense to use circular needles. You need two balls of yarn in each colour, and as only about 2½ balls are used in the scarf, there should be sufficient yarn left over to make a matching stripey hat (use the pattern on p.218)! I suggest you use a knitting needle one size bigger than recommended for the yarn when knitting this scarf as your knitted fabric will have a slightly looser 'flow' and a more drapey effect when worn.

Workshop: *Short row shaping*

This is a clever little technique for shaping your knitting so that there's more length on one side of the knitting than the other. It sounds a bit tricky, but don't worry, it will make sense when you get to it.

Short row shaping is often used on sock heels, or sometimes for subtle shaping on jumpers, cardigans and hats. My favourite way of using the technique is for a fun take on a simple scarf, as you'll see in a bit. Short row shaping is also known as 'wrap and turn' (W&T).

Here are the instructions for how to work short row shaping on a piece of garter stitch knitting. (It can be done on stocking stitch in the same way.)

ABBREVIATIONS	
K = Knit	
St(s) = Stitch(es)	
K2tog = Knit two stitches together	
W&T = Wrap and turn	
YF = Yarn forward	
Knitwise = Treat stitches as if you were about to knit them	
Turn = Turning in the middle of a row means swapping the needles around in your hands, ready to start working in the other direction	

How to wrap and turn

Knit according to your pattern instructions until you are asked to wrap and turn (W&T).

Slip the next stitch knitwise.

YF (bring the yarn to the front of the work).

Return the slipped stitch to the left-hand needle. This stitch now has the yarn wrapped around it – look closely at the base of the stitch.

Turn and work to the end. (If the next row is a purl row, bring the yarn forward

before purling to the end. If the next row is a knit row, leave the yarn at the back.)

You'll see that there is a little gap where you did the W&T.

Picking up the wrapped stitch

Knit until you get to one stitch before the gap – you'll see that is the stitch you have wrapped.

If you look very closely at the base of this stitch, you'll see the yarn you wrapped around it.

Pick up this wrap with the right-hand needle.

Then slip the wrapped stitch on to the right-hand needle knitwise. Now you have the wrap and wrapped stitch on the right-hand needle.

Insert the tip of the left-hand needle into the front of the top two stitches on the right-hand needle together.

You are now in the correct position to knit these two stitches together.

Continue knitting to the end of the row. You'll notice that the gap has been closed.

A pattern will probably tell you to work several rows with W&T in them, then pick up all the wraps in one row. As I say ... this will be a new technique to most of you and I don't want to you try and work it out until you have a pattern that uses short row shaping. It'll make sense when you get to it!

Table mat and coaster set

This pattern can be adapted to make coasters, table mats, or a twirly scarf. I know it sounds crazy to knit such unrelated projects from the same instructions, but I was designing the twirly scarf when I discovered the coaster! It works on any weight of yarn – with a thick yarn, the finished object will end up bigger than it would if knitted in a fine yarn. Experiment – it's the best way I know to discover new things and learn a lot!

Knitting isn't just for making garments and children's toys. You can make stylish additions to your home, too, such as this dinner set. This cool orange mat and coaster set is knitted using lovely self-patterning Artesano Hummingbird DK. I suggest that you knit a coaster before starting the mat.

YOU WILL NEED

(Makes 1 mat and 1 coaster)

134M DOUBLE KNIT YARN
(I used Artesano Hummingbird DK)

4MM KNITTING NEEDLES

GAUGE

This is not important for this sort of project, as it doesn't have to fit precisely.

ABBREVIATIONS

K = Knit

W&T = Wrap and turn (see Workshop: Short row shaping, p.242)

START KNITTING – COASTER

*Cast on 10sts.

Row 1: Knit 1 row.

Row 2: K8, W&T.

Row 3: Knit to end.

Row 4: K7, W&T.

Row 5: Knit to end.

Row 6: K6, W&T.

Row 7: Knit to end.

Row 8: K5, W&T.

Row 9: Knit to end.

Row 10: K4, W&T.

Row 11: Knit to end.

Row 12: K3, W&T.

Row 13: Knit to end.

Row 14: K2, W&T.

Row 15: Knit to end.

Row 16: K1, W&T.

Row 17: Knit to end

Here's what the knitting will look like after one repeat of Rows 1–17.

Row 18: Knit 1 row, picking up all wraps as you go (the wraps will be on all the stitches except for the first and last stitches).

Repeat last 18 rows a further six times (a total of seven times) to make a complete circle for the coaster*.

Here's the knitting after a total of seven repeats of Rows 1–18. It is now ready to cast off.

Cast off.

Sew up the coaster using whip stitch.

Making up the coaster. Leave a long tail of yarn, about 30cm, when you cast off. Use this tail and whip stitch (see p.156) to sew the coaster into a circle.

For a variation, knit the coaster using a textured yarn such as Stylecraft Eskimo DK, to end up with a fluffy snowflake pattern, which makes a great Christmas decoration.

START KNITTING – TABLE MAT

Cast on 30sts.

Row 1: Knit 1 row.

Row 2: K28, W&T.

Row 3: Knit to end.

Row 4: K27, W&T.

Row 5: Knit to end.

Row 6: K26, W&T.

Row 7: Knit to end.

Continue working in this way, knitting one fewer stitch before the wrap and turn on every even-numbered row.

When you have wrapped every stitch in the row apart from the first and last stitches, knit 1 row picking up all the wraps. As with the coaster, you'll have wraps on all the stitches except for the first and last stitches.

Starting from Row 1, repeat this sequence a further six times (seven in total) so you have a complete circle. Cast off and sew up the seam as for the coaster pattern.

Twirly scarf

A scarf doesn't always have to be a warm, woolly bundle of big knitting. I'm a firm believer that knitting can be used to make delicate, feminine, almost jewellery-like garments. This scarf can be knitted in anything from a fine, lace-weight yarn to a super-bulky yarn to create various effects.

YOU WILL NEED

4-PLY YARN

3.25MM KNITTING NEEDLES

This scarf has been knitted using half a ball of Araucania Ranco Solid, a beautiful sock yarn, and 3.25mm needles. (That works out to approximately 169m of any sock or 4-ply yarn.)

GAUGE

Not important for this project.

ABBREVIATIONS

K = Knit

W&T = Wrap and turn (see Workshop: Short row shaping, p.242)

START KNITTING

Follow pattern for the coaster from * to * (see p.244). Repeat until the scarf is as long as you want it to be.

Cast off.

Note to Knitters

The short row shaping shown on p.242 and the patterns for coasters, table mats and twirly scarf all use garter stitch. The technique is the same when knitting in stocking stitch; just remember that you need to knit and purl instead of knitting every row.

See the effect when you work from exactly the same pattern but using Rowan Big Wool and 10mm needles. It's worth experimenting with yarns and stitches to see what you can discover. That's how I came up with the patterns using short row shaping!

Create your own creature

I hate 'perfect' plastic dolls. As a child, my favourite teddy had no eyes! In this pattern, I've designed the basic outline of body and limbs and you have free rein to create an unlimited variety of creatures and characters.

Add personality as you create your creature.

You might find that your feline friends are fascinated by these little critters!

Hopefully these will be lots of fun to knit (as they were for me and my test knitters), so you can make a whole cast of quirky beings!

I've mostly used scraps of double knit yarn and 4mm needles, but this is a pattern where you can throw gauge-caution to the wind and use up any or all your oddments, in colour combinations of your choice. I'm a fan of colourful toys, but don't let that stop you knitting a more sober-suited character. For added charm, try putting a bell or two inside a little plastic container and sewing that into the body, wrapped in toy stuffing.

The only suggestion I might make regarding your yarn choice is washability. For children's toys, it's best to use a yarn that can be machine-washed to make life easier: I know my mum probably had to wash my favourite toys by hand whilst I was asleep.

Go forth and create!

Note to Knitters

I hope that as well as embracing the creative side of this project, it will also help you to be braver technically. This really is an opportunity for you to design your own shapes, which is a step towards really understanding the structure of knitting and understanding the 'science bit' of your work.

YOU WILL NEED

YOU CAN USE ANY SCRAPS OF YARN FOR THE BODY
I'm using double knit yarn and 4mm needles, and by scraps, I mean less than a ball. Don't feel that you have to use the same brand for body and limbs – all normal rules for knitting go out of the window with this pattern!

STRAIGHT AND DOUBLE-POINTED KNITTING NEEDLES
in the appropriate size for your yarn

DARNING NEEDLE

TOY STUFFING

ODDMENTS AND IMAGINATION TO DECORATE

Handy HINT

See the yarn label for the needle
size recommended by the
manufacturer. If you knit with
a loose tension, use a knitting
needle one size smaller than
recommended for the yarn. This
will mean that the knitted fabric
ends up with a tighter weave and
the stuffing is less likely to show
through.

ABBREVIATIONS

K = Knit	
P = Purl	
St(s) = Stitch(es)	
St st = Stocking stitch	
K2tog = Knit two stitches together	
M1 = Make one stitch by picking up the loop in between two stitches	
Cont = Continue	
Rep = Repeat	

START KNITTING

BODY

Cast on 6sts.

K 1 row.

P 1 row.

K1, [M1, K1] to end. Count 11sts.

P 1 row.

K1, [M1, K1] to end. Count 21sts.

P 1 row.

K1, [M1, K2] to end. Count 31sts.

Starting with a purl row, work in stocking stitch until piece measures approximately 8cm from beginning, ending with a purl row.

K1, [K2tog, K1] to end. Count 21sts.

P 1 row.

K2tog to last st, K1. Count 11sts.

P 1 row.

K 2tog to last st, K1. Count 6sts.

Finish with a drawstring finish.

Handy HINT

Here's an opportunity to give your character a shape of his or her own. If you work in stocking stitch for fewer than 8cm, the body will be a small, round shape. If you work for a few more centimetres, the character will be taller and skinnier. Also, you will need to knit more centimetres here if you are using thicker than double knit yarn. Another way of making the body bigger is to repeat the initial increase rows (probably best to do no more than a couple of these).

Note to Knitters

Remember that if you increase and add more stitches, you'll also need to work more decreases of [K2tog, K1] at the end of the pattern. But the main thing is not to worry and just experiment – the odder your character looks, the better, in my book. How amazing to have a knitting pattern where you simply can't go wrong!

Note to Knitters

If you've made the body bigger with more increases, simply work more decrease rows. The stitch count doesn't matter – just keep decreasing until you have 5-10sts before finishing.

Drawstring finish

Cut the yarn leaving a long tail, thread this onto a darning needle, run it through the remaining stitches, and pull tight.

Use the long tail of yarn on the darning needle to sew up the body along the seam using mattress stitch, but leave an opening of about 5cm.

Stuff the body with toy stuffing and sew up completely, stuffing the last little bit as you go.

Weave in all the ends. You can hide the ends of the yarn by poking the darning needle with the yarn end right into the body and out the other side, pulling tightly, then snipping the yarn. Then squish the body about a bit, and the end will disappear into the belly!

Limbs

Using double-pointed needles and leaving a long tail of yarn for sewing the limb to the body, cast on 7sts and knit I-cord (see p.148) until the piece is as long or short as you like.

Finish with a drawstring finish or by casting off. Fasten off and weave in the end.

Note to Knitters

Please make sure that you sew on any embellishments really securely. Little people have a reputation for prising off buttons and stuffing them up their noses, and we won't be having any of that here, please!

Make as many limbs and/or appendages as you need for the character and sew on securely.

You can add features using yarn, or by sewing on buttons or other embellishments.

Seasonal projects

Knitting isn't all about garments and keeping warm. You can use your knitting skills to knit little 'whimsies' to give as gifts or use as decorations. These also make great items to sell on stalls for your favourite charity.

Valentine's heart

Here's a fun way of using up oddments of yarn. As well as the whimsies shown below, you can sew the hearts onto clothing – they'd be so pretty on a hat or the Girls' pinafore dress (see p.186).

A little toy stuffing between two hearts makes a handy pincushion.

Here are two heart shapes sewn together, using a simple whip stitch, and then stuffed with dried lavender just before closing. With an added loop of yarn for hanging, this heart can add a soothing aroma to a bedside table, wardrobe, baby's cot or even your car.

YOU WILL NEED

ODDMENTS OF DOUBLE KNIT YARN
(I like a traditional red, but any colour will work)

3MM KNITTING NEEDLES
(I use a smaller needle than usual for DK yarn, as this makes the knitting stiffer so it can stand alone)

Handy HINT

If you'd like to use the heart as a Christmas tree decoration, you can block it for extra stiffness (see p.151).

Note to Knitters

I find it neater, on this pattern, to leave the tails of yarn a bit longer (about 20cm), so I can weave them in using a darning needle. This gives a tidier finish, as you won't have a seam to weave into. See p.164 for how to do a really neat finish.

GAUGE

Any double knit yarn and 3mm needles work with this pattern. Precise tension is not necessary.

ABBREVIATIONS

K = Knit	
St(s) = Stitch(es)	
K2tog = Knit two stitches together	
M1 = Make one stitch	
Rep = Repeat	

START KNITTING

Cast on 3sts.

K 1 row.

K1, M1, K to end. (This is tricky when you've only worked 1 row, but persevere and it will become easier the more rows you knit.)

Repeat last row until you have 16sts.

Knit 10 rows.

K8sts, turn.

Rep last row a further four times (a total of 5 rows knitted on the first half of the top of the heart).

You will now be knitting the first side of the top of the heart to completion, leaving the other side on the needle and ignoring these 8sts for now.

K2tog, K to last 2sts, K2tog.

K2tog, K to last 2sts, K2tog.

Cast off.

You've now completed one side of the heart.

Rejoin the yarn to other side. See p.163 for how to rejoin yarn.

K8sts, turn.

Rep last row a further four times (a total of 5 rows knitted on the second half of the top of the heart).

K2tog, K to last 2sts, K2tog.

K2tog, K to last 2sts, K2tog.

Cast off.

Weave in all ends.

Easter bunny egg cosy

These egg cosies are fun and practical. Chocolate Easter eggs are one of the most over-packaged items you can buy. If a child received one from his parents, grandparents and an aunt or two, that's an awful lot of waste packaging.

Instead, try giving a small chocolate egg wearing a fun and funky bunny cosy. The cosy can be used again and again, and you can also use it to cover boiled eggs for those without a sweet tooth.

The pattern is simple enough for knitters of all levels, with plenty of scope for customisation and personality.

GAUGE

Any double knit yarn and 4mm needles work with this pattern. A precise gauge is not necessary for this pattern.

START KNITTING

BODY

Cast on 24sts.

Knit every row until piece measures 5cm from beginning.

Now start decreasing for top of cosy:

[K1, K2tog] eight times. Count 16sts.

K 1 row.

[K1, K2tog] five times, K1. Count 11sts.

K 1 row.

[K1, K2tog] three times, K2. Count 8sts.

K 1 row.

Drawstring finish for top of egg cosy.

Cut the yarn, leaving a long tail. Thread this end onto a darning needle. Transfer the 8sts from the knitting needle to the darning needle one by one and pull tight.

Fold the egg cosy in half and sew up. See p.156 on sewing up garter stitch.

Weave in all ends.

EARS (MAKE TWO)

Cast on 5sts (leaving a long tail for sewing to the body).

Work in garter stitch until piece measures 3cm.

K2tog, K to end.

Repeat the last row until one stitch remains.

Fasten off.

Finishing

Pinch ears at the wide end and sew securely to the egg cosy – the pinch will add extra dimension to the ears.

Weave in all ends.

Turn your cosy into a bunny by sewing on features. I like buttons for eyes and an embroidered mouth, but use your imagination here, so that each bunny has an individual personality of its own.

Variations on the basic bunny can be made with different knitting stitches, colours and embellishments. Please note that the ears are always knitted as for the basic garter stitch bunny.

You could replace the garter stitch of the body with stocking stitch, add a ribbed border or use two-row colour stripes (see p.165). The characters don't always need ears – you could add yarn for hair and turn them into a mini-me of your favourite person. Here we have Raoul on the left and Mini-Pearson on the right. Let your imagination go wild, and don't forget to name your bunny!

Christmas tree

I love a bit of seasonal knitting. Here are some Christmas trees to get you into the holiday spirit. You can really go to town with your oddments, and it's a perfect excuse for using sparkly yarn and embellishments – not that I need an excuse. The more bling, the better!

Sew sparkly sequins and beads to a Christmas tree and use it as a tree ornament.

YOU WILL NEED

ODDMENTS OF DOUBLE KNIT YARN

3MM KNITTING NEEDLES
(I use a smaller needle than usual for DK yarn, as this makes the knitted fabric stiffer, so it can stand alone)

SEQUINS, BEADS AND SEWING THREAD FOR EMBELLISHMENT

GAUGE
Any double knit yarn and 3mm needles work with this pattern. A precise gauge and knitting tension are not necessary.

ABBREVIATIONS

K = Knit

St(s) = Stitch(es)

K2tog = Knit two stitches together

START KNITTING

Cast on 16sts.

K 1 row.

K2tog, K to end.

Repeat last row until 8sts remain.

Turn and cast on 4sts. Count 12sts.

Knit 1 row.

Turn and cast on 4sts. Count 16sts.

Knit 1 row.

K2tog, K to end.

Repeat last row until 8sts remain.

Turn and cast on 4sts. Count 12sts.

Knit 1 row.

Turn and cast on 4sts. Count 16sts.

Knit 1 row.

K2tog, K to end.

Repeat until one stitch remains.

Fasten off.

Weave in all your ends.

Use the tree to make personalised Christmas cards for your loved ones. Putting the cards together might be a fun project to do with children.

Note to Knitters

This is called a right-angled increase, as you are increasing the stitches at a sharp angle rather than one by one as with M1 or KFB.

Finishing

Block the trees by spraying them with water on both sides, then sandwich between two tea towels, cover with heavy books and leave overnight. This will help your tree to hold its shape. See the difference here between the unblocked tree on the left and the blocked tree on the right.

Use beads and sequins to decorate your tree, and make a hanging loop from a piece of black cotton.

For instructions on how to turn your tree into a Christmas card, download the free PDF from www.knittingsos.co.uk.

Note to Knitters

See p.245 for another seasonal knitting pattern – the short row snowflake.

Stitch library

In this stitch library, you will learn some new ways to use knit and purl stitches, with some clever tricks thrown in to create all sorts of beautiful and fun textures in your knitting. Some of the techniques may seem very odd at first, but if you keep calm and concentrate, it won't be long before you are able to knit way beyond the basics of stocking stitch and rib. You'll learn just how many exciting effects you can get with the craft of knitting!

Do (kn)it yourself

This stitch library can be used to learn new stitches, or for taking your first steps in simple pattern design. I'll give you the basic tools of stitches and projects, and show you how to work out your own knitting patterns for the project of your choice in the stitch and yarn of your choice. Get ready to start designing! If you follow the steps on the right, you can learn how to knit something completely unique. All it takes is a bit of vision and some 'knitting-maths'.

In the next few pages, as well as learning the stitches and how to use them in your designs, you'll see some of the projects created by my team of amazing test knitters – who are all advanced-beginner or intermediate knitters, just like you!

Step 1: *Choose a project.*

Step 2: *Choose a stitch pattern.*

Step 3: *Knit a practice square – VERY IMPORTANT!*

Step 4: *Decide on the width of knitting you need for the pattern.*

Step 5: *Do the maths to get the correct number of stitches to cast on.*

Step 6: *Start knitting!*

Step 7: *Some projects will need specific finishing techniques (you can download free PDFs on how to finish a bag, purse, cushion cover or greetings card from www.knittingsos.co.uk).*

Step 1: The projects

Here are a number of projects that you can design yourself. First, choose what you'd like to knit:

- Bag
- Purse
- Baby blanket
- Shawl/wrap/scarf
- Cushion cover
- Greetings cards
- Afghan
- **Or choose something else you'd like to make. Stick to simple shapes for now, as this is your first time designing your own knitting pattern.**

Example project: I've decided I want to knit a cushion cover.

Step 2: The stitches

Now choose which stitch you'd like to use to knit your project in:

Wrap drop stitch (p.262)

Loopy stitch (p.274)

Fireside lace stitch (p.264)

Knitting with beads (p.276)

Cable plait stitch (p.266)

Fir tree lace stitch (p.278)

Six-toed cable stitch (p.267)

Knit and purl motifs (p.282)

Cable twist stitch (p.268)

Moss zig stitch (p.283)

Bramble stitch (p.270)

Fair Isle or intarsia (p.284)

Bobble stitch (p.271)

Swiss darning (p.290)

Example project: I'd like to have a go at designing my own Fair Isle chart for my cushion cover.

Step 3: Knit a practice square

Knit a practice square in the stitch of your choice, using the exact yarn and needles you want to use for the finished project. This step is essential for figuring out the maths of the final project and to get you used to a new stitch.

Example project: I'm going to use Cascade 220, which knits up on 4.5mm knitting needles.

Example project: Here's my test square – it took a few pieces of knitters' graph paper before I got the pattern I wanted. It was tricky getting a pattern that would repeat correctly!

Example project: I measured my test square to be approximately 11cm wide.

Step 4: Decide on the width of your knitting

Example project: My cushion pad is about 40cm square, so I want my cushion cover to be about 35cm square.

Step 5: Do the knitting maths

Multiply the size of your practice square to the width you want for your finished project. You need to multiply the number of stitches you cast on in your practice square to get to the nearest approximate centimetre to your chosen final width.

Example project: If I want my final cushion cover to be about 35cm wide, that means I need to cast on approximately three times the number of stitches in my test square, and repeat my chart three times.

Handy HINT

Once you've sorted out the measurements and numbers, stop for a cup of tea! Designing knitting patterns takes a lot of maths and if you are anything like me, most of your mathematical knowledge was forgotten the day after you finished your last maths test at school. Now you have completed steps 1–5, you're nearly at the fun bit!

Handy HINT

Designing your own pattern will mean a certain amount of trial and error. When I'm designing something, I know I'll have to undo and re-knit it at least three times before getting it right! This is just part of the process of creating something completely new. There are millions of knitting patterns out there if you decide designing isn't for you, but if you give it a go I promise you will find it satisfying in the end!

Step 6: Start knitting!

You've got some lovely yarn and chosen a stitch pattern. Now there's nothing but a bit of knitting between you and a unique, personally designed piece of knitting.

If you are repeating a pattern from the stitch library, you can use markers (or contrasting bits of yarn, as shown here) to show you when to start each repeat of the pattern. This will be especially useful if you are knitting a wide piece of knitting with many repeats, such as a baby blanket.

Example project

Step 1: *I've chosen to knit a cushion cover.*

Step 2: *I'd like to use Fair Isle and design my own pattern.*

Step 3: *First of all I knit a practice square in stocking stitch with the Fair Isle design I've plotted onto a chart of knitters' graph paper (see p.281). My practice square was 24sts wide, which measured 11cm.*

Step 4: *I wanted to make a cushion cover about 35cm wide.*

Step 5: *So the maths told me to make my cast on three times the number of stitches of my practice square. That gets me to 72sts = 33cm (it's best to knit your cushion cover a bit smaller than the cushion pad so it stretches tight over the pad to best effect).*

Step 6: *I cast on 72sts and started knitting in my chosen pattern until it became square. Then I cast off and knit the back pieces of the cushion.*

Step 7: *Download a free PDF at www.knittingsos.co.uk for instructions on sewing up and finishing a cushion cover.*

Handy HINT

When knitting a new stitch, it's worth keeping a tally as you knit the rows so you always know where you are in the pattern. It's important to follow the stitch patterns accurately!

Note to Knitters

This maths is an approximate process, in that you may not get the width you planned to the exact centimetre, but only to the nearest centimetre or two. This approximation is fine for all the projects here, as they do not have to be knitted to an exact measurement.

The stitches

Wrap drop stitch

This is a great stitch to learn if you are new to stitch patterns. If you can cast on, cast off and do a basic knit stitch, then you can handle wrap drop. You don't even need to purl!

Wrap drop stitch

Cast on any number of stitches.

Knit 5 rows.

Wrap row: Wrap every stitch three times.

Drop row: Knit every stitch, dropping the wraps as you go.

Knit 5 rows.

Repeat last 7 rows until piece is as long as you want it to be.

Cast off.

Try knitting this stitch using a ribbon yarn for a very different effect from that of a traditional wool yarn. A couple of skeins of Colinette Giotto is a good ribbon yarn to try.

Knitting can be glamorous! This scarf has been knitted using Rowan Shimmer in a sparkly black. You only need 1 or 2 balls, as it goes a long way. I think that the extra-long tassels really add to the finish of this piece.

How to work wrap drop stitch

Cast on any number of stitches – 20 is a good number for a practice square. Knit 5 rows to begin with.

ROW 1 (WRAP ROW):

Pick up a stitch.

Wrap the yarn around the right-hand needle three times (back and middle three times). Use your left index finger to hold the wraps on the needle.

Complete the stitch. You'll now have 3 stitches on the right-hand needle.

Continue in the same way for the rest of the row, wrapping each stitch three times. You'll end up with three times the number of stitches you started with.

ROW 2 (DROP ROW):

Pick up the first stitch and knit it.

When you release the stitch, the extra wraps will automatically be released too. Don't worry about dropping

stitches, as only the wraps will release themselves.

Continue knitting to the end of the row, dropping the wraps as you go.

When you get to the end of the drop row, you'll see the effect of the wrap drop stitch and you'll be able to count the same number of stitches that you cast on initially. Give your knitting a little tug to even out the wrap drops.

Next knit 5 rows – this creates a garter stitch band in between the wraps to show them off to their best advantage.

Fireside lace stitch

This stitch is a simple way to start your lace-knitting career. It uses a simple repeat of YF (yarn forward) to create a very clever-looking piece of knitting and a pretty lace stitch. It can be translated into a scarf or a shawl, or if you're feeling particularly creative, why not give it a contrasting lining and make it into a cushion cover?

This glamorous evening bag has been knitted up and then inserted into a purse frame (see free PDF on www.knittingsos. co.uk for how to do this). It was lined in a contrasting colour that shows through the lace stitches.

This light summer wrap uses 5 balls of Sublime Bamboo and Pearls DK and 4mm needles. To knit it, cast on 66sts and knit fireside lace to approximately 130cm.

Fireside lace stitch

ABBREVIATIONS

YF = Yarn forward

YF2 = Yarn forward twice

YF3 = Yarn forward three times

YF4 = Yarn forward four times

Cast on a multiple of 10sts plus 6sts (for example 26sts, as I have done below).

Row 1: Knit 1 row.

Row 2: Knit 1 row.

Row 3: K6, [YF2, K1, YF3, K1, YF4, K1, YF3, K1, YF2, K6], rep to end.

Row 4: Knit the row, dropping all the extra wraps. Count to ensure you have the same number of stitches you started with.

Row 5: Knit 1 row.

Row 6: Knit 1 row.

Row 7: K1, [YF2, K1, YF3, K1, YF4, K1, YF3, K1, YF2, K6], rep to end. On the last repeat, you will end with a K1 instead of a K6.

Row 8: As Row 4.

Repeat last 8 rows until piece is as long as you want it to be, ending with a Row 2.

Cast off.

How to knit multiple yarn forwards

YF (yarn forward) is when you bring the yarn to the front of your work, as if you were about to purl (although your next stitch won't necessarily be a purl stitch).

YF2 = Bring the yarn to the front of the work, then bring it forwards again by wrapping it around the right-hand needle anti-clockwise.

YF3 = Bring the yarn to the front, then again another two times by wrapping it around the right-hand needle twice anti-clockwise. You have now brought the yarn forward a total of three times.

YF4 = Bring the yarn to the front, then again another three times by wrapping it around the right-hand needle three times anti-clockwise. You have now brought the yarn forward a total of four times.

After knitting a wrap row, you'll notice that you have lots of extra stitches bunched up on the needle – don't panic, as these will disappear after the next row.

How to drop extra wraps

When you knit the row where you drop the extra wraps, knit until you get to the wraps, and then simply push them off the left-hand needle. You'll see that they aren't proper stitches, but are just wrapped around the left needle without being attached to the work. Don't worry about dropping anything you shouldn't, as the next proper stitch to be knitted will be firmly on the needle, unlike the wraps. Don't worry if all this seems a bit daunting; remember that you'll have done all your practice on a test square before you put this stitch into a garment, so you'll be an expert by the time you start your main project!

You'll spot the proper stitch, as distinct from the wraps, by its little 'collar'. This is a small, horizontal bit of yarn at the base of the stitch, which is holding it firmly on the needle. The wraps don't have this 'collar', so they will just fall off the needle as you are knitting Rows 4 and 8.

At the end of the drop row you'll have the same number of stitches that you started with.

Note to Knitters

After working the drop row, you'll notice that the stitches and lace sections look uneven. You can fix this by gently pulling the work after each drop row. Hold the needle in one hand and pull the knitting down and away from it with the other.

Workshop: *How to cable*

A cable is a pattern that looks like a twisted section against a background of garter or stocking stitch. Once you learn how to create a basic twist, you can experiment and knit all sorts of beautiful patterns.

To do cable knitting, you need a cable needle. This is a small, double-pointed knitting needle with a V-shaped or U-shaped bend in it. Stitches are transferred on to this so that they can be knitted in a different order.

You slip the stitches on to the cable needle without knitting them, so they can be held out of the way whilst you knit the next stitches.

The two basic techniques are cable forwards (CF) and cable back (CB). The actual cable pattern itself will vary, depending on the knitting pattern, and will be written out at the beginning of the pattern; but as long as you know how to CF and CB you'll be able to follow any cable instruction.

CF (cable forward). This is when you place some stitches on a cable needle and hold them to the front of your work.

CB (cable back). This is when you place some stitches on a cable needle and hold them to the back of your work.

Cable plait stitch

Here's one of my favourite cable patterns: cable plait. It's a good starter cable pattern as you get to use CF (cable forwards) and CB (cable back), and you end up with an impressive pattern!

Note to Knitters

Both the cable patterns shown here are on a garter stitch background, so you can use them to knit scarves that won't curl up (as they would if they were on a traditional reverse stocking stitch background – this is when the purl is the right side and the knit is the wrong side of the work).

Cable plait stitch

ABBREVIATIONS

CF6 = slip 3sts on to cable needle and hold to the front of the work, knit the next 3sts, slip the 3sts from the cable needle back to the left-hand needle, knit these 3sts

CB6 = slip 3sts on to cable needle and hold to the back of the work, knit the next 3sts, slip the 3sts from the cable needle back to the left-hand needle, knit these 3sts

Cast on a multiple of 21sts (for example 21sts as I've shown here, or 42sts if you want the cable pattern repeated twice, etc.).

Row 1 (RS): K 1 row.

Row 2 (WS): K6, P9, K6 (if you are making the pattern more than one multiple, you would repeat all these instructions again from the beginning, to the end of the row).

Row 3 (RS): K6, CB6, K9. Repeat from beginning to end.

Row 4 (WS): As Row 2.

Row 5 (RS): K 1 row.

Row 6 (WS): As Row 2.

Row 7 (RS): K9, CF6, K6. Repeat from beginning to end.

Row 8 (WS): K6, P9, K6. Repeat from beginning to end.

Repeat last 8 rows until piece is as long as you want it to be, ending with a RS row.

Cast off on the WS of your work in pattern.

This pretty scarf is knitted using two repeats of the cable plait pattern with a cast-on of 42sts, and 2 balls of Sirdar Click DK.

Aneeta's six-toed cable stitch

Designing your own cable stitch isn't something I recommend, but I couldn't resist having a go, and after lots of maths, undoing and re-knitting, here it is. I'm calling it Aneeta's six-toed cable stitch and no, I don't have six toes – I just thought it would be a funny name as the cable has six strands to the pattern. It's a more complicated-looking cable design, which I think is pretty and very satisfying to knit. As I've put it on a garter stitch background and not a reverse stocking stitch, as is traditional for cable patterns, this stitch won't curl and would make a great scarf.

This bag was knitted with 1½ balls of Debbie Bliss Cashmerino DK and two repeats of the stitch pattern (that's a cast-on of 48sts). Download a free PDF from www.knittingsos.co.uk for instructions on how to sew on bag handles.

This stitch takes a bit of extra concentration, so I suggest you work a practice square before you start.

Aneeta's six-toed cable stitch

ABBREVIATIONS

CF4 = slip 2sts onto cable needle and hold to the front of the work, knit the next 2sts, slip the 2sts from the cable needle back to the left needle, knit these 2sts

CB4 = slip 2sts onto cable needle and hold to the back of the work, knit the next 2sts, slip the 2sts from the cable needle back to the left-hand needle, knit these 2sts

Cast on a multiple of 24sts (for example 24sts, as I've shown here, or 48sts if you want the cable pattern repeated twice, etc.).

Row 1 (RS): K 1 row.

Row 2 (WS): K6, P12, K6. Repeat from beginning to end

Row 3 (RS): K6, CF4, CF4, CF4, K6. Rep from beginning to end of the row, depending on how many repeats of the pattern you're knitting.

Row 4 (WS): As Row 2.

Row 5 (RS): K 1 row.

Row 6 (WS): As Row 2.

Row 7 (RS): K8, CB4, CB4, K8. Rep from beginning to end.

Row 8 (WS): As Row 2.

Repeat last 8 rows until piece is as long as you want it to be, ending with a RS row.

Cast off on the WS of your work in pattern.

Knit a cosy snood from approximately 1½ balls of Rowan Big Wool and 12 mm knitting needles. Cast on 24sts and repeat the pattern for 60 cm, then cast off. Sew into a tube.

Cable twist stitch

This stitch gives the impression of a very fine cable, but it's knitted without using a cable needle. I have to say that this is one of my favourite stitches to knit, as it's a really simple process to get such a pretty result. I'm planning to knit a delicate baby's blanket using cable twists.

Note to Knitters

As this stitch is based on a 2 x 2 rib pattern, you can use it for any project that has a 2 x 2 ribbed border – it would make a pretty addition to socks.

Cable twist

ABBREVIATIONS

CT = Cable twist

Cast on a multiple of 4sts plus 2sts (for example 22sts, as I have done below).

Row 1 (RS): K2, [P2, CT], rep to last 4sts, P2, K2.

Row 2 (WS): P2, K2, rib to end – you will start and end this row with P2.

Row 3 (RS): K2, P2, rib to end – you will start and end this row with K2.

Row 4 (WS): P2, K2, rib to end – you will start and end this row with P2.

Repeat last 4 rows until piece is as long as you want it to be.

Cast off in pattern.

This scarf has been knitted using an amazing hand-dyed yarn from Prick Your Finger. You can really experiment with your yarn choices when using the Stitch library.

How to knit cable twist

Knit 2sts together, but DON'T release the two stitches from the left-hand needle.

Insert the right-hand needle into the top stitch on the left-hand needle (one of the two you just knitted together).

Knit that stitch.

Then release both of the two original stitches that you knitted together.

Bramble stitch

Bramble stitch is surprisingly quick to knit once you get the hang of it, and really shows the limitless options for what you can create once you can knit and purl.

See the free PDF at www.knittingsos.co.uk for how to finish a purse using a frame.

Bramble stitch

ABBREVIATIONS

MB = Make bramble

P3tog = Purl 3sts together

Cast on a multiple of 4sts plus 2sts (for example 22sts).

Row 1 (RS): P 1 row.

Row 2 (WS): K1, [MB, P3tog], rep to last st, K1.

Row 3 (RS): P 1 row.

Row 4 (WS): K1, [P3tog, MB], rep to last st, K1.

Repeat last 4 rows until piece is as long as you want it to be.

Cast off.

This pretty scarf is knitted in 4-ply Araucania Ranco Solid. You only need half a ball for a cute kiddy scarf.

How to make a bramble

Pick up the stitch and knit it, but DON'T release the stitch from the left-hand needle.

Bring the yarn to the front of the work.

Purl into the same stitch again, and again DON'T release the stitch from the left-hand needle.

Take the yarn to the back of the work and knit into the same stitch again.

Now that you have knit, purl, knit into the same stitch, you can release that stitch from the left-hand needle.

Then purl the next 3sts together. This means that you will have the same number of stitches at the end of the row that you had at the beginning of the row. Remember to count them!

Bobble stitch

Knitting bobbles into your knitting can turn a simple project into something instantly zany. Whilst I'm not sure I'll be knitting all my jumpers with bobbles on them, I definitely think they work as a fun twist on a simple scarf, or as a border to a pair of gloves. You can add a bobble anywhere you wish in your knitting, on any number of stitches or any stitch background – use your imagination!

Cast on 29sts using Debbie Bliss Cashmerino DK for this cool 'dragon-skin' bobble scarf.

Bobble stitch

ABBREVIATION

MB = Make bobble

I've knitted my test square on a garter stitch background. This means the knitting won't curl up and would work nicely as a scarf.

Cast on a multiple of 7sts plus one stitch (for example 22sts, as I have done here).

Row 1 (WS): K1, [K3, MB, K3], repeat to end.
Rows 2, 3, 4, 5, 6: Knit these rows.
Row 7 (WS): MB, [K6, MB], repeat to end.
Rows 8, 9, 10, 11, 12: Knit these rows.
Repeat last 12 rows until piece is as long as you want it to be, ending with a Row 8.
Cast off.

How to make a bobble

To make a bobble, you have to knit into the same stitch five times. You do this on the WS of the work, so the bobble appears on the other side.

Handy HINT

Remember that you can make the bobbles as close together or as far apart as you like. You can even take the challenge of making a chart and adding bobbles to create a letter, name or motif. This would work really well on a garter stitch scarf.

First, knit into the front of the stitch as if it were a regular knit stitch – but DON'T release the stitch from the left-hand needle.

Then, knit into the back of the same stitch (see section on knitting into the front and back of a stitch, p.143) and DON'T release the stitch from the left-hand needle.

Then knit into the front of the stitch again without releasing the stitch from the left-hand needle.

And then knit into the back of the same stitch again (this is the fourth time you've knitted into the original stitch).

Finally, knit into the front of the stitch (this is the fifth time you've knitted into the same stitch).

This time, release the stitch from the left-hand needle.

This is how your knitting will look when you've knitted into the front, back, front, back, and front of the same stitch.

Turn the work and knit those 5sts.

Turn the work and purl those 5sts.

Then turn and knit the 5sts and finally turn and purl the 5sts.

To complete the bobble, with the WS of the work facing you, take the yarn to the back and then one by one, lift the 4 extra stitches you knitted over the stitch at the top of the right-hand needle – as if you were casting them off one at a time.

You'll see that once you've lifted all 4sts over the top stitch on the right-hand needle, you are left only with only one stitch instead of the 5sts you started with.

Handy HINT

Poke your finger into the back of the bobble at this stage to make sure it's facing the right way – this is, away from you and towards the RS of the knitting.

Then simply continue working until you are ready to make another bobble.

Questions & Answers

Is there a way of knitting this stitch so that the bobbles appear on both sides of the knitting?

Yes! Instead of knitting 5 plain knit rows in between the bobble rows, knit 4 rows (or any even number). That way, the bobbles will alternate from one side of the work to the other.

Loopy stitch

OK … I know it's a bit mad and 70s, but I couldn't resist showing you how to do loopy stitch. I don't really think it would work on an entire cardigan or jumper (but please feel free to try this out if you dare: my sister and I had matching pink loopy cardigans back in the day!) – how about using it for the border of a scarf, gloves or jumper? First person brave enough to knit a bathmat wins a prize!

Loopy stitch

ABBREVIATIONS

ML = Make loop

YF = Yarn forward

Cast on any number of stitches (for example 12sts, as I have done here).

Row 1 (WS): Knit 1 row.

Row 2 (RS): ML, repeat to end, making a loop in every stitch.

Repeat last 2 rows until piece is as long as you want it to be.

Cast off on the wrong side.

These glamorous gloves have been knitted with a loopy stitch border instead of rib (see p.210 for glove pattern) and require 154m double knit yarn (the pretty pair pictured used about half a skein of self-patterning Manos del Uruguay Silk Blend). They are so luxurious!

How to make a loop

Knit the stitch but DO NOT release it from the left-hand needle.

Bring the yarn to the front of the work in between the needles (YF).

Wrap the yarn clockwise around your thumb (as you look at it from the top) and take it to the back of the work in between the needles.

Now knit into the same stitch again and release it from the left-hand needle. You'll be left with 2 stitches on the right-hand needle.

Lift the first (lower) stitch over the second stitch (as if you were casting it off). This holds the loop securely in place.

Repeat this process for every stitch. When you get to the end of the row, I suggest you give a quick tug to every loop to straighten them out.

I know this stitch feels a bit odd to knit, but persevere – I think it's a fun one to impress your knitting or even non-knitting friends.

Knitting with beads

Knitting beads in with your yarn really adds an extra dimension to your fabric and can be used to great decorative effect on any of your classic projects.

Here's a handy glasses case. See the free PDFs at www.knittingsos.co.uk for how to finish your knitting with a purse frame.

Knit with beads

ABBREVIATIONS

YF = Yarn forward

YB = Yarn back

PB = Place bead

SL1P = Slip one stitch purlwise

To knit the square below, I threaded 36 beads on to the yarn. You can use any yarn. Choose beads with a hole that is the right size to allow them to slide on to the yarn easily.

For this square I started by casting on 20sts.

Starting with a knit row, work in stocking stitch for 6 rows, ending with a purl row.

Row 1 (RS): K3, YF, PB, SL1P, YB, [K5, YF, PB, SL1P, YB], rep to last 4sts, K4.
Row 2 (WS): P 1 row.
Row 3 (RS): K4, YF, PB, SL1P, YB, [K5, YF, PB, SL1P, YB], rep to last 3sts, K3.
Row 4 (WS): P 1 row.
Row 5 (RS): K5, YF, PB, SL1P, YB, [K5, YF, PB, SL1P, YB], rep to last 2sts, K2.
Row 6 (WS): P 1 row.
Row 7 (RS): K6, YF, PB, SL1P, YB, [K5, YF, PB, SL1P, YB], rep to last st, K1.
Row 8 (WS): P 1 row.
Repeat last 8 rows until piece is as long as you want it to be.
Cast off.

How to place a bead in your knitting

Before you start knitting, you must thread all the beads you need on to the yarn. This can be a tricky process – try using something called a big eye needle, which you can find in bead shops. Also be sure to use a bead that slides on to the yarn easily.

Using this method, you can place beads wherever you wish on your knitting. They can make a pattern, be randomly scattered, or even carefully placed to form a letter or a shape.

Knit until you are ready to add a bead.

Bring the yarn to the front of your work (YF).

Slide the bead down so it rests on the knitting (PB).

Slip the next stitch as if you were purling (SL1P).

Take the yarn to the back of the work (YB), making sure you hold the bead to the front.

Continue knitting, making sure that you knit the first stitch after the bead firmly.

Handy HINT

If the bead shows on the wrong side of the work, you may not be knitting the first stitch after the bead firmly enough. You can remedy this by simply poking the bead through to the right side of the knitting, where it should stay neatly in place.

You can scatter a mixture of beads (and sequins) anywhere you fancy as you are knitting. Just remember that all embellishments have to be threaded on to the yarn first.

See www.knittingsos.co.uk for how to make and finish a cushion cover.

Fir tree lace stitch

This lace pattern is a little more advanced. It will take some dedication, but the end result is very satisfying. I know that some of you will look at this pattern and think, "Argh! Run for the hills!" But don't panic ... Just take each stitch and each row at a time, work slowly, mark off the rows as you work them and remember the Four Rules of Knitting. You'll be fine!

Handy HINT

Lace is best knitted with a great deal of care and patience. If you are feeling tired, pick up some simpler knitting and save the lace for when you have more energy. There's no point in struggling with it. And it's definitely not a project to be knitting after a glass or two of wine!

Fir tree lace

ABBREVIATIONS

YO = Wrap the yarn around the right-hand needle clockwise

P2SSO = Pass two slipped stitches over

SK2 = Slip a stitch knitwise, then slip the next stitch knitwise

SSK = Slip, slip, knit (see p.142)

Cast on a multiple of 10sts plus one stitch (for example 21sts, as I have done below).

Row 1 (WS): P 1 row.

Row 2 (RS): K1, *[YO, SSK] twice, K1, [K2tog, YO] twice, K1. Rep from *. Count to ensure you've got the same number of stitches you started with – they'll look twisted, so take care to count accurately.

Row 3 (WS): P 1 row.

Row 4 (RS): K2, *[YO, SSK, YO, SK2, K1, P2SSO, YO, K2tog, YO, K3]. Rep from * (on the last repeat you'll end with K2 instead of K3). Count to ensure you've got the same number of stitches you started with.

Repeat last 4 rows until piece is as long as you want it to be.

Cast off.

This beautiful shawl, with a cast-on of 201sts, was made with 2½ skeins of Manos del Uruguay Fairtrade lace yarn – and it nearly doubled in size after blocking (see p.151). It was pinned out to measure 50 x 125cm, then steam-blocked. The first time that you block lace, the difference in size and texture will amaze you!

How to work fir tree lace stitch

YO: wrap the yarn around the right-hand needle clockwise.

P2SSO: pass 2 slipped stitches over.

Handy HINT

Don't forget to mark off each row as you've done it. It will be hard to keep track of where you are otherwise.

Handy HINT

See p.161 for how to do a saver row. I found this was invaluable when I insisted on watching telly at the same time as knitting fir tree lace. When I made a mistake through a lapse of concentration, it saved me from having to undo the knitting all the way back to the beginning.

Note to Knitters

After working a lace row, the stitches will look a bit wonky. Take care to knit these carefully. Sometimes the stitches will look crossed over – this is where you did a YO. Sometimes the stitches will look as if they are twisted. In this case, roll them towards you as the stitches on the top are the correct ones.

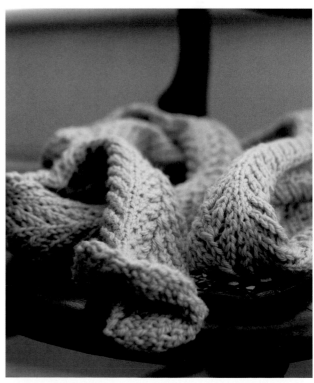

This scarf, knitted with 2 balls of Debbie Bliss Cashmerino DK, hasn't been blocked, so you can see the curled-up effect of this stitch.

How to follow a chart

Stitch and colourwork patterns (any means of incorporating colour, such as with stripes, Fair Isle or intarsia) are often shown on a chart, as well as being written out. Following a chart can seem daunting, but it's really very simple if you follow a few basic rules:

1. Read a chart from the bottom up.
2. Read knit rows from right to left.
3. Read purl rows from left to right.

Start reading a chart from the bottom and work your way up. (Please note that the grey squares are just for information.)

4. Tick off rows as you do them, so you always know where you are.
5. Remember to count your stitches carefully, so you follow the pattern accurately.

The chart for the heart motif below has 21sts and 29 rows. The pattern starts on stitch 11 of Row 7 – this is a knit row, so you read it from right to left.

If you were working this pattern in colourwork, you would use intarsia, with three separate bobbins of yarn: one for the heart and two for the background to the left and right of the heart. When you get to the top of the heart where there's a patch of background between the two 'bumps' of the heart; here you would add a third bobbin for the background. (For instructions on intarsia, see p.287.)

If you were working this pattern in Swiss darning (see p.290), you would start by knitting the background square, casting on 21sts and working in stocking stitch for 29 rows. The heart motif would then be sewn on top.

	1	2	3	4	5	6	7	8	9	10	11	12	13	14	15	16	17	18	19	20	21	
K																						29
P																						28
K																						27
P																						26
K																						25
P						X	X								X	X						24
K					X	X	X	X						X	X	X	X					23
P				X	X	X	X	X						X	X	X	X	X				22
K				X	X	X	X	X	X				X	X	X	X	X	X				21
P				X	X	X	X	X	X	X		X	X	X	X	X	X	X				20
K					X	X	X	X	X	X	X	X	X	X	X	X	X					19
P					X	X	X	X	X	X	X	X	X	X	X	X	X					18
K						X	X	X	X	X	X	X	X	X	X	X						17
P						X	X	X	X	X	X	X	X	X	X	X						16
K						X	X	X	X	X	X	X	X	X	X	X						15
P							X	X	X	X	X	X	X	X	X							14
K							X	X	X	X	X	X	X	X	X							13
P								X	X	X	X	X	X	X								12
K								X	X	X	X	X	X	X								11
P										X	X	X										10
K										X	X	X										9
P											X											8
K											X											7
P																						6
K																						5
P																						4
K																						3
P	→																					2
K	←																					1

Handy HINT

When I'm designing a chart, I like to start the contrasting colour pattern on a knit row. It makes it easier to add the new colour.

Handy HINT

Three things to remember when reading a chart:
1. Start reading the chart from the bottom.
2. Knit (RS) rows are read from right to left.
3. Purl (WS) rows are read from left to right.

Note to Knitters

Your knitting pattern will give a key to the squares and symbols on the chart. This key will vary from chart to chart.

Blank knitters' graph paper

Use this to design your own motifs.
Simply photocopy it and start designing!

Side	Grid	Row
K		29
P		28
K		27
P		26
K		25
P		24
K		23
P		22
K		21
P		20
K		19
P		18
K		17
P		16
K		15
P		14
K		13
P		12
K		11
P		10
K		9
P		8
K		7
P		6
K		5
P		4
K		3
P	→	2
K	←	1

Columns: 1 2 3 4 5 6 7 8 9 10 11 12 13 14 15 16 17 18 19 20 21

Knit and purl motifs

You all know how to knit and purl. These are very basic techniques that you learnt many patterns ago. Now I want to show you how simple combinations of knit and purl can produce far from simple effects. You can use them to create complicated patterns and images, and even to put messages in your knitting. You can use charts to create motifs, and here you can really use your imagination to personalise your knitting.

Rule Number One of knitting (see p.158) will be, as always, invaluable with knit and purl patterns. Remember to count your stitches at the end of every row!

Knit and purl motifs

Using the heart chart on p.280 you can work in knit and purl combinations to create any image you like. This is a more subtle way of adding an image into your knitting than colourwork. I've made my image in stocking stitch on a garter stitch background. This makes the pattern stand out nicely, and the knitting will not curl up (so it would be perfect for a scarf, or alternatively a baby's blanket).

This chart is the same as would be used for Swiss darning or intarsia. Follow the key carefully to knit the stocking stitch heart on a garter stitch background.

Use the heart chart but follow this key to knit your heart motif.

☐ = Knit on RS and knit on WS

X = Knit on RS and purl on WS

 Handy HINT

The main thing you have to remember is:

When you knit, the yarn is at the back.

When you purl, the yarn is at the front.

 Handy HINT

Here is a tip from my test knitters: to keep an eye on the rows, you can use a stitch counter – or do as I do and remember to tick off the rows as you work them. Accuracy is important when following a chart.

You can work knit and purl patterns into garments, or make charming little coasters or greetings cards with small squares of knitting.

Moss zig stitch

This stitch started off as the moss zigzag that I give my advanced beginners to knit to practise their stitch skills. One of these knitters took it a step further and decided that she wanted diagonal stripes rather than a zigzag ... and that's a great example of how you can design your own stitches using only knit and purl. It doesn't take years of knitting to start designing – all you need is an idea and a willingness to experiment!

MOSS ZIG STITCH

Cast on a multiple of 9 stitches (18sts is a good number to practise with).

Row 1 (RS): K4, P1, K1, P1, K1, P1, repeat from beginning to the end of the row.

Row 2 (WS): P1, K1, P1, K1, P1, K1, P3, repeat to end.

Row 3: K2, P1, K1, P1, K1, P1, K2, repeat to end.

Row 4: P3, K1, P1, K1, P1, K1, P1, repeat to end.

Row 5: P1, K1, P1, K1, P1, K4, repeat to end.

Row 6: K1, P4, K1, P1, K1, P1, repeat to end.

Row 7: P1, K1, P1, K4, P1, K1, repeat to end.

Row 8: K1, P1, K1, P4, K1, P1, repeat to end.

Row 9: P1, K4, P1, K1, P1, K1, repeat to end.

Row 10: K1, P1, K1, P1, K1, P4, repeat to end.

Row 11: K3, P1, K1, P1, K1, P1, K1, repeat to end.

Row 12: P2, K1, P1, K1, P1, K1, P2, repeat to end.

Row 13: K1, P1, K1, P1, K1, P1, K3, repeat to end.

Row 14: P4, K1, P1, K1, P1, K1, repeat to end.

Row 15: K1, P1, K1, P1, K4, P1, repeat to end.

Row 16: P1, K1, P4, K1, P1, K1, repeat to end.

Row 17: K1, P1, K4, P1, K1, P1, repeat to end.

Row 18: P1, K1, P1, K1, P4, K1, repeat to end.

Repeat the last 18 rows until the piece is as long as you want it to be, ending on any RS row.

Cast off in pattern on the WS of your work.

For instructions on how to make and finish a knitted cushion cover, see the free PDFs at www.knittingsos.co.uk.

The front of the cushion is moss zig, and the back with the buttons is in moss stitch (K1, P1 on an odd number of stitches).

Fair Isle and intarsia knitting

In Fair Isle and intarsia knitting you use more than one colour in each row to create a design or motif in a piece of stocking stitch knitting.

In Fair Isle, the design is small or intricate and the yarns of various colours are carried behind the work until they are needed.

In intarsia, the motif is worked in bigger blocks of colour to create bolder images, and as it would be impractical to carry the yarn over large areas at the back of the knitting, the yarn is wound on to bobbins for each separate part of the pattern.

You can slip a bit of Fair Isle or intarsia into any piece of stocking stitch knitting. Perhaps you could use it on the border of a cardigan, or turn the Men's bulky jumper (p.180) into a jolly winter pressie, or how about using it to add a bit of zing to a simple hat pattern? You can really unleash your creativity here.

You can use these techniques on any stocking stitch piece of knitting. Here you can see how effective the techniques are on cushion covers. Go to www.knittingsos.co.uk for free instructions on how to finish a knitted cushion cover.

Really practise using two fingers to hold the strands of yarn when knitting Fair Isle – it will be tricky at first, but you'll get the hang of it.

Fair Isle

Try this simple Fair Isle pattern, which uses two colours to create a decorative design. Fair Isle is often worked in the round, but it can be knitted on straight needles too. The yarn is carried over small areas at the back of the work.

KEY

□ = Knit on RS and purl on WS

X = Knit and purl using the contrasting colour

	1	2	3	4	5	6	7	8	9	10	11	12	13	14	15	16	
K																	23
P																	22
K																	21
P																	20
K																	19
P																	18
K		X		X		X		X		X		X		X		X	17
P	X		X		X		X		X		X		X		X		16
K		X		X		X		X		X		X		X		X	15
P																	14
K																	13
P																	12
K																	11
P																	10
K	X		X		X		X		X		X		X		X		9
P		X		X		X		X		X		X		X		X	8
K	X		X		X		X		X		X		X		X		7
P																	6
K																	5
P																	4
K																	3
P																	2
K																	1

Work in stocking stitch for 6 rows (starting with a knit row and ending with a purl row) until the start of the Fair Isle section.

For a refresher on how to read a chart, see p.280.

Join the new colour of yarn without cutting the original yarn.

Knit the first stitch in the new colour (following the chart).

Knit the second stitch in the original colour.

Handy HINT

You can wrap each of the two colours of yarn around your right index and middle finger and use each finger to knit in turn. If you find that this is too tricky, simply pick up each colour as you need it. As there is only a small distance between each colour change in Fair Isle, you don't need to worry about twisting the yarns at the back of the work as you work along the row, as you would with intarsia.

Continue the row, knitting each stitch in a different colour according to the chart.

Here's what your work will look like after the first row of the Fair Isle chart.

At the start of the next row – the purl row – twist the two strands of yarn at the beginning of the row, at the back of the work.

Purl across the row using the opposite colour for each stitch. For example, here I use the blue to purl a pink stitch and vice versa.

Here's how your knitting will look after you've worked a knit row and a purl row of the Fair Isle chart.

There will be a few loose ends at the back of the work where you've joined the new colour. Ensure that you weave these into the back of the work neatly and securely.

Intarsia

For this practice pattern, I drew out a bold shape on knitters' graph paper.

 Handy **HINT**

You have the option of winding small amounts of yarn on to bobbins, but I sometimes find these to be a bit unwieldy and prefer to have long strands of yarn hanging from the back of my knitting. I add more long strands as I need them. I find that this makes for fewer tangles at the back of the work. Have a go with bobbins or long strands and see which you prefer.

Start by winding some of the yarn into separate balls, or on to a bobbin if you wish. This is so you can work each side of the pink background from two different balls of yarn, rather than carrying the yarn across the back of the blue shape, which would be untidy.

KEY

□ = Knit on RS and purl on WS

X = Knit and purl using the contrasting colour

	1	2	3	4	5	6	7	8	9	10	11	12	13	14	15	16	17	18	19	20	
K																					27
P																					26
K																					25
P																					24
K																					23
P										X	X										22
K									X	X	X	X									21
P								X	X	X	X	X	X								20
K					X	X	X	X	X	X	X	X	X	X							19
P						X	X	X	X	X	X	X	X	X							18
K						X	X	X	X	X	X	X	X	X							17
P					X	X	X	X	X	X	X	X	X	X	X						16
K						X	X	X	X	X	X	X	X	X	X						15
P						X	X	X	X	X	X	X	X	X	X						14
K						X	X	X	X	X	X	X	X	X	X						13
P						X	X	X	X	X	X	X	X	X							12
K						X	X	X	X	X	X	X	X	X							11
P						X	X	X	X	X	X	X	X	X							10
K								X	X	X	X	X	X								9
P									X	X	X	X									8
K										X	X										7
P																					6
K																					5
P																					4
K																					3
P																					2
K																					1

Work until you get to the start of the blue shape and join the blue yarn.

Knit the blue stitches as marked on the chart, then join the pink yarn from the ball that you previously wound into a separate ball.

Complete the row with the pink yarn from the separate ball.

On the next row, purl until you get to the place where the blue starts.

Twist the blue yarn under and then over the pink yarn, and work the next stitches as shown on the chart.

When you get to the next pink section on that row, twist the pink yarn from the other side under and over the blue and work the rest of the row.

Continue working the rows and following the chart, making sure that you twist the yarn every time there is a colour change. You'll soon see the pattern start to emerge.

The back of your work will look quite messy at this stage. Don't worry: we'll sort it out at the end. If, at any stage, the yarn from the separate ball runs out, simply wind off some more yarn and join it in the usual way.

When you get to the end of the blue shape, you can cut one of the pink yarns so that you are now only knitting with one ball of pink again to complete the chart.

When you have finished, you'll see that there are several loose strands of yarn at the back of the work. These loose ends can be neatened by weaving them into the back of the work.

Questions & Answers

Why do I need to twist the yarn at a colour change?

If you don't, there will be a gap in the knitting between the colours. When you knit with a new piece of yarn, you need to make sure you are knitting as if the yarn were joined together for a continuous piece of knitting.

The strands at the back of my work are all tangled!

Don't worry: if you get into too much of a snarl simply cut the yarn, leaving ends long enough to be woven in, and join a new piece of yarn to work with.

Handy HINT

I suggest you leave the loose ends fairly long, so that you can weave them in using a darning needle rather than a crochet hook, as this is a bit easier to do.

Handy HINT

Take your time over weaving in. My mother always taught me that the inside of your work should be as tidy as the outside – this is good advice for all neat crafters!

Questions & Answers

Help! I forgot to twist the yarn and I have a hole in my knitting.

Don't panic: you can usually correct this by sewing up the hole from the inside. Use loose ends of yarn or matching sewing thread for a subtle repair.

Swiss darning

So this isn't officially knitting, but I couldn't resist including it. Swiss darning isn't seen much these days, but I foresee a comeback for this simple, clever technique for adding colour patterns and motifs into your knitting.

Swiss darning is a way of sewing a colour pattern on to a piece of stocking stitch knitting. It has a similar look to intarsia or Fair Isle, but is infinitely simpler to produce than knitting with all those strands of yarn. Personally, I like the effect of intarsia and Fair Isle, but I really don't enjoy the process and I'm a firm believer that a crafter must enjoy the process as much, if not more, than the final product!

If, like me, you prefer the simple life, try Swiss darning to add colour and pattern to your knitting. You can use it on any stocking stitch knitting. It would work well on a cushion cover, for instance, or on small squares of knitting to turn into greetings cards.

Here I've added a fun bit of Swiss darning to the Gloves on p.210.

You can personalise any stocking stitch knitting, such as the Versatile kiddies' jumper on p.192: add any motif you like!

There are so many possibilities once you master this new technique. Have fun experimenting.

How to do Swiss darning

To start with, you need a plain background of stocking stitch. This practice piece features a heart. Cast on 21sts and work in stocking stitch for 29 rows. End with a RS row and cast off on the WS of the knitting.

Note to Knitters

See p.280 for how to read a chart. The same charts can be used for intarsia, Fair Isle, Swiss darning or knit and purl motifs.

You are now ready to follow the chart. I suggest that you start from the bottom point of the heart and work your way upwards. If you've ever done counted cross stitch, it's a similar process – each stitch is represented by a square on the chart.

You are going to sew the heart design on top of the stocking stitch background, by following the line of each stitch. The best way to do this is by following the 'V' of the stitch. Each square of the chart is the 'V' of a stitch.

Start by threading the yarn onto a darning needle and pulling it from the back of the work to the front, at the point where you want to start sewing. Leave a long tail at the back and use it for weaving in later.

Pick up the two sides of the 'V' of a stitch just above where you want to start sewing.

Insert the needle back into the point at which you started.

You can see that you've exactly covered the original pink stitch of the background with a blue stitch.

Then work your way up the chart to create the heart motif.

Handy HINT

Here's a tip from my testers: you'll find it easier if the background piece of knitting is a light or bright colour. You'll be able to see the structure of the stitches more easily than when working on a very dark background – especially the first time you try this technique.

Sometimes it will be easier to sew if you turn your work to hold it an angle. Don't be afraid to turn your work in all directions to make it easier to sew! Work across each row, making sure you cover the 'V' of each stitch for each square on the chart.

When you've finished your Swiss darning, make sure you take time to weave in all the ends neatly.

Handy HINT

When you've finished sewing, take care to weave the ends into the back of your work. Try and weave each colour into itself rather than weaving the blue yarn into the pink knitting, for example.

Note to Knitters

Be sure to use the same make and model of yarn for the darning as you did for the base square, so it is the same thickness. This will ensure that the darning yarn will cover each stitch neatly.

The stitch-library scarf afghan

Sounds like the title of a novel, eh? But no – it's my way of knitting a blanket or afghan.

New knitters often tell me that they want to knit a blanket out of squares as they think it will be easy. I almost always discourage this! My reasoning is: squares can be dull and samey to knit, and you'll need an awful lot of them; plus the sewing-up process will take forever and never look as tidy as you want. Both of these reasons can be disheartening, and I don't want anyone to be put off knitting due to one badly thought-out project.

So … you still want to knit a blanket? Try what I call my 'scarf-blanket' technique. It has plenty of scope for creativity and personalisation, and it will be much more satisfying to knit and sew up than squares. Another benefit of this technique is that you won't end up lugging around a huge and heavy knitting project, as each scarf is of course very portable.

YOU WILL NEED

I suggest a chunky-weight yarn on 7 or 8mm needles, as this will be quicker to knit and warm to snuggle under. I've used Rowan British Sheep Breeds Chunky Undyed, as it comes in lovely natural, neutral shades. I used around 18 balls for this afghan and knitted each scarf to be 150cm long, but of course your blanket can be as big or small as you choose. (You can use the same principles for knitting an afghan on finer yarn and needles to knit a baby blanket.)

Look at the stitch pattern library (or any stitches you fancy) and choose the ones you want in your afghan, then knit some practice squares.

Once you've chosen your stitch patterns, knit several scarves, using one stitch pattern per scarf. Alternatively, mix and match as many or as few stitch patterns as you wish, to create the texture of your choice.

I chose to start and finish each side of my scarves with a few rows of contrasting coloured garter stitch, as I wanted the edges to be neat. You could choose to knit a few rows in a stitch or colour of your choice, to work as a border.

This project is ideal for group knitting. If you're knitting this as a gift, you and your friends could knit a scarf each and sew them up into a single blanket. This would make a great gift for a baby shower, a housewarming or to donate to charity.

Making up

Lay out your scarves in the order you like best (I'm not giving you very detailed instructions here as I want this to be designed to your own taste rather than a prescribed pattern), and sew them up along the long edges.

You can use mattress stitch; if you get confused when sewing up all the different stitches, just remember that the general rule of thumb when sewing up with mattress stitch is to look for a horizontal bar on both sides of the knitted fabric.

One of the great things about this pattern is that you can keep adding to your afghan until it's as big as you want!

Farewell and good luck!

Woo hoo! Congratulations. If you've made it this far then you are well on the road to becoming an accomplished knitter, with not just the technical skills to add finesse to your knitting, but the experience and understanding to add flair and creativity to any knitting pattern you choose. I hope you've enjoyed the ride and will use this book as your stepping stone as you travel deeper into the Wonderful World of Knitting.

Appendix
Conversion charts

KNITTING NEEDLE SIZES	
2mm	(UK14/US0)
2.25mm	(UK13/US1)
2.75mm	(UK12/US2)
3mm	(UK11/US n/a)
3.25mm	(UK10/US3)
3.5mm	(UK n/a/US4)
3.75mm	(UK9/US5)
4mm	(UK8/US6)
4.5mm	(UK7/US7)
5mm	(UK6/US8)
5.5mm	(UK5/US9)
6mm	(UK4/US10)
6.5mm	(UK3/US10½)
7mm	(UK2/US n/a)
10mm	(UK000/US15)
12mm	(UK n/a/US17)
15mm	(UK n/a/US n/a)

CENTIMETRES TO INCHES	
Centimetres	Inches
1	0.39
5	1.97
10	3.94
15	5.9
20	7.87
25	9.84
30	11.8

METRES TO YARDS	
Metres	Yards
1	1.0936
2	2.1872
5	5.468
10	10.936
25	27.34
50	54.68
75	82.02
100	109.36
500	546.8
1000	1093.6

YARN WEIGHT	
Grams	Ounces
25	0.88
50	1.76
75	2.65
100	3.5
150	5.29
200	7.05
250	8.81

YARN	
UK	USA
2 Ply	Lace weight
4 Ply	Fingering
Double knit	Sport/Double knit
Aran	Worsted
Chunky	Bulky

Abbreviations

[ ]	Sequence of instructions in square brackets is to be repeated as stated
Approx.	Approximately
Circ	Circular needle
Cont	Continue
Dpn(s)	Double-pointed needle(s)
K	Knit
K2tog	Knit two stitches together
K2tog tbl	Knit two stitches together through the back of the loops
KFB	Knit into the front and back of a stitch
Knitwise	Treat stitches as if you were about to knit them
M1	Make one stitch
P	Purl
P2SSO	Pass two slipped stitches over
P2tog	Purl two stitches together
P2tog tbl	Purl two stitches together through the back of the loops
PB	Place bead
PM	Place/pass marker
Purlwise	Treat stitches as if you were about to purl them
Rem	Remaining
Rib	Work in rib stitch as specified
RS	Right side
SKP	Slip, knit, pass
SKPO	Slip, knit, pass over
Sl	Slip
Sl1P	Slip one stitch purlwise
SM	Slip marker
SSK	Slip, slip, knit
St(s)	Stitch(es)
W&T	Wrap and turn (short row shaping)
WS	Wrong side
YF; YF2; YF3; YF4	Yarn forward: bring the yarn to the front of the work as if you were about to purl it (although next stitch will not necessarily be a purl stitch); yarn forward twice; yarn forward three times; yarn forward four times
YO	Yarn over: wrap the yarn around the right-hand needle clockwise

Stockists

Artesano www.artesanoyarns.co.uk
Quality yarns from ethical producers.

Colinette www.colinette.com
Beautiful hand-painted luxury yarns.

Debbie Bliss www.debbieblissonline.co.uk
Gorgeous yarns, stylish patterns and more!

Get Knitted www.getknitted.com
Terrific shop and online store with some hard-to-find yarns as well as all the favourites, and knitting accessories.

HCS Crafts www.hcscrafts.co.uk
Family-run craft store. Great for bulk buys for craft groups.

Hip Knits www.hipknits.co.uk
Luxurious hand-painted yarns and fibres.

I Knit London www.iknit.org.uk
Shop and sanctuary for knitters.

John Lewis www.johnlewis.com
Good selection of favourite yarns and accessories.

Loop www.loopknittingcom
London yarn boutique with knitting supplies sourced from all over the world.

Prick Your Finger www.prickyourfinger.com
Yarn shop and gallery in East London specialising in natural and hand-spun fibres.

Rowan www.knitrowan.com
Yarns, patterns, knitting books, workshops and much more.

Sirdar www.sirdar.co.uk
A terrific source for yarn and accessories – look out for their amazing novelty yarn selection.

Stylecraft www.stylecraft-yarns.co.uk
Yarns and patterns to suit all tastes.

Yarnbox www.yarnbox.co.uk
Online shop for beautiful yarns and accessories.

Yarnscape www.yarnscape.co.uk
Luxurious hand-spun and hand-dyed yarns.

Index

abbreviations 126, 295
adding yarn 23, 163
angled edges 154–155

backstitch 38
basket weave stitch 120–121
beads 276
binding off 21, 51, 144–146
blocking 151
bobble stitch 271
bramble stitch 270
buttonholes 64, 149

cable plait stitch 266
cable twist stitch 268
cables 78–79, 266–268
casting off 21, 51, 144–146
casting on 17–18, 136–137
changing colour 23, 163, 165
charts, how to follow 280
choosing yarn 11, 15, 134
circular needles 218–221, 240
conversion charts 126, 294
counting rows 166

darning needle 38
decreasing 36–37, 141
designing your own knits 258–261
double-pointed needles 227–229
drawstring finish 56, 144
drop shoulder 192, 194
dropped stitch 28–29

easing in 157

Fair Isle 284–286
fastening off 144
finishing 62–65, 148–151
fir tree lace stitch 278
fireside lace stitch 264
following a pattern 164

frogging 158–160
fully fashioned angled edges
    154–155

garter stitch 20, 139
gauge 10–11, 132–133
grafting 146
graph paper 281

holes 164, 215, 238, 289

I-cord 148
increasing 58–59, 142
intarsia 284, 287–289

Kitchener stitch 146
knit stitch 19, 138
knitwise 141
knots 23

lace stitches 116, 264, 278
left-slanted decrease 141
loopy stitch 274

markers 167
mattress stitch 39–40, 152–154
mistakes 27–29, 158–160
modified drop shoulder 192, 194
moss stitch 51, 140
moss zig stitch 283
motifs 280, 282, 284–291

needles 14

patterns, how to follow 167
pick up and knit 149
pom-poms 56–57
purl stitch 25–139
purlwise 141

raglan sleeves 154–155, 172

recognising rib 160
rejoining yarn 23, 163, 175
ribbing, or rib stitch 49–50, 140,
    160
right-angled increase 257
right side 22, 165
right-slanted decrease 141
rules of knitting 19, 20, 32, 158

saver row 161
sewing-up 38–40, 152–157
shaping 140–142, 242
short rows 242–243
six-toed cable stitch 267
slipknot 16
soup and scoop method 58–59
stitch markers 167
stocking stitch 26, 139
stockists 128, 295
stripes 112–115, 165
substituting yarn 134
Swiss darning 290

tassels 35
tension 10–11, 132–133
three-needle bind-off 145
thumb method cast-on 137
turning 163
two-needle cast-on 136

undoing knitting 158–160

washing 132
weaving in ends 24, 164
whip stitch 156
winding yarn 33
wrap and turn 242–243
wrap drop stitch 262
wrong side 22, 165

yarn 11, 15, 134